A DREAM OF GLORY

A DREAM OF GLORY
FANHUA MENG

a Chinese play by Wang Yun

Translated, with introduction and annotation, by Qingyun Wu
(With the original Chinese text edited by Qingyun Wu)

The Chinese University Press

A Dream of Glory **(Fanhua meng)***: A Chinese Play by Wang Yun*
Translated, with introduction and annotation, by Qingyun Wu
(With the original Chinese text edited by Qingyun Wu)

ISBN 978–962–996–309–5

THE CHINESE UNIVERSITY PRESS
The Chinese University of Hong Kong
SHA TIN, N.T., HONG KONG
Fax: +852 2603 6692
+852 2603 7355
E-mail: cup@cuhk.edu.hk
Web-site: www.chineseupress.com

Printed in Hong Kong

CONTENTS

Part Two. The Original Chinese Text

FOREWORD

This edition of Wang Yun's *A Dream of Glory*, the first full-length *chuanqi* play by a Chinese woman, represents a double contribution to literary history. The original preface and other lyrical attachments to the play have been known and studied since the time of its composition, but the play itself had been largely lost to sight until rediscovered and published in the present volume by Professor Qingyun Wu. The translation of the play, moreover, offers to Western readers a rich source of information concerning Chinese social and esthetic concepts during the eighteenth century.

Both similarities and differences inherent in Oriental and Occidental cultures may be perceived in plays such as *A Dream of Glory* that sharply reveal significant Chinese and European attitudes toward the realities of life as well as perceptions of the supernatural. The plot of this drama, reflecting the interaction of religious mythology and ordinary human circumstances, is, nevertheless, sparse and simple. A young girl from a socially privileged family, after a physical and psychological transformation into a young man, sets out on a trip in this masculine identity, during which he makes contact with two virgins of a slightly lower caste, whom he takes on as concubines. He subsequently encounters a female of his own social status, and with whom he weds. These basic elements also constitute the framework of the most famous Chinese work of fiction of all time, *The Dream of the Red Chamber* (also translated as *Story of the Stone*), which was not published until 1792 and not known in the West until the middle of the next century. This novel of extraordinary length combines elements of nearly every genre of narrative fiction, including the basic elements of the bildungsroman, aspects of which resemble *A Dream of Glory*. Although its male protagonist does not travel, he presides as the scion of a privileged family over a lavish compound inhabited by a number of nubile and talented females who vie for his attention. Both texts, the drama and the novel, portray individual reactions to the psychological and physical conflicts inherent in sexual relationships of traditional Chinese society during past generations, but relevant also to evolving Western standards of the present.

Although *The Dream of the Red Chamber* was not translated into any European language until the late nineteenth century, long after its publication in China, just as the present edition of *A Dream of Glory* embodies its first

English translation, two other Chinese literary texts had been translated and become relatively well known in Europe as early as the eighteenth century. The first of these, a drama of the thirteenth century, *The Orphan of the House of Zhao*, by Ji Junxiang, was translated by a French Jesuit, Joseph de Prémare, and published by Jean-Baptiste du Halde. An English version of the play was shortly produced by William Hatchett and one in Italian by Metastasio. Its most noted European reincarnation, however, came in the form of a greatly revised imitation by Voltaire in 1755 under the title of *L'Orphelin de la Chine* [*The Orphan of China*], which was, in turn, adapted by Arthur Murphy for the English stage in 1759. Whether in its original form or in its various modifications, this play has very little in common with *A Dream of Glory*. Essentially a realistic historical drama concerning the effect of the conquest of China by the Tartars as revealed in the fortunes of a noble Chinese family, which succeeded in maintaining the ancient traditions of China despite the military superiority of the invaders, the play has none of the mystical aura or intimate psychological analysis connected with the dream vision.

The second Chinese literary work to be introduced to European readers was a prose narrative belonging to an established genre endemic to China known as the scholar-beauty romance. Little is known about the origin of this work, *Haoqiu zhuan*, except that it is anonymous and that it originally appeared around the middle of the seventeenth century. About a century later, in 1761, it was edited and published in English by a literary bishop of the Church of England, Thomas Percy, under the title, *The Pleasing History*, and in a separate translation by an employee of the East India Company in 1829 under the title, *The Fortunate Union, A Romance*. A French translation based on Percy's appeared in 1765, a German in the same year and a Dutch in 1767. Considerable international attention was drawn to the work in 1766 by a well-known French literary critic, Melchior Grimm, who in his widely circulated *Correspondance Litteraire* praised it effusively for its moral excellence and penetrating portrayal of Chinese chivalry and feminine virtue.

A Dream of Glory shares with *The Pleasing History* the standard ingredients of the scholar-beauty romance, a young student who excels in the governmental examinations and as a moral obligation devotes himself to the protection of a beautiful maiden to whom he is betrothed, meticulously observes every caution to preserve her chastity from the least danger. The protagonist of *A Dream of Glory* also wins first place in the examination process and becomes the suitor of a lovely virgin, but his dedication seems artificial and manipulated rather than sincere and genuinely morally determined. Occasional references throughout the play to Confucian and

Buddhist concepts seem platitudinous, moreover, while the general ambiance together with the speech and behavior of the young man and his feminine consorts suggests incipient sexual desire rather than internal restraint. *The Pleasing History* portrays the application to real life of an accepted philosophical system while *A Dream of Glory* consists primarily of myth and fantasy.

Had *A Dream of Glory* been available to Western readers during the eighteenth century, it probably would not have enjoyed the success of either *The Orphan of the House of Zhao* or *The Pleasing History* because of the literary and philosophical system then prevailing throughout Europe. This was the period of the Enlightenment, the Age of Reason, when fantasy and myth were outmoded and almost entirely abandoned in favor of realism, authenticity, physical science, and related philosophies. Supernaturalism had been superseded by the religion of nature. *A Dream of Glory* has much more in common with the Elizabethan period in English literature when the mystical and fanciful vied with the realistic, and readers accepted unhesitatingly Shakespeare's pronouncement, "we are such stuff/as dreams are made on" (*The Tempest*, 1611). Even today, Western parallels to passages in *A Dream of Glory* may be discerned in fantasies and allegories such as those in *A Midsummer Night's Dream* and *The Tempest*, works suggesting eroticism, splendors of natural scenery and psychological speculation. Western literary involvement in the mythical and magical was revived in the Romantic period, which produced many works of sheer fantasy, for example, John Keat's *Endymion*, the poetic narrative of a shepherd falling in love with the moon goddess Cynthia. While visiting her on the moon, he meets a real woman, Phoebe, and transfers his affections to her, but she turns out to be another incarnation of Cynthia, who possesses him for eternity.

The dream motif aroused great interest in Europe from ancient times until late in the seventeenth century and then faded out until the advent of Proust in the late nineteenth century. The early periods used dreams as a forecast of the future, the latter as clues to the past. The Renaissance is replete with dream works forecasting one thing after another. A more serious treatment is given in a Spanish play of the same period, *La vida es sueño* [*Life is a Dream*] by Calderón de la Barca. The protagonist, a member of a royal family, is kept in solitary confinement, then is suddenly elevated to the throne and freedom, but is again placed in confinement, making him believe that all his memories are dreams, not actual experience. The situation resembles that of Zhuang Zhou in the fourth century BC. who could not decide whether he was dreaming about a butterfly or the butterfly dreaming about him, a parallel also to the situation in *A Dream of Glory* as pointed out by Professor Wu in her introduction. Among the plethora of Western parallels to the other major theme of the play, is that of metamorphosis, by the turning of human beings into various animal forms and even into material objects such as coins, sofas, and articles of apparel. The outstanding example of a change of gender is Tiresius in ancient Greece who was turned into a female by the gods because he struck with a stick two coupling snakes and when he did it a second time was turned back into a man. When Zeus and Hera asked him which sex had the greater pleasure by means of physical sex, he indicated the female.

Western history also contains a famous personage, the Chevalier d'Eon, a French aristocrat of the eighteenth century, who lived alternately as a male and a female. Whether this individual was a homosexual or a hermaphrodite, however, has never been established. Some eminent female novelists of the West, moreover, have published under masculine names: Mary Ann Evans of England became George Eliot; A. A. Lucie Dupin of France became George Sand; and in America, Pearl S. Buck, who had won fame as a female writer on life in Asia, published five novels about small town America under the pen name of John Sedges.

Six major motifs apart from the scholar-beauty theme have been associated with *A Dream of Glory*: metamorphosis, homosexuality, transvestism, lesbianism, feminism, and religion. These are obviously alternate relationships in the action that cannot all exist concurrently. If the protagonist's metamorphosis is complete and he no longer remains conscious of his former identity, there is no basis for assuming transvestism. Only if the protagonist's metamorphosis is incomplete, moreover, can her relations with female companions be linked to lesbianism although its elements could be considered as present among the other female characters. Regardless of how the protagonist's sex change is interpreted, however, no basis exists for assuming male homosexuality. Clear examples of the combination of transvestism and male homosexuality, by contrast, may be perceived in some modern dramatic works presented on both stage and screen, such as *M. Butterfly* and *Farewell to My Concubine.*

The varied themes of *A Dream of Glory* do not easily blend. The nature of the glory that is celebrated in the title is ambiguous with at least three different or conflicting connotations. Its ingredients variously consist of becoming a top scholar, attaining a pleasurable sex-life, and conforming to a rigorous moral code. The scholar-beauty paradigm is depicted as Wang takes first place in the civil examination and weds the lovely Lady Xie, a "marriage of talent and beauty." The delights of fulfilled sex drive are suggested through most of the action in the play. Despite the "official gauze cap," symbol of Confucian ethics, Wang determines to "seize the day," as translated by Professor Wu to suggest the concept of carpe diem in Western Epicureanism. The exigencies of the rigorous moral code, however, are not displayed until the conclusion of the play when Wang returns to her original female status. Most of the dialogue throughout the play reflects sex and drunkenness.

The author plays tricks on the reader or auditor by not revealing until the denouement that Wang's metamorphosis is an imaginary event and the play not a biographical portrayal of an actual human being. Only on brief occasions does Wang recognize her double identity and not until the denouement is she restored to her original status and taken in charge by the female Immortal Magu in a condition between life and death. The reader is at a loss to understand what has actually taken place. Has Wang spent twenty years of her life as a male or, as a recent scholar suggests, has she merely dreamed "an entire lifetime of blessings and happiness" during a period of only a few minutes in duration.* In only one of the poems attached to the play does the theme of gender inequality come to the fore although there do exist a few ripples in the primary text. Wang, in this poem, condemns Heaven for "creating chaos and letting the female be born handicapped" and reveals resentment for the lack of appreciation awarded to "talented ladies through the centuries." But this anger does not appear anywhere in the play itself. None of the female characters, wives, mothers, courtesans, concubines, or servants, reveals any major discontent with the social system. The only female character expressing discontent bases her hostility upon old age, not the conventions of society. Despite problems such as this, inherent in *A Dream of Glory*, it offers a fascinating view of both ideal and actual human relations in eighteenth-century China. Readers are greatly indebted to Professor Wu for her meticulous editing as well as translation that unites both the lyrical and metaphorical beauties of the original.

A. Owen Aldridge
Winter 2004

* Paul S. Ropp, "Love, Literacy, and Laments: The Themes of Women Writers in Late Imperial China," *Women's History Review* 2, no. 1 (1993): 126.

ACKNOWLEDGMENTS

I am very grateful to Professor A. Owen Aldridge, a world renowned comparatist, who had read my manuscript with interest and written a foreword for the work shortly before he passed away in January 2005. He will remain my inspiration for pursuing truth and beauty in East-West comparative studies. This project started in 2003 when I felt very encouraged after attending the symposium, "Daring to Imagine: Women's Voices in Drama and Politics in Imperial China," sponsored by the UCLA Center for Chinese Studies on October 18, 2003. Participants of the symposium, especially Yenna Wu, Ying Hu, Joan Judge, Susan Mann, and Kathryn Lowry, gave me their support and comments with enthusiasm. I am indebted to Ellen Widmer and Joan Judge, who read early drafts of the manuscript and made valuable suggestions. The challenging yet constructive comments made by several academic readers significantly enriched the contents of the introduction to the play. I would also like to express my deep gratitude to Professor Robert Hegel, who guided me kindly through my revisions of the manuscript with his profound knowledge in drama, printing history, and cultural milieu of Imperial China. I am also indebted to Paul Ropp, the pioneering scholar in the study of Wang Yun, whose generosity made me feel free to ask or discuss anything with him in the course of my research. I would say that the book would not come out as it is without the timely help from the scholar-poet Zhang Cuo and drama critic Hua Wei. With Zhang Cuo's assistance, Hua Wei mailed her two essential books on Ming Qing women's drama promptly from Taiwan. In a word, what I have learned from my colleagues and other scholars and friends is far beyond my expectations. Finally, I would like to thank the National Library of China, Beijing, for their permission to reproduce several images of the original woodblock print of *Fanhua meng* (Huaiqingtang Treasure Edition, 1778). I would also like to express my great appreciation to *Renditions* for publishing my translation of the four scenes of the play with a short introduction in 2005 and my indebtedness to the editors of The Chinese University Press in Hong Kong, who have worked so hard to bring this bilingual project to completion.

Qingyun Wu
October 2007, Los Angeles

A NOTE ON THE TRANSLATION

This translation is based on the original woodblock print of *Fanhua meng*, a Huaiqingtang Treasure Edition first published in the year of 1778. The play can be classified as a verse drama, with its libretto consisting of dialogue, verses, and arias. The original play was printed in two parts, with each part subdivided into two volumes. In this translation, I placed the first part as Act One and the second part as Act Two. The names of poetic tunes or singing tunes are all placed in brackets [ ]. If a *ci* tune or an aria appears more than once in the same scene, its frequency will be indicated by roman numerals in superscript. See Index to *Ci* Tunes and Index to Arias for more information. Following the original text, all singing in this play will be in bold print. The play is translated with its original prefaces and postfaces.

In classical Chinese plays, stage directions are assigned to performers such as "*sheng*" (leading male role), "*xiaosheng*" (young male character), "*dan*" (young leading female role), "*xiaodan*" (secondary female role), "*jing*" (older male role), "*mo*" (secondary male role), and "*chou*" (male role, clown, comic), because one performer often has to take on more than one role in the same play. To avoid confusion, I have assigned directions to the respective characters instead. Since each major character in the play is often addressed by more than one name, I provide a list of characters for handy reference.

In this play, as observed by Cyril Birch about other classical Chinese plays, "It is not very usual for the venue to change within a single scene but if it does the characters will indicate this by taking a few steps, perhaps circling the stage, and then announcing their arrival at the new location."* The stage direction "turn aside" means turning to the audience or talking to oneself rather than to anyone on the stage.

---

* Cyril Birch, trans., "Preface to the Second Edition," in *The Peony Pavilion: Mudan ting* (Bloomington: Indiana University Press, 2002), xiii.

ILLUSTRATIONS

1. The Front Cover Page. (Permission from the National Library of China, Beijing)

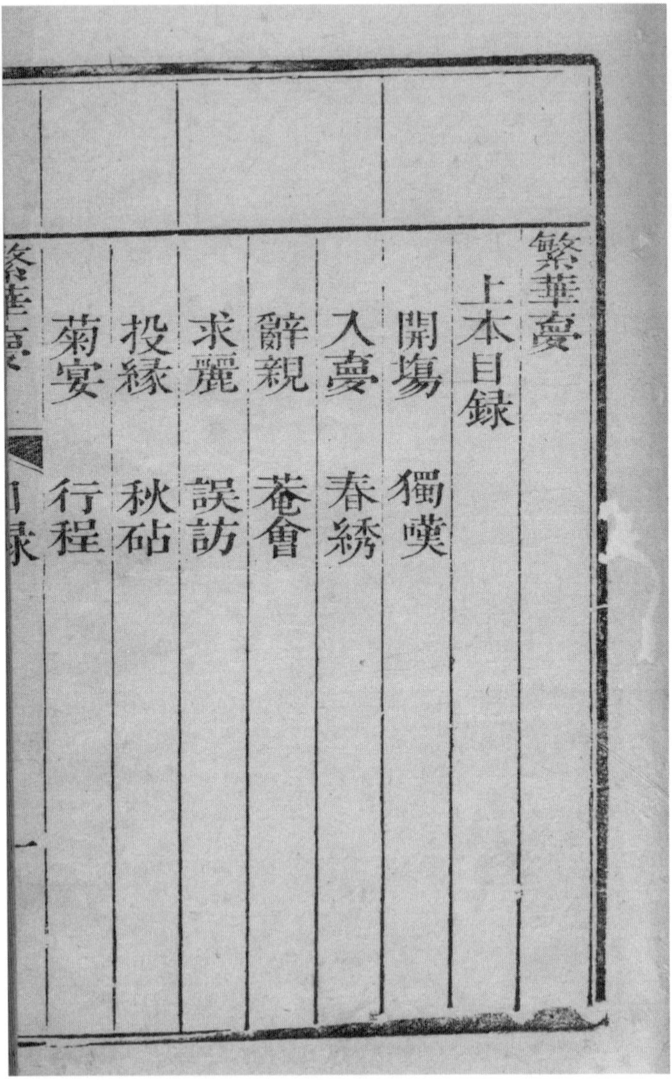

繁華夢

上本目録

開場　獨嘆

入夢　春綉

辭親　菴會

求麗　誤訪

投緣　秋砧

菊宴　行程

2. The Content Page Showing Act One. (Permission from the National Library of China, Beijing)

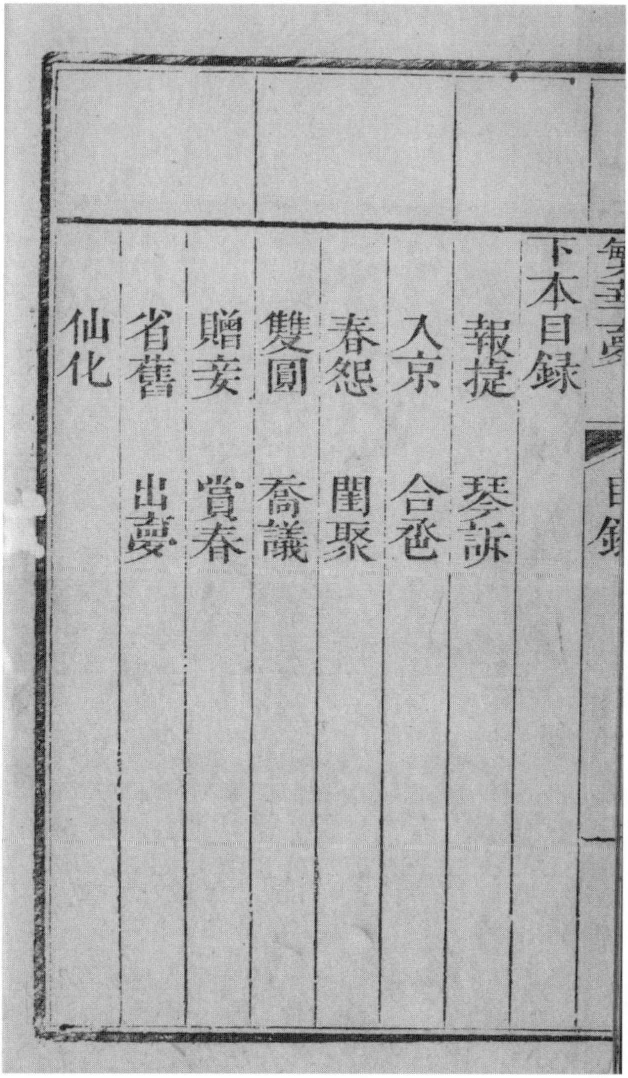

下本目録

報提 琴訴

入京 合巹

春怨 閨聚

雙圓 喬議

贈妾 賞春

省舊 出夢

仙化

3. The Content Page Showing Act Two. (Permission from the National Library of China, Beijing)

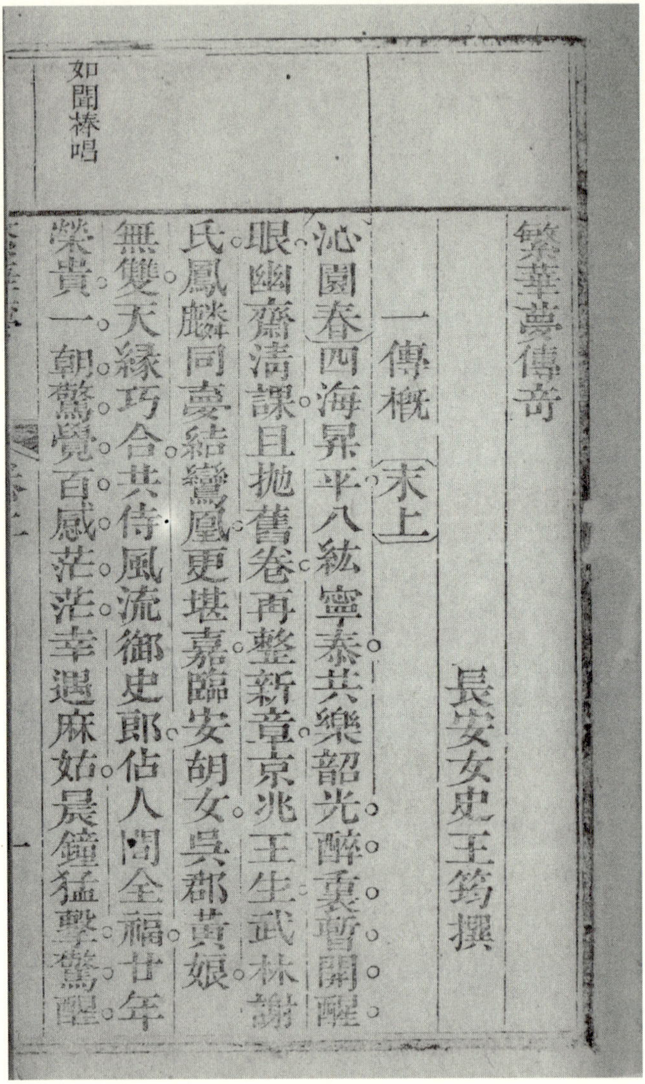

如聞棒喝

繁華夢傳奇

長安女史王筠撰

一　傳概　（末上）

（沁園春）四海昇平八紘寧泰共樂韶光醉裏曾開醒眼幽齋清課且拋舊卷再整新章京兆王生武林謝氏鳳麟同夢結鸞凰更堪嘉臨安胡女吳郡黃娘無雙天緣巧合共侍風流御史郎佔人間全福廿年榮貴一朝驚覺百感茫茫幸遇麻姑晨鐘猛擊驚醒

4. The First Page of Scene 1. (Permission from the National Library of China, Beijing)

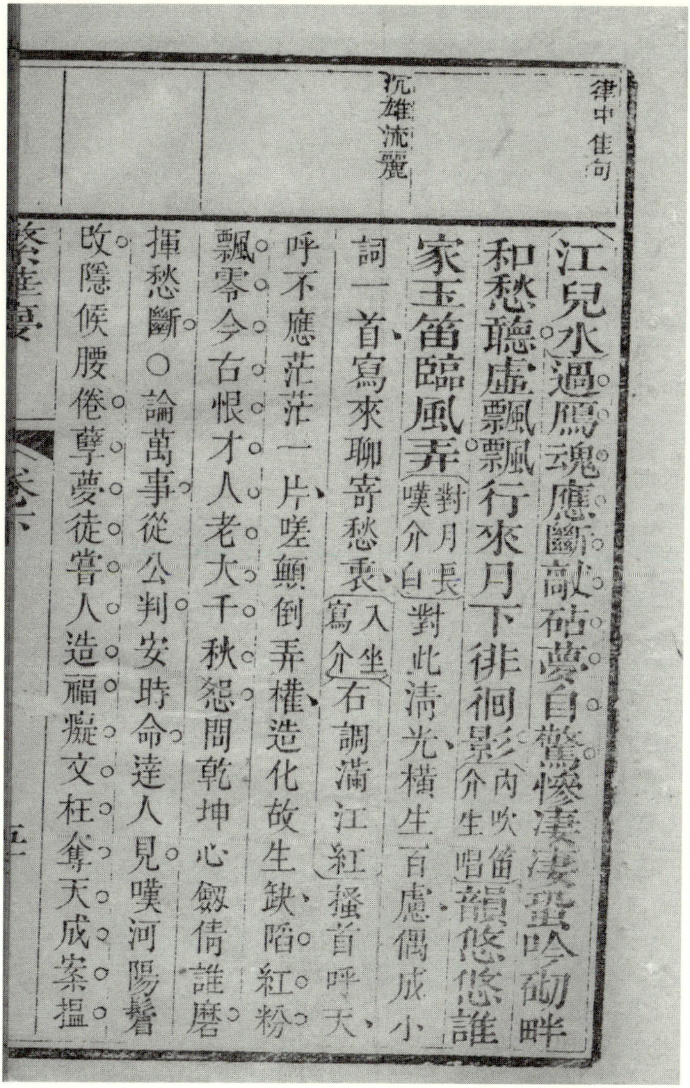

律中佳句

沉雄流麗

〔江兒水〕過鴈魂應斷敲砧夢自驚慘凄凄蛩吟砌畔和愁聽虛飄飄風行來月下徘徊影（內吹笛介生唱）韻悠悠誰家玉笛臨風弄（對月長嘆介白）對此清光橫生百慮偶成小詞一首寫來聊寄愁衷（入坐寫介）右調滿江紅搔首呼天呼不應茫茫一片嗟顛倒弄權造化故生缺陷紅粉飄零今古恨才人老大千秋怨問乾坤心緒倩誰磨揮愁斷〇論萬事從公判安時命達人見嘆河陽鬢改隱侯腰倦孽蔓徒嘗人造福癡文枉奪天成案揾

5. A Page from Scene 25 with Wang Yuanchang's Comments in the Head Margin. (Permission from the National Library of China, Beijing)

INTRODUCTION[1]

Wang Yun, a native of Chang'an (present-day Xi'an), was born in 1749. She wrote under the name Songping and was known by the sobriquet Lüchuang nüshi (Lady of the Green Window).[2] Her father Wang Yuanchang and her son Wang Bailing attained the academic rank of *jinshi*[3] respectively in 1748 and 1802. They both served as magistrates in Zhili[4]. In spite of her widowhood, Wang Yun continued her creative writing until her death in 1819. Over two hundred of her poems were published as the *Huaiqingtang ji* (Huaiqingtang Collection) and some were printed in *Xiyuan banxiang ji* (Fragrant Petals of the Western Garden) as a volume in a shared collection with her father's and son's poems. Wang Yun wrote three plays: *Fanhua meng* (A Dream of Glory, 1769), *Quanfu ji* (Full Happiness, 1779), and *Youxian meng* [A Dream Visit to the Immortals, n.d.; also known as *Huixian ji* (Meeting the Immortals)]. Well-known as a poet and dramatist during her lifetime, Wang has also received critical attention in contemporary China.

Chinese classical drama has had a considerable impact on the West since the eighteenth century. However, the tradition familiar to the West is primarily that of the male dramatists and their plays. At least twenty-five women dramatists appeared in late Imperial China from 1600 to 1911, with nineteen plays remaining extant in complete form.[5] Yet these women's works

---

[1] Part of this introduction was published in Wu Qingyun's article, "Daring to Dream: Wang Yun and Her Play *A Dream of Glory*," *Renditions*, no. 64 (Autumn 2005): 83–95.

[2] Xu Fuming, *Yuan Ming Qing xiqu tansuo* (Hangzhou: Zhejiang guji chubanshe, 1986), 271.

[3] *Jinshi* (presented scholar) was a successful candidate in the national imperial examination during the Ming and Qing dynasties.

[4] Zhili, meaning "directly ruled (by the imperial court)," was the name of Hebei province. It completely surrounded Beijing and Tianjin municipalities (which also border each other). Wang Yuanchang served as the county magistrate (*zhixian*) in Wuyi and Yongqing. Wang Bailing served as the county magistrate in Xincheng and prefecture magistrate (*zhizhou*) in Yanqing and became the city magistrate (*zhifu*) of Baoding before his retirement in 1819.

[5] See Hua Wei, *Ming Qing funü zhi xiqu chuangzuo yu piping* (Taipei: Zhongyang yanjiuyuan Zhongguo wenzhe yanjiusuo, 2003).

are little known in the West. Of these, Wang Yun's much praised *Fanhua meng*, previously assumed to have been lost,[6] deserves special attention. In 1993, while doing research on women's *tanci* novel,[7] I found the complete script of *Fanhua meng* in the National Library of China, Beijing, and was later fortunate enough to obtain a copy of the full text—a woodblock edition first carved by Huaiqingtang in 1778. It formed the basis for my study and translation of the play.

Due to lack of resources, Wang Yun has been understudied in Western scholarship, even though passing comments on her have been frequently made.[8] There is no index of Wang Yun in *Writing Women in Late Imperial China* published in 1997.[9] In 1999, Paul S. Ropp co-contributed the entry on Wang Yun in the monumental anthology *Women Writers of Traditional China*[10] and published an essay titled "'Now Cease Painting Eyebrows, Don a Scholar's Cap and Pin': The Frustrated Ambition of Wang Yun, Gentry Woman Poet and Dramatist" in *Ming Studies*. Ropp provided some biographical information on Wang Yun as well as analyzed her poems through his refined translation. But he also assumed that the extant script of *Fanhua meng* was mere fragments and the play, like Chen Duansheng's (1751–1796) *Zaisheng yuan* (The Destiny of the Next Life, 1796), was a woman's cross-dressing fantasy.[11] In mainland China, although Wang Yun has been discussed as a playwright and included in the studies of Ming Qing

[6] In 1930, the Chinese scholar Tan Zhengbi praised *Fanhua meng* as a feminist play, but he assumed that the complete script was no longer in existence. Some Western scholars have accepted Tan's assumption. See Tan Zhengbi, *Zhongguo nüxing wenxue shi*, 3rd ed. (Tianjin: Baihua wenyi chubanshe, 2001), 333.

[7] *Tanci*, a popular literary genre, belongs to the traditional category of telling-singing literature. *Tanci* novel is written in poetic form, resembling an ancient epic. Many *tanci* novels are over a thousand pages and are intended for reading. Some are also adapted as performing *tanci* and plays.

[8] Not to be confused with Wang Yun (1784–1854), a prominent male classical scholar and etymologist, from Anhui, Shandong.

[9] Ellen Widmer and Kang-i Sun Chang, eds., *Writing Women in Late Imperial China* (Stanford, CA: Stanford University Press, 1997).

[10] See Kang-i Sun Chang and Haun Saussy, eds., *Women Writers of Traditional China: An Anthology of Poetry and Criticism* (Stanford, CA: Stanford University Press, 1999), 532.

[11] See Paul S. Ropp, "'Now Cease Painting Eyebrows, Don a Scholar's Cap and Pin': The Frustrated Ambition of Wang Yun, Gentry Woman Poet and Dramatist," *Ming Studies*, no. 40 (Fall 1998): 89.

women playwrights by scholars such as Wang Yongkuan and Xu Fuming since the 1980s,[12] the study of Wang Yun and her plays remains largely introductory and there are no reprints of her plays in contrast to the modern republications of *tanci* novels by Ming Qing women. Taiwan scholar Hua Wei has devoted herself to the studies of Ming Qing women's drama since her graduate days in Berkeley. In 2003, she published her pioneering study, *Ming Qing funü zhi xiqu chuangzuo yu piping* (Drama Works and Criticisms by Ming Qing Women), and a valuable anthology of Ming Qing women's plays.[13] The critical volume includes her insightful analysis of Wang Yun's *Fanhua meng* and *Quanfu ji*. The texts of Wang Yun's two plays occupy half volume of her anthology. Both volumes, published in Chinese by Academia Sinica, are not easily accessible to the public and scholars outside Taiwan. Although Hua Wei used the same woodblock copy from the National Library of China as I did, her text omits one woodblock page from Scene 8, containing 157 characters. The voluminous English volume, *The Red Brush: Writing Women of Imperial China*, offers a hasty introduction of Wang Yun and her play *Fanhua meng*, which has several avoidable errors.[14] Its authors' assumption that Chinese women playwrights "may have preferred drama to prose fiction because of the higher status of drama (*zaju* and *chuanqi*) in the eyes of literati" does not really apply to Wang Yun.[15]

[12] See Xu Fuming, *Yuan Ming Qing xiqu tansuo*, 271; Wang Yongkuan, "Qingdai Shaanxi nüqujia Wang Yun," *Shaanxi shifan daxue xuebao* (Zhexue shehui kexue ban), no. 1 (1981): 109–112; Zhang Hua, "Qingdai nüzuojia Wang Yun," *Xi'an wanbao*, March 6, 1987; Zhou Miaozhong, "Ming Qing jutan nüzuojia," *Gudai xiqu luncong*, no. 1 (July 1983): 57–61; and Guo Mei, "Zhongguo gudai nüqujia de chuangzuo shijian ji xintai," *Gudai jindai wenxue yanjiu*, no. 8 (August 1995):41–45.

[13] Hua Wei, ed., *Ming Qing funü xiqu ji* (Taipei: Zhongyang yanjiuyuan Zhongguo wenzhe yanjiusuo, 2003). Also see n. 5.

[14] Wilt Idema and Beata Grant, *The Red Brush: Writing Women of Imperial China* (Cambridge, MA: Harvard University Asia Center, 2004), 677–685. Some errors found on p. 680 include: "Zhang Zhao" should be "Zhang Zao"; Wang Yun's father and son wrote postfaces, not prefaces; it was Zhang Fengsun, not his younger sister, who put up the money to have the play published. Moreover, it would not be accurate to call Wang Yun's protagonist in *Fanhua meng* a cross-dressing heroine. See my discussion on cross-dressing and cross-gender below.

[15] See Idema and Grant, *The Red Brush*, 677.

Fanhua meng is a rare full-length play by a Chinese woman of the eighteenth century. Wang Yun's authentic self-exploring voice and her unique theatrical representation of women of her time have sustained my enthusiasm in translating and editing the play into a book with two parts: the English part contains the annotated translation of *Fanhua meng*, with translated original prefaces and postfaces, a bibliography of Ming Qing women playwrights and references; the Chinese part includes the edited texts of *Fanhua meng* with the original margin comments by Wang Yuanchang (now placed in footnote format) and the original prefaces and postfaces. Together with this introduction of mine, this volume hopes to make a contribution to the reading, teaching, and researching of Wang Yun's *Fanhua meng* and addresses the needs of general readers as well as scholars.

Women Playwrights and the Eighteenth-Century Milieu for Women's Writing

Chinese drama is a multimedia art form consisting of arias, lyrics, speech, vocal and instrumental music, and acting that may include dance, mime, and acrobatics. Its style ranges from highly refined poetic diction in verses to crude street language in dialogues. In spite of the complex nature of opera music, six women writers had stepped into the drama arena by the end of the Ming dynasty.[16] Chinese women dramatists adopted the "Northern drama" (*zaju*) as their favorite form.[17] Wang Yun's *Fanhua meng*, however, is a "Southern drama" (*chuanqi*).

Chuanqi, as described by Cyril Birch, is "a long lyrical work with a cavalcade of scenes. Such plays, or rather operas, were intended for performances before an elite audience, usually in a private household, often during the leisure days of a festival."[18] *Zaju* is a drama genre of one to four

[16] These women dramatists include: Ma Shouzhen (1604–1649), Ruan Lizhen (late Ming), Ye Xiaowan (1613–1657?), Liang Xiaoyu (late Ming), Liang Mengzhao (Ming), and Jiang Yujie (late Ming). For more about these dramatists, see the "Women Playwrights of the Ming and Qing Dynasties" section in the Bibliography.

[17] Xu Fuming, *Yuan Ming Qing xiqu tansuo*, 265.

[18] See Cyril Birch, trans., "Preface to the Second Edition," in *The Peony Pavilion: Mudan ting* (Bloomington: Indiana University Press, 2002), xii.

regular acts[19] and has a fixed order of arias with a single lead role singing in each act; whereas the genre *chuanqi* breaks the rigidity of *zaju* with a free choice of arias, multiple singers, and chorus and utilizes more percussion rather than string instruments. Writing *chuanqi*, rather than *zaju*, allowed Wang Yun to stage her dreams in a more extensive and flexible dramatic form.

To understand Wang Yun as a dramatist and to appreciate the significance of *Fanhua meng*, we need to understand the political, cultural, and literary environment for women's writing in the eighteenth century. According to Dorothy Ko, women's voices of the seventeenth-century China surfaced in historical records especially with urbanization, commercialization, and print culture.[20] Susan Mann noted a pen/brush shift from the hands of late Ming courtesans to the hands of Qing *guixiu* (ladies of the boudoir), including wives and widows. About half of the extant works by over three thousand women writers are from the High Qing period (1683–1839).[21] During this period, the education of daughters grew in importance. The famous poet and educator Yuan Mei (1716–1798) not only openly accepted women as his students but also published their poems.[22] The debates between conservative and liberal scholars on women's education and their writing marked the eighteenth century as the age of the *querelle des femmes*.[23]

Meanwhile, promotion of Confucian ideal gender codes and the "widow chastity cult" by the Manchurian government reinforced female seclusion within home and intensified learned women's desire to break out of their immobility through imagination. This accounts for the rise in popularity of

[19] In *zaju*, any act could be preceded by an introduction to the main action or a brief extension of it known as a "wedge."

[20] Dorothy Ko, *Teachers of the Inner Chambers: Women and Culture in Seventeenth-Century China* (Stanford, CA: Stanford University Press, 1994).

[21] See Susan Mann, *Precious Records: Women in China's Long Eighteenth Century* (Stanford, CA: Stanford University Press, 1997), 83–94.

[22] At least ten volumes of women's poems were published under Yuan Mei's influence. See Yuan Mei, comp., *Suiyuan nüdizi shi, Suiyuan quanji* (N.p.: Wenming shuju, n.d.); and Yuan Mei, *Suiyuan shihua*, 2 vols., ed. Gu Xuexie (Beijing: Renmin wenxue chubanshe, 1982).

[23] "Querelle des femmes" means "debate about women." For the debate between Yuan Mei and Zhang Xuecheng (1738–1801), see Susan Mann, "Learned Women in the Eighteenth Century," in *Engendering China: Women, Culture, and the State*, ed. Christina K. Gilmartin et al. (Cambridge, MA: Harvard University Press, 1994), 27–46.

caizi jiaren (scholar-beauty) romances and cross-dressing plays and *tanci* novels.[24] Xu Wei (1521–1593) established the pro-feminist drama tradition with his famous *Ci Mulan tifu congjun* (Female Mulan Joins the Army in Her Father's Stead, ca. 1556) and *Nü zhuangyuan cihuang defeng* (The Female Number One Scholar Declines a She-Phoenix and Gets a He-Phoenix, 1577–1579),[25] while Tang Xianzu (1550–1616) anticipated the Qing celebration of *qing* (love/passion) in his masterpiece *Mudan ting* (The Peony Pavilion).[26] In addition, the eighteenth century also witnessed the circulation of Chen Duansheng's *tanci* novel *Zaisheng yuan*[27] and Cao Xueqin's (1715–1763) *Honglou meng* (The Dream of the Red Chamber, 1791).[28] The former is a strong feminist fantasy while the latter presents a fresh appreciation of women and female values. All this contributed to the climate in which Wang Yun wrote her play *Fanhua meng*.

In the long history of Imperial China, women had never been allowed to compete with men for official ranks and titles through civil service examinations. Wang Yun, a woman with extraordinary talent and ambition, had been stifled throughout her life with the restrictions imposed on her by cultural gender norms. Although mainstream Confucian culture enshrined Huang Chonggu and Hua Mulan as female models, Wang Yun was intelligent enough to see that this paragon system was an unrealistic trap for women. Instead of being encouraged, women were torn between the

---

[24] For a sample analysis of scholar-beauty romances, see Martin W. Huang, *Desire and Fictional Narrative in Late Imperial China* (Cambridge, MA: Harvard University Asia Center, 2001), 206–235. For the cross-dressing tradition in Chinese drama, see Siu Leung Li, *Cross-dressing in Chinese Opera* (Hong Kong: Hong Kong University Press, 2003).

[25] Xu Wei, *Ci Mulan tifu congjun*, in his *Sisheng yuan, Gedai xiao (fu)*, ed. Zhou Zhongming (Shanghai: Shanghai guji chubanshe, 1984), 44–59; and Xu Wei, *Nü zhuangyuan cihuang defeng*, in ibid., 62–106.

[26] For an insightful discussion of Xu Wei and his two plays, see Ann-Marie Hsiung, "A Feminist Re-vision of Xu Wei's *Ci Mulan* and *Nü zhuangyuan*," in *China in a Polycentric World: Essays in Chinese Comparative Literature*, ed. Yingjin Zhang (Stanford, CA: Stanford University Press, 1998), 73–89. For an analysis of *The Peony Pavilion*, see Tina Lu, *Persons, Roles and Minds: Identity in Peony Pavilion and Peach Blossom Fan* (Stanford, CA: Stanford University Press, 2001).

[27] Chen Duansheng, *Zaisheng yuan* (Zhengzhou: Zhongzhou shuhuashe, 1982).

[28] The best translation is by David Hawkes. See David Hawkes, trans., *The Story of the Stone: A Chinese Novel*, 5 vols. (New York: Penguin, 1973–1986).

traditional duties of a virtuous lady and the demands of such legends, and were often frustrated and beset with an inferiority complex. Wang Yun's strong resentment over her fate as a woman and her yearning for equal opportunity in public service as well as in private life compelled her to write *Fanhua meng* as wish fulfillment.

The question of how Wang Yun was able to write *Fanhua meng* at the age of twenty during the eighteenth century leads to an exploration of the progression of women's development from spectator, reader, performer to playwright. According to Xu Muyun,[29] during the period of the Three Kingdoms, *youren*, professional male actors, began to wear women's attire and act the female parts. During the Tang dynasty, the imperial troupe Liyuan (Pear Garden)[30] consisted of two groups: male performers and female performers. In the Jin period (1115–1234), courtesans were so involved in acting that the scripts they used were known as *yuanben*,[31] which became the name for the principal form of Jin dynasty theater. Ming women dramatists Ma Shouzhen and Liang Xiaoyu were both courtesans. During the seventeenth century, Shang Xiaoling, a famous actress of Hangzhou in the Ming Chongzhen period, became so involved in the role of Du Liniang, the heroine of *Mudan ting*, that she literally died on stage during the scene "Pursuing the Dream."[32] Women constituted a major portion of audiences and readers of Chinese dramas, especially dramas of romance. It is striking that *Mudan ting* reached near-cult status among young women spectators and readers, similar to the impact of Goethe's *The Sorrows of Young Werther* (1774) upon young male readers in eighteenth-century Europe. During the

[29] See Xu Muyun, *Zhongguo xiju shi* (Shanghai: Shanghai guji chubanshe, 2001), 11.

[30] Under the patronage of Emperor Xuanzong (r. 712–756), over three hundred young entertainers were selected to form a prototype drama academy, known as the Pear Garden, for performing dharma melodies and Buddhist moralities shows. Today, the term "Pear Garden" refers to theater or drama troupes and "Disciple of the Pear Garden" (*liyuan zidi*) refers to a play performer.

[31] The people of Jin addressed courtesan courts as *hangyuan*. Therefore, *yuanben* stands for the scripts used for performing in *hangyuan*. See Xu Muyun, *Zhongguo xiju shi*, 42. But some scholars assume that *hangyuan* was where theatrical troupes stayed. *Yuanben* were *zaju* scripts they used after Jin took Beijing as its Capital. See Yu Qiuyu, *Zhongguo xiju shi* (Shanghai: Shanghai jiaoyu chubanshe, 2006), 86.

[32] See Yu Weimin, ed., *Zhongguo gudai sida mingju* (Nanjing: Jiangsu guji chubanshe, 1998), 100.

seventeenth century, the passion that women had for writing commentaries on the play, in addition to several female deaths, has drawn scholarly interest in exploring "the unprecedented intensity of the female reactions to *The Peony Pavilion*."[33] The ways women finally made the transition from readers and commentators of drama to writers for the stage are a fascinating, if not well-documented, process.

According to Xu Fuming, most Qing women dramatists were either wives or relatives of dramatists. Wang Yun, however, was not directly related to the professional drama world. Her knowledge of arias largely came from her experience as a spectator and reader of plays. With extensive readings in Yuan *zaju* and Ming Qing *chuanqi* and frequent visits to theater, Wang Yun wrote over thirty commentary poems on various plays, all collected in *Xiyuan banxiang ji*. Wang Yun was not only a passionate spectator but was also acquainted with actresses from the Xi'an theater. She once praised their performance as the best of the Pear Garden and their singing and expression as "superbly natural."[34] It is therefore not surprising that Wang Yun could flexibly employ over sixty arias in her play. Her talent can also be seen in the casual verses in *daobai* (spoken sections in a play), which she employs with the sophistication of the classical dramatists.

Fanhua meng and *Zaisheng yuan*

Fanhua meng is Wang Yun's first play. Choosing the right title is like "dotting the eye in drawing a dragon." The title *Fanhua meng* is the eye of the play. In English, "dream" is unquestionably the equivalent of "*meng*." But the word "*fanhua*," with its frequent appearances throughout the text, has three layers of meaning: (1) worldly success, desire-fulfillment, and the related luxury and extravagance; (2) the best or the apex; (3) beauty, grandeur, and magnificence. It is difficult to find an English word that encompasses all these meanings. The obvious choices are "glory" and "splendor." The former captures the story and sheds light on Wang Yun's portrayal of the protagonist Lady Wang's dream of glory as human vanity at the end of the play. However, the word "splendor" conveys the last two meanings better. Although this is the story of

[33] See Judith T. Zeitlin, "Shared Dreams: The Story of the Three Wives' Commentary on *The Peony Pavilion*," *Harvard Journal of Asiatic Studies* 54, no. 1 (June 1994): 129.

[34] See *Zhongguo xiqu zhi · Shaanxi juan* (Xi'an: Zhongguo xiqu zhi, Shaanxi juan bianweihui, 1985), 700.

one lady's dream, the play itself is a splendor created from Wang Yun's imagination and brush. At the end of Scene 19, Wang Yun celebrates Lady Wang's academic and romantic successes with the happy line, "We've won the first beacon of splendor in our land." Similarly, with her play *Fanhua meng*, Wang Yun attempts to achieve the first place in a contest for literary accomplishment. Disillusionment made Wang Yun realize that the only escape from the claustrophobia of her boudoir was through writing. She believed that the splendor of her play might give her a possible immortality. On the whole, *A Dream of Splendor* might be a title that better conveys the essence of the play. However, I have chosen the title *A Dream of Glory* because it encapsulates the movement from fantasy to an awakening to reality.

Wang Yun's *Fanhua meng* tells the fascinating story of a woman in love with three other women and with success in a man's world. Its plot is cleverly conceived: In her studio, Wang Menglin[35] feels frustrated because she cannot be a military commander such as Ban Chao (33–103) or an immortal poet such as Li Bai (701–762). She does not even have an opportunity to emulate the female legends of Hua Mulan and Huang Chonggu.[36] Since she is deprived of the right to excel through the civil service examinations, she can only express her feelings in the form of a dream. In her frustration she turns her attention to a portrait of a beautiful lady. Her attraction to the lady reminds her of her longing for two other beauties, Lady Hu and Lady Huang. Her love for the three ladies compounds her frustration over her fate of being a woman. Overwhelmed by boredom, she falls asleep. In her dream she is transformed into a male. With this male body, she can realize her ambition to pursue both an official career and a free love life.

To seek the ladies of his heart, Wang Menglin leaves for West Lake and there he becomes engaged to Lady Hu of Hangzhou and Lady Huang of Suzhou. As his plans for marriage hinge upon his official success, Wang travels to the Capital, where he achieves first place in the national imperial examination. He begins to serve at the court alongside his father. Wang worries over his engagement to the two ladies because he has not yet secured

---

[35] Wang is the family name of the playwright; "*meng*" means dream and "*lin*" means unicorn. The unicorn is traditionally a male image, similar to the dragon, suggestive of luck, nobility, and success. The name conveys the intent of Wang Yun's alter ego in the play.

[36] For more information on Ban Chao, Li Bai, Hua Mulan, and Huang Chonggu, see Scene 2, n. 1 to n. 4.

parental permission. Meanwhile, his mother arranges his engagement to Lady Xie, the lady in the painting, who, to his surprise, surpasses both Lady Hu and Lady Huang in beauty, intelligence, and family background. To please Lady Xie, he agrees to annul his previous engagements. But after admonishing him playfully, Lady Xie accepts Hu and Huang as his concubines. Later on, Wang buys two singing girls for his brother as a token of gratitude. This causes a dramatic misunderstanding from his three wives, who fear that the girls will become Wang's concubines as well. Wang gives the two girls to his brother, and then finds a wife for his servant Yaoqin. Everyone in the mansion lives in perfect happiness. However, after twenty years of marital bliss, he awakens at a party to find himself having been changed back into a female, complete with a skirt and hairpins.

Restored as a woman, Wang finds it hard to accept that the loss of her wealth, fame, and love is simply caused by returning to her original gender. Finally, the Immortal Magu[37] relieves Wang from her extreme perplexity and pain by revealing the emptiness of worldly fame, wealth, and love. The play ends with Wang's negation of her dream and fantasy with the message:

> A woman as well as a man needs
> A wakening return from a life gone astray.

Wang Yun's *Fanhua meng* is the most significant play, as Chen Duansheng's *Zaisheng yuan* is the most significant *tanci* novel, produced by an eighteenth-century woman. It is important to compare the two works and their authors to appreciate their different visions under a similar utopian impulse. Chen Duansheng was born in 1751. She and Wang Yun coincidentally started writing in the same year of 1769. Chen finished first sixteen books by the time she was twenty and added another book at the age of forty-two. She left her work, an epic of over a thousand pages, unfinished upon her death in 1796. Although both Chen and Wang turned to writing as a wish fulfillment to escape the secluded boudoir life through utopian fantasies, Chen adopts the tactics of cross-dressing while Wang employs a framework that relies on a bodily gender change. Cross-dressing allows Chen Duansheng to preserve a female identity under a male guise so as to raise questions about gender inequality and to project radical feminist ideas, whereas the cross-gender change enables Wang Yun to see through the concept of glory based on male values. Although Meng Lijun, the protagonist

[37] See Scene 1, n. 4.

of *Zaisheng yuan*, and Lady Wang of *Fanhua meng* both strike into the masculine world and earn first place in the national imperial examinations, Meng Lijun spurns sexual and romantic love for a career in politics and power. She even rejects her parents in order to retain her position as the prime minister of the country. Even though Meng Lijun lives with a woman as her husband and challenges the notion that a woman cannot marry another woman, her seemingly lesbian position is more a transient strategy to disguise her female gender than a political critique. But Lady Wang's dream of success in the masculine world is kindled by her passion for three women. She always values love over career even after she gains fame and wealth as a man. Reluctant to allow Meng Lijun to be restored to her feminine role, Chen Duansheng left her novel unfinished at the point where her protagonist risks death rather than yield to the intimidation of the emperor who wants to possess her as a concubine. In contrast, Wang Yun deconstructs her dream of glory after exhausting its possibilities and questions the practical value of such cross-dressing fantasies that became almost stereotyped in drama and popular fiction during her time. In addition to stressing the desire to be successful in academic and court careers, Wang Yun equally emphasizes the fullness of a woman's love life, so dependent on wealth and power in her society. The essential difference between *Zaisheng yuan* and *Fanhua meng* indicates different choices of life a woman could have in a utopia unrestricted by gender difference.

Cross-dressing and Cross-gender

From the seventeenth century to the end of Imperial China, cross-dressing plots in popular fiction and drama were prevalent. In the women's favorite genre of *tanci*, according to *Tanci xulu*, fifty-three out of two hundred *tanci* novels involve the plot of cross-dressing.[38] In twelve novels, men wear female clothing to escape danger. But ironically, female garments throw those men into unexpected dangers of being kidnapped, shut into deep palaces, and forced to become concubines or maids. No matter how capable a man is, once he assumes female clothing, he instantly becomes humiliated, powerless, immobile, and above all a sexual prey. Female clothing embodies the cultured gender that bears patriarchal prejudices against women and social codes imposed on women. On the contrary, a woman's cross-dressing, no matter

[38] Tan Zhengbi and Tan Xun, *Tanci xulu* (Shanghai: Shanghai guji chubanshe, 1981).

how banal, has been her attempt to steal equal opportunities with men. Not surprisingly, Xu Wei's two cross-dressing plays *Ci Mulan* and *Nü zhuangyuan* were received as empowering plays for women during Wang Yun's time.[39] However, Wang Yun was not much influenced by Xu Wei. She chose a transsexual or cross-gender strategy for her protagonist to maneuver in the masculine arena.

Wang Yun did not originate the notion that a female body be transformed into a male one. The idea might have come from the play *Wusheng xi: Bian nü wei er pusa qiao* (Silent Show: A Female Turns Male by a Buddhist Miracle) written by the famous playwright Li Yu (1611–1680),[40] reflecting the Mahayana Buddhist belief that a female apostle can achieve Buddhahood through metaphorical sexual transformation. However, Wang Yun is the first and only playwright who employs such a cross-gender device to purposely set a woman free with all her desires from her oppressed social and psychological state.

The essential difference between cross-dressing and cross-gender as a dramatic means to liberate women can be seen through the differences between Xu Wei's and Wang Yun's attitude toward the prototypes of Mulan and Chonggu. Hua Mulan, a legendary girl who took her aged father's place and fought twelve years in male disguise, first appeared in "Mulan shi," a folk ballad of the Northern Wei dynasty. As soon as the war ends, Mulan removes her male garments and retires to her boudoir. In contrast, Huang Chonggu, the daughter of a Tang commander, cross-dressed as a boy since childhood and served as an officer. A prefecture governor called Zhou Xiang wanted to marry her daughter to Chonggu for his exceptional intelligence and ability. Chonggu replied with a poem, including the line: "I wish Heaven soon turns me into a man," and signed her title as *jinshi*. Chonggu remained single all her life but unfortunately never had opportunity to earn an academic title. Xu Wei embraced these two prototypes heartily. In *Ci Mulan*, he amplifies the dutifulness of Mulan and adds his male anxiety over her masculinization as well as his obsession with female chastity. Mulan worries about how to restore

[39] See Hsiung, "A Feminist Re-vision of Xu Wei's *Ci Mulan* and *Nü zhuangyuan*," 73–89.

[40] See *Li Yu quanji* (Hangzhou: Zhejiang guji chubanshe, 1992). Pu Songling (1640–1715) and Yuan Mei (1716–1798) also wrote strange tales of a female turning male. For detailed discussion, see Charlotte Furth, "Androgynous Males and Deficient Females: Biology and Gender Boundaries in Sixteenth- and Seventeenth-Century China," *Late Imperial China* 9, no. 2 (December 1988): 16–18.

the size of her lotus feet for marriage and the first thing after the war to report to her parents is that she has kept her virginity. In *Nü zhuangyuan*, Xu Wei elevates the historical Chonggu to *zhuangyuan* (higher than *jinshi*) and even lets her serve as a capable government official for over three years. However, Chonggu appears meeker than the average woman with the revelation of her sexual identity as if she needs to atone for the cross-dressing crime by returning to the kitchen. Xu Wei's Mulan and Chonggu are, like their prototypes, empowering women. But by upholding marriage as a woman's ultimate goal and molding each to a potential dutiful wife and good mother, Xu Wei undeniably confines them firmly within the patriarchal social and moral order.

Wang Yun might not, like our scholars today, have the critical insight of feminist subversion as well as patriarchal containment embodied in Xu Wei's plays, but she was obviously intelligent enough to see through the Mulan-Chonggu paragon system as an unrealistic trap for women. Instead of being inspired, a woman, torn between the traditional duties of a virtuous lady and the demands of those super models, was often mired in an alienation complex.

In Scene 2 of *Fanhua meng*, Wang Menglin laments in a poem:

> Buried deep in the boudoir for a dozen years,
> I can be neither an official nor an immortal.
> Every reading rouses my admiration for Ban Chao;
> Holding a wine cup, I chant the poems of Li Bai.
> In spite of my soaring ambition,
> I am not fated to be a Mulan or a Chonggu.
> Since I have no share in the Jade Court and Golden Steed,[41]
> I can only pour my fantasies into a dream.

The sixth line of this poem not only states that the emulation of Mulan and Chonggu is not in her fate but also implies that her ideal self differs from them. The best way to view those differences is through analyzing the differences between *Fanhua meng* and *Ci Mulan* and *Nü zhuangyuan*.

Cross-dressing limits the masculine assertiveness of Xu Wei's Mulan and Chonggu by being exigent, temporary, and transitory. Mulan's disguise as a male warrior is justified by a national crisis and the inability of her aged father

[41] After Tang and Song, the Jade Court (Yutang) refers to the Hanlin Academy. In popular culture, it also refers to wealth and position. The line means that born as a woman, one is denied the opportunity to be either a scholar or a commander.

and underage brother to serve while Chonggu's usurpation of the *zhuangyuan* title and governing office under male guise is driven by poverty and livelihood. Although they surpass men in those fields considered masculine, Xu Wei makes certain that their true identities are always feminine. Before embarking on her adventures, Mulan thinks about marriage after the war and Chonggu declares that she will withdraw from the masculine arena as soon as she makes enough money. For such heroines, masculinity serves as mere garments; cross-dressing is an exigent means; and acting as a man is only a transitory phase in life. But Wang Yun, as a woman playwright, thought differently. She insisted that masculinity can be a woman's true identity, and regarded herself as a masculine soul trapped in a female body. Her ideal models, as shown in the above poem, were Ban Chao and Li Bai. She despised her fate of being a woman simply because a woman of her time was "born handicapped."[42] The boudoir, like an extended female body or jailhouse, imprisoned her ambition and wasted her talent. In her old age, Wang Yun summed up her womanly life as "a bird with tied up feathers and culled wings." This explains why she chose the strategy of a cross-gender identity rather than cross-dressing to dream the impossible. Cross-gender transformation by becoming a man, or his absolute equal, is her life desire, permanent struggle, and ultimate goal.

In the first stage of feminist wakening in history, a woman's imitation of a successful man is inevitable, because our civilization has generally accredited positive human qualities such as intelligence, strength, bravery to men and negative qualities such as frailty, vileness, and jealousy to women. A man has ambition and glory whereas a woman can only have virtue and feminine charms. What makes Wang Yun a playwright for women is her honesty in handling female masculine desire. Wang Menglin's cross-gender transformation is not caused by any exigency or external factor but driven by her own ambition and lesbian passion. In a sense, Wang Yun ignores the patriarchal moral order. On the contrary, Xu Wei ignores masculinity as innate part of an androgynous woman. To Wang Yun, masculinity is not necessarily the birthright of a man but is certainly an essential part of an ideal being. It is not surprising that Wang Yun demands a *sheng* (a young male lead) to play her protagonist in *Fanhua meng*, whereas Xu Wei limits his Mulan or Chonggu to *dan* (a young female lead). In Chinese drama, it does not matter

---

[42] Brief quotations that are not noted are either from the play *Fanhua meng* or its prefaces and postfaces; they can be easily located in this book.

whether *sheng* is acted by a man or a woman. But *sheng* must represent on stage the image of a dashing young male with handsome vitality and masculine spirit. Such a young male is the idealized image for many strong women such as Wang Yun.

Insistence on chastity in *Ci Mulan* and *Nü zhuangyuan* reveals a patriarchal male desire to have absolute control over female sexuality. Surprisingly, as early as in the eighteenth century, Wang Yun, being an elite learned lady, was not only quite open with female sexual desire but also unscrupulous enough to profane female chastity on stage. Her play breaks the convention of monogamous lesbian love and is transparent with sexual imageries such as the pounding of washing and erotic longing.

Chinese classical drama tradition requires a play, especially a *chuanqi*, to end in a *da tuanyuan* (grand reunion) scene where everybody falls into the proper space prescribed by the Confucian system. *Ci Mulan* and *Nü zhuangyuan*, known for their innovative subject matter, turn rather conservative with such banal happy endings. The former ends with Mulan's marriage by her father's arrangement while the latter ends with the nuptial match of Chonggu with the prime minister's son. Wang Yun's *Fanhua meng* radically breaks away from this tradition. Instead of a grand reunion, things completely fall apart. In drama, cross-gender, like cross-dressing, is after all a mere literary device for exercising utopian imagination. The awakened Wang Menglin cannot find her proper place with the sudden disappearance of fame, position, and love. But she refuses to reconcile with a woman's fate as prescribed by the convention. Her spiritual crisis, with doubled alienation, culminates into a poetic protest in the last scene:

> Scratching my head, I complain to Heaven.
> The vast void sends back no response.
> Why should you abuse your power in
> Creating chaos and letting the female be born handicapped?
> Can't you explain the deep-rooted resentment of a woman,
> Whose fate has been scattered like Pink Powder?
> Can't you appreciate the sorrows of
> talented ladies through centuries?
> Heaven and Earth, may I ask
> Who can sharpen the fine sword of the heart?
> Please cut off my sorrows and frustrations!

This last scene poem and the second scene poem I quoted earlier well reflect Wang Yun's resistance as a marginal member of the patriarchal society.

Capturing her personal experience with inkstone, brush, and paper, Wang Yun's play, though with bursts of frustration and melancholia, reveals the subjectivity or autonomic quest of an ambitious lady imprisoned in the boudoir. Even with the assumed loss of the script, critics have hailed *Fanhua meng* as a feminist play because of these two thematic poems that have never ceased circulation in over two hundred years.

Wang Menglin's cross-gender transformation and endeavor toward masculine glory is reminiscent of a twelfth-century Japanese novel, *The Changelings*.[43] It is known as the world's first cross-gender novel. Its story actually contains no physical change but a swap of gender roles between a sister and a brother. Sister Chonagon grew up as a tomboy, better suited for male life, whereas her brother grew up effeminate, preferring to live a female life. But eventually Chonagon has to withdraw from her court service as warrior general due to an accidental pregnancy, and her brother has to remove feminine garments and replace her as the general. But due to the swapping experience, both siblings were improved; the behavioral difference between the male and the female was narrowed. This novel demonstrates that a person's gender character is defined by a composite of innate personality and cultural and social environments. Likewise for Wang Menglin, cross-gender change supports her androgynous identity and justifies her struggle for opportunities in the masculine world. However, love in *The Changelings* is conventionally male-centered and heterosexual. In contrast, in *Fanhua meng*, Wang Menglin's cross-gender transformation intends to fulfill her lesbian desire more than her desire for masculine success.

Lesbian Desire and Women-Centered Polygamy

Although just as Xu Wei's Chonggu, Wang Menglin successfully obtains the title of *zhuangyuan* and serves at the imperial court equally with her father, Wang Yun does not focus on her performance in politics or office but emphasizes her emotional life in the domestic world. Wang Yun values *qing* over fame, wealth, and career. She did not write *qing* as those frustrated male literati in order to compensate for their career setbacks. She is similar to her contemporary, Cao Xueqin, who originally conceived *Honglou meng* as a

[43] Rosette F. Willig, trans., *The Changelings: A Classical Japanese Court Tale* (Stanford, CA: Stanford University Press, 1983).

chuanqi play rather than a novel. Cao Xueqin and Wang Yun were both influenced by the celebration of *qing* in Tang Xianzu's *Mudan ting*. They adhered to the late Ming liberal treatment of *qing* and *yu* (lust/desire) as a central discursive site to reformulate self-identity.[44] As a woman writing a play about a woman and her world, Wang Yun's redefining *qing* as the passion of a woman for women is significant. A woman's love is supposed to be centered for a man; such love has produced innumerous "boudoir love-sick" (*guiyuan*) poems. By celebrating lesbian *qing*, Wang Yun's protagonist discards her boredom and passivity and becomes an active agent pursuing her fantasy world.

By imagining a gender reversal achieved through physical transformation rather than mere clothing change, Wang Yun legitimizes lesbian desire and creates the possibility to fulfill this desire on stage. Some readers feel it difficult to accept *Fanhua meng* as a lesbian play, because Wang Menglin becomes a man and behaves like a man after body transformation. But one cannot ignore the fact that Wang's gender change is dominantly driven by her desire to fulfill her love for three beautiful ladies. Even after her cross-gender change, in the eye of the audience, she is always a woman on stage.

Although Chinese women writers tend to reveal love for their own sex, the best lesbian representation in Chinese classical literature is *Jinyu yuan* (Romance of Gold Fish), a long *tanci* novel by Sun Deying published in 1871.[45] In Chen Duansheng's *Zaisheng yuan*, Meng Lijun never shows passion for men but expresses desire for her maid Su Yingxue. After they get married as man and wife, they live a happy life. However, Su Yingxue loves Shaohua, a handsome young man, at first sight. The marriage with Meng Lijun on her part may not be completely satisfactory. In Sun Deying's *Jinyu yuan*, Qian Shurong, in male attire, marries Li Yu'e. The two women love each other passionately. After Shurong becomes *zhuangyuan* and minister of punishment, she is able to retain her male masquerade with the support of Yu'e. After a fulfilling active life, she retires to West Lake with Yu'e. Meng

[44] For detailed discussion of *qing* during the Ming and Qing, see Huang, *Desire and Fictional Narrative in Late Imperial China*, 1–85; and Maram Epstein, *Competing Discourses: Orthodoxy, Authenticity, and Engendered Meanings in Late Imperial Chinese Fiction* (Cambridge, MA: Harvard University Asia Center, 2001), 61–119.

[45] Sun Deying, *Huitu Jinyu yuan* (Shanghai: Shanghai shuju, Qing Guangxu Guimao [1871]).

Lijun's unfulfilled dreams are all realized by Shurong through a lesbian bond. Although there is no historical evidence of her intimate contact with other women, Sun Deying rejected all marriage proposals in her life and hid in the boudoir reciting Buddhist Sutra and writing. In a sense, we may say that Sun Deying fled to a life of nunnery to escape heterosexual love and submerged her lesbian desire. Similarly there is no historical evidence that Wang Yun was a lesbian. As she gave birth to Wang Bailing at the age of twenty-two, she must have been facing marriage or just married when she wrote *Fanhua meng* at the age of twenty. Possibly her uneasiness for marriage or her alienation from her newly wedded husband enhanced her subconscious desire for female companionship. In *Fanhua meng*, there are quite a few female same-sex love overtures. Lady Huang and Lady Hu become intimate as they live together daily. Jokingly, Lady Hu removes Lady Huang's hand from her shoulder. Madam Wang expresses compassion at the first sight of Lady Hu. Lady Xie thinks that it would be fortunate for one to have a beauty like Lady Huang or Lady Hu and admires her husband who can have beauties in pairs. Through the wishes of Madam Wang and Lady Xie, Wang Yun coveys the message that every woman is seeking the "Golden Orchid" (*jinlan*) of her heart; to put it in a modern term, every woman is lesbian in some corner of her heart. In Scene 24, Wang Menglin is heartbroken because of the loss of her three ladies rather than her masculine glory. She sings:

> Back then you were my true love of the Golden Orchid
> Who understood the music of my heartstrings.

The term "Golden Orchid" stands for the deep friendship between sworn brothers or sisters. It came from *Yi jing* (The Book of Changes), "If the two are of one heart, their sharpness can cut gold; if their words are from the same heart, their fragrance smells of orchids." Chinese women of the past and today particularly like to use the phrase "Golden Orchids of Sisterhood" to refer to their lesbian bond.

Fanhua meng draws much from Wang Yun's personal experience and observation. She not only incorporated the Locust Hall (Huaiqingtang), her Wang Clan,[46] as well as her family members into the play but also modeled the portrait of Wang Menglin after herself. According to the margin comments in the script, other characters such as Lady Hu and Lady Huang

---

[46] Wang Yun's *Fanhua meng* was published by Huaiqingtang and she mentioned the Locust Hall in Scene 9, "In the old Locust Hall,/ The Wang Clan has a long list of honor."

were drawn from women living in her neighborhood. Yaoqin, which with its apparent feminine connotation appears inappropriate for a butler's name, was actually the name of a young housemaid who died from illness. Wang Yun simply named the man housekeeper Yaoqin in memory of her maid. Although the play has a surreal dream framework, it mirrors the women's world of her time. Restricted by the social reality, a woman who crosses gender and becomes a man can only play the role of a patriarchal man in relation to other women. She can serve at the court and move in and out of the house freely whereas all other women must remain deep in the house. Their daily activities are embroidering, playing music, and, at best, taking walks in the garden or writing poetry. The polygamous bliss that Wang Menglin enjoys is based on sexual double standards. No wonder Chinese critics such as Wang Yongkuan blame Wang Yun for her stereotyping of other women and especially for her advocating of polygamy. This simplistic criticism shows no insight into the play as a play written by a woman for playgoers who were predominantly women.

During the eighteenth century, a woman's emulation of a successful man indicated her pro-feminist consciousness. One can easily comprehend why Wang Menglin, after borrowing a male body, must succeed as the Number One Scholar in the nation. But why does Wang Yun let her imitate a male debaucher, flirt with ladies, wallow in polygamy, and even purchase girls as a gift to her brother? A comparison of *Fanhua meng* with *The Female Quixote*, an eighteenth-century English novel by Charlotte Lennox, will provide some insight.

Lennox wrote *The Female Quixote* in 1752.[47] Like *Fanhua meng*, it is a fantasy conceived by an eighteenth-century woman about an eighteenth-century woman. Parodying the style of Cervantes, Lennox creates the portrait of the female Quixote, Arabella. She challenges the gap between the reality of powerless women in society and the all-powerful women in romantic tradition by an insistence on implementing such female power in real life through Arabella, a lady forced into seclusion from the world by her misanthropic father. From a literal reading, Lennox seems to be supporting the male patriarchal status quo by bending her Arabella to the dictates of society and behavior, but a closer reading reveals the authorial support for the power held by the fictitious princesses of Arabella's fancy as well as by the

[47] Charlotte Lennox, *The Female Quixote or the Adventures of Arabella*, ed. Margaret Dalziel (Cambridge: Oxford Classics, 1998).

quixotic Arabella herself. Despite being mocked as a ridiculous madwoman, Arabella manipulates the world of men by her intelligence, honesty, and disarming charm. The examples of Arabella and Wang Menglin indicate that a woman can construct a world of her own in which women, who in reality were helpless, hold power. However, the historical conditions of the eighteenth century made both stories end in disillusionment. While the Immortal Magu leads Wang Menglin to nowhere, the pious and learned Doctor, a prototype of a psychiatrist, cures Arabella of her fantasies and leads her submissively to a traditional marriage — the death of utopian imagination in both plays. But the ending cannot revoke their political messages, because the reader and the audience are fully aware of their gender identity; Arabella or Wang Menglin can only be a dame Quixote or a female Don Juan. Their imitation is aimed at mocking the absurdities of tradition rather than women. For instance, Wang Menglin could not help mocking herself for her flirtation with Lady Huang who was actually inferior to Lady Hu in both talent and appearance. Brother Wang ridicules him, "What would you do if you meet another Lady named Liu?" Wang Yun's father comments on the scene of Wang Menglin's near capture by a sixty-three-year-old prostitute, "It serves him right." It is through such observations that a sensitive reader finds an ironical satire on established patriarchal depravity.

The original prefaces and postfaces of *Fanhua meng* contain no inference of lesbian love. The commentators were not bothered by the motif of a woman in love with three other women. They possibly took it as a theatrical device to bring three more women onto the stage. We can easily interpret *Fanhua meng* as a female community settled with various women. Lady Xie is the epitome of a virtuous wife in the model of Meng Guang.[48] Lady Hu is a self-centered narcissist even though she has to accept her social and financial confinement. Lady Huang is a love-centered Du Liniang, preoccupied with her passion and desire for an ideal man. Wang Menglin is a woman with a desire to be a male and the ambition to succeed like a man. They are all talented women trained in literature, music, and calligraphy. In addition to these four women, *Fanhua meng* features two strong widows: Grandma Wang and Mother Hu. This female community enables Wang Yun to capture the attitudes of different women in dealing with socio-psychological issues such as polygamy and female jealousy.

[48] See Scene 9, n. 3.

According to Keith McMahon's investigation of Chinese polygamy in the eighteenth century, Wang Yun has put the best face of polygamy in *Fanhua meng*. She portrays her protagonist Wang Menglin as a benevolent and potent polygynist. He is a successful scholar/official and enjoys the assemblage of wife of the same or higher class and concubines who are beautiful and sensual from the lower social classes.[49] All of the women in the play are connected in this idealized polygamous system. Wang Menglin's behavior suggests that a woman should be like a man, enjoying sexual freedom and not being restricted by monogamous love. Mother Hu offers her daughter to be a concubine for it is the only way to be free from poverty and achieve social advancement. Polygamy enables Lady Huang to realize her romantic love under the moon and Madam Wang to accept her son's free choice of lovers without parental consent. Wang Yun employs polygamy as a compromise between parental arrangement and individual choice in marriage. In the case of Wang Menglin, she seems to be neutral or leaning toward parental arrangement since Lady Xie, who was chosen by Madam Wang, turns out to be superior either in talent or appearance or status. But to Wang Menglin, feelings of the heart are more important and she always feels more intimate with the ladies of her own choice. However, Wang Yun's representation of polygamy was not intended for criticizing or challenging the system. Like many women *tanci* writers of her time, she thought of the possibility of making use of polygamy as an opportunity for sisterhood and collective female power.

Ninety percent of *tanci* novels, even women's *tanci*, end with polygamy. Polygamy is generally portrayed as male-centered and the number of wives represents a man's success in life. But in some women's *tanci*, polygamy has been revised into a utopian type in which women are the center. Either through a woman in male guise or by other self-inspired means, a group of sisters are eventually married to the same man who is usually feminized. In *Mengying lian* (Romance of Dreams and Shadows) by Zheng Danruo, twelve women after their death are married to one man, who sometimes liked to dress in lady's clothing before he entered heaven. They live a pastoral life happily ever after. In their polygamous utopia, there is no power, wealth, or love associated with male supremacy. The unfinished *Jifang yuan* (The Garden of Gathering Flowers) by a nameless country woman, who wrote in

[49] Keith McMahon, *Misers, Shrews, and Polygamists: Sexuality and Male-Female Relations in Eighteenth-Century Chinese Fiction* (Durham: Duke University Press, 1995), 7.

the quiet hours when her children were away at school and the landlord did not come to press for rent, plans to end the story with twelve women married to one man and their settlement in the utopian Garden of Gathering Flowers. It is shocking how those women writers upheld polygamous utopia. It is certainly impossible to establish such a Garden of Eden without first ridding the earth of male supremacy. This literary phenomenon can only be interpreted as a tactic to legitimize a utopian female community within the patriarchal system by using man as a token linkage.

In *Fanhua meng*, after Wang Menglin transforms into a man, Wang Yun decentralizes her on stage by shifting the focus to other female characters and, by doing so, diminishes her newfound male supremacy. Several scenes are devoted to Lady Hu, Lady Huang, and Lady Xie. The male Wang Menglin is portrayed as a laughingstock in the brothel and a Don Juan type of debauchee in the romantic seduction of women. In order to undermine his male supremacy, Wang Yun lets Lady Xie torment him through a well-designed trial until he completely yields. Then polygamous bliss is given to him by Lady Xie only as a gesture of mercy. Clearly, Lady Xie suffers from female jealousy and Lady Huang suffers from emotional alienation, as a consequence of polygamy. Through Madam Wang and Lady Xie, Wang Yun advises women to overcome female jealousy for the sake of women. Historically, female jealousy has always taken women as the object of persecution. Instead of resenting other women or rivaling with each other, Wang Yun suggests that women should form alliances and even lesbian bonds within a polygamous structure. Not surprisingly, she entitles the scene in which Lady Xie accepts Lady Hu and Lady Huang into the house as "The Female Union" and the scene in which her husband teases all the wives over the issue of two purchased pretty girls as "A Fair Consultation." Wang Yun also gives mothers the highest power and privilege in the play. Wang Menglin only regains stage centrality and finds her powerful voice after she is changed back to a woman. It is indeed a play of women for women.

A Parody of Handan Dream and Quest for Self-Identity

Fanhua meng is a literary dream. The dream genre was a favorite device shared by women playwrights during the Ming and Qing periods.[50] Ye Xiaowan

[50] See Xu Fuming, *Yuan Ming Qing xiqu tansuo*, 274.

(1613–1657?), Wu Lanzheng (1778–1806), and Liu Shuzeng (Qing)[51] each wrote a play entitled *Yuanyang meng* (Dream of Mandarin Ducks). Other titles include *Menghu yuan* (Dream of a Meeting a Tiger) by Ruan Lizhen (late Ming)[52]; *Mengjue guan* (The Pass between Dream and Wakening) by Zhang Lingyi (Qing)[53], *Lihua meng* (The Pear Blossom Dream) by He Peizhu (ca. 1819–?), and Wang Yun's third play, *Youxian meng*. There are also dream plays without the word "dream" in their titles. Women playwrights of the Ming and Qing were dreamers of fantasies who dared to explore possibilities of a different existence. Through literature, they were able to imagine their potentialities that have been suppressed in their society.

It is important to note that each woman playwright's dream is different according to her specific life experience and desire. Wang Yun's *Fanhua meng* can be called a female Handan Dream (*Handan meng*). But instead of interpreting her play as a conventional Handan Dream, readers with a current critical sensibility and consciousness will be able to appreciate how she consciously or unconsciously parodied such a genre.

According to Linda Hutcheon, parody becomes ubiquitous in modern art but it by no means is a new phenomenon. Parody involves the imitation of previous works but it is a form of imitation "characterized by ironic inversion." It "establishes difference at the heart of similarity" and is "transformational in its relationship to other texts." The process of communication is central to the understanding of parody.[54] In the case of *Fanhua meng*, the communication between Wang Yun and her audience/reader is critical to understanding her play as a parody. *Fanhua meng* contains ironic imitations of many previous drama texts and tropes. For instance, falling in love with a beauty in a painting by a man often appears in previous plays, including *Mudan ting*. By convention, the painting of a beauty is for the viewing of men. In *Fanhua meng*, Wang Menglin, as a female, falls in love with the beauty in a painting, thus creating an ironic twist of the familiar. Her

[51] For more about Liu Shuzeng, see the "Women Playwrights of the Ming and Qing Dynasties" section in the Bibliography.

[52] For more about Ruan Lizhen, see the "Women Playwrights of the Ming and Qing Dynasties" section in the Bibliography.

[53] For more about Zhang Lingyi, see the "Women Playwrights of the Ming and Qing Dynasties" section in the Bibliography.

[54] Linda Hutcheon, *A Theory of Parody: The Teachings of Twentieth-Century Art Forms* (New York: Methuen, 1985), 1–25.

calling the beauty as "Yunying" could remind her audience of the seductive fairy dwelling in a cave by a bridge over the Blue Stream, the legend of Pei Hang meeting Yunying in the cave or of the Ming play titled *Lanqiao ji* (The Romance of the Blue Bridge). Her parodied erotic longing would certainly tantalize her audience as well as keep them at a critical distance.

Wang Yun starts her female Handan Dream with Wang Menglin falling in love with two ladies in Handan and then she makes quite a few references to Handan and the character Lu Sheng throughout the play. The Handan Dream, also known as the Golden Millet Dream, originates from a Tang tale called "Zhenzhong ji" (The Dream inside a Pillow) by Shen Jiji (ca. 750–ca. 797). In Shen's tale, the protagonist Lu Sheng was napping in a Handan inn while the innkeeper was cooking millet. In his dream, Lu Sheng enjoyed all fame and wealth of this world. When he woke up, everything was gone but the millet was not yet well cooked. This dream, which suggests emptiness and the transitory nature of human glory, awakens Lu Sheng to his Daoist transcendence. Tang Xianzu's play *Handan ji* (The Dream of Handan), derived from this tale, had an obvious influence on Wang Yun.[55] But in drawing from her personal experience, Wang Yun transformed this genre into a quest for a woman's self-identity.

It is said that Ye Xiaowan was the first pioneer of autobiographical play writing. But her play, focusing on her memory and longing for her two lost sisters, expresses a woman's strong desire for *zhiyin* (bosom friends) who can offer everlasting friendship and love just as an ideal brotherhood. It is not a concentrated reflection on female fate and a woman's life as in Wang Yun's *Fanhua meng. Fanhua meng* presents a fantasized self-portrait of Wang Yun. From this portrait, we find no descriptions of feminine appearance or traits. She is simply a prodigy with a desire for glory as a man. Wang Yuanchang states in his postface, "My daughter Yun was born with exceptional talent. From childhood, she could comprehend a book or a historical record well enough after a single reading. Out of a long-brooded regret for being a female, she wrote the play *Fanhua meng* to express her fantasies." In *Fanhua meng*, Wang Yun focuses her representation of a woman as a subject of desire and a subject in discourse. In an ironically imitated dream world, her personal wishes and fantasies come true. One may say that the process of parodying the traditional Handan Dream itself becomes a form of female wish fulfillment.

---

[55] Tang Xianzu, *Handan ji*, in his *Linchuan simeng*. The work was collected in *Nuanhongshi huike chuanqi*, vols. 17–20 (repr., Yangzhou: Jiangsu Guangling guji keyinshe, 1979).

In the quest for self-identity, all women in the play are shadow characters to help Wang Yun figure out a woman's true identity. Those various roles—a passionate tomboy Wang Menglin who succeeds like a man, a love-detached but self-centered woman like Lady Hu, a Du Liniang type of love-centered woman, a Meng Guang type of virtuous wife, and a strong mother/widow—are multi-selves of a woman or possibilities for a lady of twenty at the crossroads of life. Ironically, Wang Yun died a strong widowed mother. What makes *Fanhua meng* different from other woman-imitating-man stories is its final negation of such a dream of glory. Even if a woman succeeds as a man and fulfills her sexual desire as a man, so what?

Wang Yun's perplexity is well reflected through her alter ego Wang Menglin's inner struggle. Although the Butterfly Dream is not obviously present in *Fanhua meng*, Wang Yun employed Zhuangzi's mysticism to unfold her protagonist's spiritual development.[56] In her dream, Wang Menglin undergoes a butterfly transformation; upon wakening, she does not know whether she is the female who longs for the love of the three ladies or the butterfly who has fulfilled her dream as a man. The perplexity has turned a Zhuangzi Butterfly Dream into a self-reflexive device that leads to the eventual awakening. Borrowing the vision of Immortal Magu, Wang Menglin comes to see that her life as a confined woman and her fantasized glory as a successful man are nothing but a dream. Madame Bi understood the message so well that she wrote an insightful prefatory poem for the play in 1778:

> Don't be a whale rider on the sea;
> Turn into a butterfly-person among flowers.
> Fantasies and real life are all one dream;
> Who can find true identity in one's past-present-future lives?

By the end of the play, Wang Yun tries to pass her message to all women as well as to all men who need to awaken from lives gone astray.

---

[56] See Burton Watson, trans., *The Complete Works of Chuang Tzu* (New York: Columbia University Press, 1968), 49: "Once Chuang Chou dreamt he was a butterfly, a butterfly flitting and fluttering around, happy with himself and doing as he pleased. He didn't know he was Chuang Chou. Suddenly he woke up and there he was, solid and unmistakable Chuang Chou. But he didn't know if he was Chuang Chou who had dreamt he was a butterfly, or a butterfly dreaming he was Chuang Chou. Between Chuang Chou and a butterfly there must be *some* distinction! This is called the Transformation of Things."

Wang Yun and Daoist Enlightenment

The original Handan Dream ends with Lu Sheng's Daoist transcendence. In *Fanhua meng,* Wang Menglin admits that she is unable to become a transcendental immortal like Lu Sheng. But since Wang Yun ends her female Handan Dream with Wang Menglin's ambiguous awakening at Magu's enlightening, one is tempted to ask how serious Wang Yun takes to the Daoist path.[57] Wang Yuanchang sees her Daoist transcendent ending as a helpless gesture:

> After she wakes up from the dream, she is thrown into a struggle between life and death in a state of madness and drunkenness. She has resorted to a Daoist ending. It is rather a meaningless dead end of imagination.[58]

However, Wang Yun seemed to be quite serious about Daoist pursuit at the time of her writing and in her struggle with love and career. In her commentary poem to the play *Huichun meng* (Dream of a Returning Spring) by Gu Sen (Qing),[59] she writes:

> Awakened from a dream, you appreciate the meaning of Handan
> And spend the rest of your life by Buddhist light or Zen lamp.[60]

But in reality, Wang Yun never gave up her dream of glory. According to her son Wang Bailing, because of the impossibility of realizing her own ambition at court, Wang Yun educated him personally from an early age and told him, "You must study hard to fulfill my ambition." When Wang Bailing, at the age of twenty-three, could not afford to travel to take the imperial examination, Wang Yun said, "I have eaten poor food and worked hard since joining the family. My only wish, a daughter of a *jinshi,* is to become the mother of a

[57] In *Fanhua meng,* Wang Yun offers a mixture of Chinese popular religions. In Scene 3, she uses a Buddhist miracle for cross-gender sexual transformation. In Scene 6, she mentions "the melody of solitude in a Zen woods." But the final scene is dominated by Daoism, with Magu as a Daoist immortal.

[58] Wang Yunchang's first head-margin comment on Scene 25 of *Fanhua meng.*

[59] Gu Sen (Qing), having a pen name "Yun'an laoren" (Old Man of the Cloud Temple), experienced many setbacks in life. He wrote the play *Huichun meng* (a Handan-type of fantasy) as a wish fulfillment in his old age. He also authored the *Yun'an zalu* (Miscellaneous Writings of the Cloud Temple).

[60] Cai Yi, ed., *Zhongguo gudian xiqu xuba huibian* (Jinan: Qilu shushe, 1989), 3: 2055.

jinshi."[61] Thus her father Wang Yuanchang sees the play *Fanhua meng* as an outlet for her unfulfilled desire for glory. In 1802, Wang Bailing finally gained the title of *jinshi.* Overjoyed with her son's success, Wang Yun momentarily forgot her own fate and praised Heaven for its infallible judgment:

> Through a hundred kinds of hardship you traveled to Peking,
> For a fifth try in the heart-breaking examination stalls.
> Today you are honored in the Jade and Gold Horse Halls,
> Now we see the infallible judgment of the Heaven's Way.[62]

This poem does not prove that Wang Yun changed her position against Heaven over a woman's fate in *Fanhua meng.* It reminds us to draw a line between Wang Yun the writer and Wang Yun as the practical gentry woman and a strong widowed mother. Daoist enlightenment for her is largely a literary or spiritual consolation.

The play *Fanhua meng* raises the question: "What does Wang Yun gain beyond conventional Daoist enlightenment?" Lee R. Edwards observes, "Dreamer's agents, necessary fictions, heroes enact our sleeping visions in the world in daylight. We dream our heroes. In exchange, our heroes alter us."[63] Through her alter ego, the heroine Wang, Wang Yun obtained a glimpse of Daoist transcendence. But after relinquishing the obsession and vanity behind female love and masculine glory, the author and her heroine again face a dead-end. She felt inexpressible pain caused by the sudden disappearance of all of her achievements due to the restoration of her original gender. It is this pain that called for a Daoist salvation. In *The Classical Chinese Novel,* C. T. Hsia discusses Baoyu's becoming a monk as a questionable separation from the intolerable sufferings of the author as well as his protagonist.[64] Many intellectuals and poets in Chinese history have turned to Daoism as a utopian escape. It is thus not surprising that Wang Yun wrote her third play, *Huixian*

[61] From Wang Bailing's postface in Wang Yun's *Fanhua meng.*

[62] Translation adapted from Ropp, "'Now Cease Painting Eyebrows, Don a Scholar's Cap and Pin': The Frustrated Ambition of Wang Yun, Gentry Woman Poet and Dramatist," 103.

[63] Lee R. Edwards, *Psyche as Hero: Female Heroism and Fictional Form* (Middletown, CT: Wesleyan University Press, 1984), 3.

[64] C. T. Hsia, *The Classical Chinese Novel: A Critical Introduction* (New York: Columbia University Press, 1968).

ji, when she reached middle age.[65] According to Zhou Miaozhong, "*Huixian ji* is a sequel to *Fanhua meng*. It portrays the life of Wang Menglin after she becomes an immortal. The play reflects the inescapability of real life. Its thematic concerns are still about equality between man and woman and a woman's pursuit for liberation and an ideal life."[66]

Fanhua meng as a Stage Script

The renowned scholar Zhu Gui (1731–1807), in his preface to *Quanfu ji*, stated that since *Fanhua meng* was somewhat "cold" (*leng*) for performing on festival and banquet occasions, Wang Yun wrote *Quanfu ji* the following year.[67] The term "cold" is a technical word for categorizing Chinese plays. A "cold" play is one that is called *moben* (ink book or closet drama), famous for its poetic nuances but intended for reading rather than for performing. However, Wang Yun wrote *Fanhua meng* as a *taiben* (stage script), with the intention of actual performance. It is "cold" because of the content of the play rather than for its technical aspects. Audiences during the Imperial period were accustomed to grand reunion happy endings. Wang Yun's *Fanhua meng*, which ends with a heartbroken woman in spiritual crisis, is obviously unsuitable for merry-making festival occasions. However, *Fanhua meng* contains comic elements and theatrical humor. Wang Yun even plays out a farce with Pipa Qian in Scene 8. Although lyrics and arias are hard to follow for modern readers, audiences of her time, including women and average theatergoers, should have been receptive. In *Quanfu ji*, Wang Yun portrays a strong woman called Shen Huilan. In order to marry her ideal man, Wen Yan, she dresses herself as a man and achieves the title of *jinshi* in order to be equal to Wen Yan. However, Wen Yan is portrayed as being superior over all women. He wins the title of *zhuangyuan*, marries two wives, and has everything possible in the world: fame, wealth, and family bliss. Even the emperor admires him and presents him with a plaque inscribed with two characters "Quanfu" (Full Happiness), hence, the play's title. But in spite of

---

[65] See *Zhongguo xiqu zhi · Shaanxi juan*, 700.

[66] See Zhou Miaozhong, *Qingdai xiqu shi* (Zhengzhou: Zhongzhou guji chubanshe, 1987), 297. There is no indication whether or not Zhou has seen the actual text of this third play.

[67] See Wu Mei, *Zhongguo xiqu gailun* (Hong Kong: Taiping shuju, 1964), 38. Hu Wenkai misread Wu's term 冷 (cold) as 泛 (extensive but shallow); for more see Hu Wenkai, *Lidai funü zhuzuo kao*, rev. ed. (1957; repr., Shanghai: Shanghai guji chubanshe, 1985), 246.

the affirmation of the male hierarchy, the play does encourage women to play sexual politics and maneuver within the patriarchal system. *Fanhua meng* ends in late autumn with chilly cries whereas *Quanfu ji* ends with a happy outing in spring. Zhu Gui in his preface described *Fanhua meng* as "chilly wind and rain" and *Quanfu ji* as "warm spring sunshine." Although *Quanfu ji* is a realistic play with refined lyrics, it fails to sever itself from the "stereotyped," as observed by Wu Mei.[68]

The structure of *Fanhua meng* as an acting script gives insight into the double rehearsals in Scenes 9–10 and weddings in Scenes 19–21, which might seem redundant for today's readers. Although the romantic meeting and introduction of a talented scholar and a beauty in Scene 9 may be expected, its repetition in Scene 10 with a less attractive lady would provoke laughter from the audience. (Wang Yuanchang noted their difference by emphasizing Scene 10 as a self-initiated love in contrast to a parental arrangement as in cases of Lady Xie and Lady Hu.) The wedding ceremonies and banquets are not as interesting to read but would be entertaining to watch on the stage. The first wedding (Scene 19) is for Wang and Lady Xie and the second wedding (Scene 21) is for Wang's servant, Yaoqin, and a maid. Yaoqin justifies his right to have a wife by questioning a wealthy man's giving women away as a gift of concubines. Wang Yun's awareness of women as disadvantaged citizens connects her with the poor and the servants. *Fanhua meng* gives attention not only to the servants but also to talented women of disadvantaged widow's and widower's families.

Publication History and Commentators' Response

The original copy of *Fanhua meng* in the National Library of China is a woodblock edition by Huaiqingtang and dated as the year of Wuxu during the reign of Qianlong (1778). The play was printed in two parts, with each part subdivided into two volumes. Although Inspector Zhang Xipu[69] is the identified editor, Wang Yuanchang wrote the comments printed in the head margins of the text. The preface and commentary poems before the text were contributed by Zhang Fengsun of the Stone Lake, Madame Bi or Zhang Zao of the Suzhou Riverside, and Cao Renhu of Jiading. Wang Bailing and Wang

[68] Wu Mei, *Zhongguo xiqu gailun,* 38. Wu Mei did not make comments on *Fanhua meng.* It seems that he never saw the script of the play.

[69] Zhang Xipu is another name for Zhang Fengsun.

Yuanchuang wrote the postfaces. The commentary poem written by Zhu Gui was incorporated into the play as its ending. Given that Wang Yun's son Wang Bailing was hardly ten in 1778 and his postface included in *Fanhua meng* was written in 1804, the woodblock copy in the National Library of China would have been printed in 1804, even though it was carved or first published in 1778.

According to Wang Yuanchang's postface, after he wrote the margin comments, he stored the manuscript of *Fanhua meng* away in a small box. Years later, in 1778, he happened to show it to Inspector Zhang Fengsun (*jinshi* in the Qianlong reign), who shared it with his younger sister Madame Bi. They were so excited over reading the play that Zhang Fengsun wrote a preface and Madame Bi composed a commentary poem. Madame Bi's maiden name was Zhang Zao and she was the mother of the famous scholar-official Bi Yuan (1730–1797), who "headed a houseful of talented women: his mother, his wife, and his eldest daughter were all accomplished poets."[70] Since Madame Bi greatly valued talent in women, she recommended immediate publication of *Fanhua meng*.[71] The money for publishing was donated by Zhang Fengsun.

The published women's works in Imperial China often raised the concern of male authorship/patronage. In 1738, Shi Zhenlin published *Xiqing sanji* (West Green Random Notes), of which the poems by the woman writer, He Shuangqing, constituted over twenty percent.[72] Although in the twentieth century, those poems have been published several times under the name of He Shuangqing, the authenticity of authorship as well as the existence of He Shuangqing as a woman remains an academic controversy.[73] The truth of Ruan Lizhen as the author, at least the co-author, of the famous play *Yanzi jian* (The Swallow Letter) will hopefully be established by scholarship. It is likely that her father Ruan Dacheng (1587–1646) simply took the play as his own and used it to advance his career in the Ming court. Later, under the Qing rulers, he married off Ruan Lizhen as a concubine to a Manchu lord for his advancement, which eventually led to her death by poisoned wine at the

[70] See Mann, "Learned Women in the Eighteenth Century," 35.

[71] For detailed information, see Hu Wenkai, *Lidai funü zhuzuo kao*.

[72] See Elsie Choy, *Leaves of Prayer: The Life and Poetry of He Shuangqing, a Farmwife in Eighteenth-Century China* (Hong Kong: The Chinese University Press, 1993).

[73] See Paul S. Ropp, *Banished Immortal: Searching for Shuangqing, China's Peasant Woman Poet* (Ann Arbor: University of Michigan Press, 2002).

hands of his jealous wife.[74] This could be a striking example of male appropriation of female talent. Wang Yun's father edited *Fanhua meng* but, fortunately, Wang Yun did not lose the recognition as the sole author.

Wang Yun, as the author of *Fanhua meng*, is also attested by the four commentators who offered spontaneous reactions as the play's readers. Apart from their shared recognition of the play's imaginative plot and theatrical qualities, Zhang Fengsun responds to Wang Yun's protest against the Heaven for her misfortune of being born a woman by saying that "A foot can be short and an inch can be long. A talented being is not born handicapped." Through the examples of famous female talents such as Xie Daoyun (317–342), he attributes Wang Yun's frustration and protest to her "momentary bias." By the end of his preface, Zhang Fengsun is reminded of his own failure as a male in contrast to the heroes of ancient times, thus feeling a vicarious release. Similarly, Cao Renhu gains a deeper sense of life's regret. From the bitter tears of an unfortunate male scholar in blue gown, he understands why an ambitious female in her boudoir should have more complaints. Madame Bi, who especially appreciates female talent, observes that although the genre of Southern drama used by Wang Yun is not popular among other playwrights at the time, *Fanhua meng* with its rare beauty of songs and lyrics can be compared to *Yanzi jian* and *Taohua shan* (The Peach Blossom Fan). She appreciates Wang Yun's awakening from the dream of glory but warns her and the readers of *Fanhua meng* of the arduousness in setting foot upon the path to the Daoist paradise, Penglai. Zhu Gui, in his commentary poem, implies that audience of the play would be confined to women, but from the responses by Zhang Fengsun and Cao Renhu, we know the play was of interest to men as well.

Zhu Gui compared Wang Yun's talent with that of two most famous women poets, Xie Daoyun and Li Qingzhao (1084–ca. 1151). Like Madame Bi, he also ranked *Fanhua meng* with the mainstream *chuanqi* plays *Yanzi jian* and *Taohua shan*. Madame Bi even suggested the possibility that a woman playwright like Wang Yun could have been better than the famous male playwrights Tang Xianzu and Xu Wei if she had the opportunity:

> Your warbling was so in harmony with the palace tunes
> Even Yuming and Tianchi had a hard time to imitate.

[74] See Tan Zhengbi, *Zhongguo nüxing de wenxue shenghuo* (1931; repr., Yangzhou: Guangling guji chubanshe, 1998), 352–358. Although Tan Zhengbi was quite certain about Ruan Lizhen as the originator of *Yanzi jian*, the authorship of Ruan Lizhen has not been recognized today due to insufficient scholarship.

The Value and Influence of *Fanhua meng*

Wang Yun's *Fanhua meng* was not just complimented by her commentators. As a play of poetic beauty and bold imagination, Hua Wei believes that the publication of *Fanhua meng* made Wang Yun quite famous and the play was at least performed in some private courts.[75] Jiao Xun (1763–1820), a Qing drama critic, mentioned the scene acting changes in *Jushuo* and he quoted from Li Tiaoyuan (1734–1803):

> It is indeed rare for a woman to compose *chuanqi*. Lady Wang Yun of Chang'an loved books from childhood and regretted her fate of being a woman. She wrote *Fanhua meng* to express her wish-fulfilling fantasy. Let Lady Wang, a woman, come on the stage first and *sheng* appear on the second scene. This is an example of stage change.[76]

Li Tiaoyuan also mentioned that since people were surprised that a woman could write drama, Wang Yun became instantly known as "*nücaizi*" (a talented female writer).[77]

Fanhua meng is a valuable historical text to study alongside other women's publications during the period, such as the *Suiyuan nüdizi shi* (Poems by Female Students of the Sui Garden, 1796), which was compiled and published by the renowned scholar and women's educator Yuan Mei.[78] We also can examine it in light of Zhang Xuecheng's (1738–1801) influential essay "Fuxue" (Women's Learning, 1796).[79] Zhang Xuecheng astutely attacked Yuan Mei and negated the poems written by his female students through the affirmation of famous women such as the Han scholar Ban Zhao (ca. 49–ca. 120)[80] and the Song poet Li Qingzhao. His critique indeed smacks of negating the present by elevating the past. Although there is no evidence of Wang Yun's contact with other women in her creative activities, her lyrics on

---

[75] Hua Wei, *Ming Qing funü zhi xiqu chuangzuo yu piping*, 114.

[76] Jiao Xun, *Jushuo*, vol. 5, in *Zhongguo gudian xiqu lunzhu jicheng*, vol. 8 (Beijing: Zhongguo xiju chubanshe, 1959), 196.

[77] Li Tiaoyuan, *Yucun shihua*, vol. 3.

[78] For a sample from Yuan Mei's collection, see poems by Xi Peilan, Dai Lanying, and Qu Bingyun in Chang and Saussy, *Women Writers of Traditional China*, 27–46.

[79] See "Fuxue" (Women's learning) translated by Susan Mann, discussed in Chang and Saussy, *Women Writers of Traditional China*, 784–799. Also see Mann's "Learned Women in the Eighteenth Century" for an analysis of Zhang Xuecheng's "Fuxue."

[80] She was the sister of Ban Gu (32–92) and Bao Chao (33–103).

nature and personal sentiments in *Fanhua meng* share similarities with the poems written by the Sui Garden sisters; the latter repelled Zhang Xuecheng as the product of indecent idleness. Wang Yun's arias and lyrics challenging the Heaven in protest of female fate, with an indignant tone or a desperate cry of frustration, would fall short of Zhang Xuecheng's moral and aesthetic criteria. Along with Chen Duansheng and pen sisters from the Sui Garden, we may say that women's creative writing in the eighteenth century was more inspired by Yuan Mei's concept of *xingling* (native sensibility) that advocates spontaneous artistic expressions of personal character, experience, and feelings rather than being confined by archaic aesthetic criteria and conventional moral standards.

In the history of Chinese women's drama, Wang Yun's *Fanhua meng* should be valued as a seminal text. Its influence upon Wu Zao's (1799–1862) famous play *Yinjiu dusao* (Drinking Wine and Reading "Encountering Sorrow") is evident. Like Wang Yun, Wu Zao uses the protagonist as her own fair shadow. But instead of admiring another woman's portrait, she looks at her own portrait as a cross-dressed scholar, imagining living a male-debauchee type of life by selling wine while indulging in drinking and reading poetry. While reading Qu Yuan's (ca. 340–ca. 278 BC) poem "Li sao" (Encountering Sorrow), she laments the fact that Qu Yuan as a man gains literary immortality through his disciples' preservation of his poems whereas as a woman, her poems will be discarded without a trace in history. This echoes Wang Yun's yearning for fame and literary immortality.

He Peizhu developed Wang Yun's ambiguous lesbian motif into a five-act play titled *Lihua meng*. Drama critic Yan Dunyi analyzed *Lihua meng* in his *Yuan Ming Qing xiqu lunji* (Essays on Yuan Ming Qing Drama) and noted "a rather serious lesbian tendency" in the play.[81] Hua Wei, in her analysis of the play, detects the influence of *Fanhua meng*. Both Wang Yun and He Peizhu's lesbian desire reveals a Chinese woman's admiration for other women and her longing for an alternative love and friendship beyond heterosexual love. This desire stresses "the same mind" (*tongxin*) or free communication of the two minds.[82]

It does not seem to be incidental that Wu Zao developed the image of female imprisonment from Wang Yun's being "born handicapped," or "a bird with tied up feathers and culled wings" into "a sick crane in a cage." Like

[81] Yan Dunyi, *Yuan Ming Qing xiqu lunji* (Zhengzhou: Zhongzhou shuhuashe, 1982).

[82] See Hua Wei, *Ming Qing funü zhi xiqu chuangzuo yu piping*, 13.

Wang Yun, Wu Zao and He Peizhu both let *sheng* play the role of the protagonists, even though they are merely cross-dressed heroines. Those women playwrights openly rejected traditional feminine traits and assumed a daring masculine voice by means of dramatic cross-gender change or cross-dressing. The most obvious evidence of Wang Yun's influence on Wu Zao and He Peizhu lies in the ending of their plays. Both *Yinjiu dusao* and *Liuhua meng* adopt the ending aria "Qing jiang yin" of *Fanhua meng*. While *Fanhua meng* ends with the line "A woman as well as a man needs a wakening return from a life gone astray;" *Yinjiu dusao* ends with "The shadow as well as the body undergoes the same transformation;" and *Lihua meng* ends with "The female as well as the male appears the same [in the land of the immortals]." *Fanhua meng* reveals Wang Yun's central concern with gender equality, whereas *Yinjiu dusao* demonstrates Wu Zao's wish for a complete merging of the shadow (the ideal self) with the body (the present self) and *Lihua meng* emphasizes an ideal androgynous identity/love. Wang Yun's influence upon her sister playwrights reinforces the importance of *Fanhua meng* in the historical growth of female consciousness and exploration through the form of drama.

Wang Yun's *Fanhua meng* is not just a woman's play for women. It is an important play for studying the correlation between modern play and classical Chinese drama. In spite of its conventionalities, *Fanhua meng* comes close to a modernist monologue. Through the composite character of Wang Menglin as the heroine, the playwright inside the play, and Wang Yun herself, *Fanhua meng* resonates with modern self-reflexivity, especially authorial self-reflexivity. By composing and demolishing the dream of glory, one may say that Wang Yun's enlightenment lies more in her insight into the function of writing rather than Daoist transcendence. It is interesting to note that the 2000 Nobel Laureate Gao Xingjian's reasons for engaging in literature[83] are not that novel. Wang Yun anticipated him in questioning the futility of writing to delve in social politics as a means of defeating the enemy or running state affairs. Just as Gao Xingjian, she also recognized the restricted function of creative writing as being limited to wish fulfillment, psychological release, aesthetic pursuit, and historical reflection. Wang Yuanchang understood his daughter so well that he regarded the publication of *Fanhua meng* as "a

[83] See Gao Xingjian's Nobel lecture titled "The Case for Literature," delivered in Börssalen at the Swedish Academy in Stockholm, December 7, 2000. Also see Gao Xingjian, *Meiyou zhuyi* (Hong Kong: Cosmos Books, 2000).

satisfying consolation" to Wang Yun who should "no longer regret having been born a female." It is true that only through the brilliance of her brush could Wang Yun have achieved her expected literary immortality:

> With tears on my dress and the soul-stirring
>   fragrance of the grass,
> I will recapture the splendor of this dream of glory and
> Turn it into a manuscript of mad passion, which
>   will last until
> Heaven becomes a wasteland and Earth meets its doomsday.[84]

With historical reflections of social reality such as polygamy, the story of Wang Yun's *Fanhua meng* seems to be dated. But it is still a play with concerns of interest to modern readers, such as liberating female sexual desire, questioning a woman's dream of masculine glory, and exploring a playwright's self-reflexivity. *Fanhua meng* is still producible. It can be also adapted from a verse drama into a modern play. Since the problems Wang Yun confronted as a woman have not yet been resolved in many parts of the world, *Fanhua meng* will continue to be thought-provoking to audiences.

---

[84] See Scene 24.

Part One · The Translated Text

ZHANG FENGSUN'S PREFACE

The sea is boundless; yet Jingwei[1] is determined to fill it. When the sky collapsed, it was Nüwa[2] who mended it. Since *yin* and *yang*, fire and ashes came into being, the differentiation between flowing and blocking, gathering and dispensing never ceased to exist. A foot can be short and an inch can be long. A talented being is not born handicapped. Some are born two feet and others with wings. Can we talk about unfairness in the creation of those forms? Due to momentary bias, one might feel the Heaven has created the chaos and thus harbor resentment. Such feelings are strong and vast, difficult to eliminate.

There were three locust trees[3] in the door shade[4]. They were born with noble elegance, absorbing eight subterraneous waters, and grew like the lustrous pearls. Like the willow catkins blown by the wind to the court, Lady Xie's[5] name soared high with her ode to the snow. Like the seasoning pepper plate for wine,[6] Lady Liu's poem on the New Year reveals her special talent.[7] Listening to the zither, a lady could distinguish the subtle music of the seven strings. Writing history, she completed the eight chronicles.[8] Why were

---

[1] According to an ancient Chinese myth, Nüwa 女娃, the daughter of Tiandi (God), was drowned in the Eastern Sea. She turned into a bird called Jingwei and vowed to fill up the sea with twigs and pebbles that she brought with her beak.

[2] Nüwa 女娲, the goddess who created human beings from mud, mended the sky when one of the pillars supporting the sky was broken due to men's fighting. Although 女娃 and 女娲 are both pronounced "nüwa," the former simply means a female child and the latter refers to the image of goddess Nüwa with a woman's head and a coiled snake tail.

[3] The three locust trees (*sanhuai*) refer to the three talented ladies in the following text. *Sanhuai*, forming a tripod, refers to top officials and ministers of the court.

[4] Door shade (*menyin*) implies the favor resulting from inherited virtues or service.

[5] Refers to Xie Daoyun (317–342).

[6] The plate for serving pepper to season the wine on the first day of the first lunar month is called *jiaopan*.

[7] During the Jin dynasty, the wife of Liu Zhen offered her "Jiaohua song" as an ode to the Chinese New Year on the first day of the first lunar month.

[8] Refers to Ban Zhao (ca. 49–ca. 120) or Cai Wenji (177–?); both are famous women scholars and historians.

such great talents all born in the hidden boudoirs? They are far superior to those immortals of Peng and Ying.[9]

The play begins with a fantasy that leads to a dream. A miracle occurs and the female body is transformed. The hero succeeds at the imperial examinations and meets beautiful ladies. Accompanied by spring orchids and autumn chrysanthemums, the hero tours lakes and hills. Dancing dresses float with singing fans, what a romantic pleasure.

Suddenly the morning bell rings, the dreamer is startled awake. All illusionary vicissitudes are within the claws of Magu, who awakens the dreamer from the pillow of Lu Sheng.[10]

Composing *Fanhua meng*, the author attempts to seek the causes and effects of her past, present, and future. The profusion of her lyrical talent splashes from a blooming brush.[11] Her rhythmical tunes echo around the beams. Following the beats of *hongya*[12], the performers change their cloaks and move from scene to scene; the stage action seems to be quite proper. To enhance the beauty of the hair, the author matches the dark hue with the white color. Every description looks natural. This is indeed a splash of her poetic elegance, which can be compared with the best of lyrics of past and present.

Alas! The water of the Penglai Sea, how shallow or deep one cannot possibly imagine! The constellation of Moxie[13] (Capricorn) foretells setbacks ahead. It seems one has to be engaged completely in one's pursuit in order to be released. It is difficult to disentangle oneself from earthly concerns. This play has helped set off a series of reflections upon my own life. The wealth and fame in this world is nothing but a desire for the Twelve Golden Hairpins.[14] The immortals of the paradise are merely three thousand *li* of soft water[15]

---

[9] Penglai and Yingzhou, Daoist fairylands beyond the seas.

[10] See Scene 25, n. 1.

[11] It is said that Li Bai (701–762) had a dream in which flowers bloom from his brush. Later he became the immortal poet. Therefore, a talented brush is called "shenghua bi" or "bi shenghua."

[12] *Hongya* is a musical instrument used to keep time.

[13] Moxie or Mojie, one of the twelve zodiacal signs. A person born under the Mojie sign is supposed to have a hard, tortuous fate.

[14] See Scene 20, n. 1.

[15] Soft water (*ruoshui*) is either too shallow or too remote for sailing. It is said that the Abode of the West Queen Mother is surrounded by soft water.

away. Admiring the manly heroes of the ancient times, I regret having achieved nothing at such an old age. By reading the play written by this lady doctor[16], I seek some vicarious release.

Zhang Fengsun of the Stone Lake
Spring 1778, aged 73

[16] The lady doctor (*nüboshi*) refers to an exceptionally talented lady. During the Warring States, Qin, and Han periods, *boshi* was the title for a high-ranking official. During the period of Three Kingdoms, Empress Zhen of Wei Wendi was said to be an omnivorous reader in her maidenhood. Her brother laughed at her, saying, "You should keep to your women's work. What's the use of learning? Are you going to become a lady doctor?" See *Ci yuan*, 0396.

MADAME BI'S COMMENTARY POEM

The Goddess of the Qin Platform loved playing flute;[1]
But she left with the phoenix, leaving an empty stage.
The lady of a boudoir has succeeded this noble career;
Her clear voice sings the music from beyond the lofty clouds.

Swallow Letter and *Peach Blossom Fan* are plays of superb lyrics,[2]
Pity, only a few authors still know the southern style drama.
Heaven has now reversed his way of distributing literary talents:
Bestowing them on a woman rather than on a man.

Don't be a whale rider on the sea;
Turn into a butterfly-person among flowers.
Fantasies and real life are all one dream;
Who can find true identity in one's past-present-future lives?

In the former life you must have been a wondrous *luan*[3].
You copied rhymes daily at court, forgetting your meals.
Your warbling was so in harmony with the palace tunes
Even Yuming[4] and Tianchi[5] had a hard time to imitate.

---

[1] The Qin Platform (Qintai) is also known as the Phoenix Platform (Fengtai or Fengnütai). According to the legend, during the Spring and Autumn period, Duke Mu of Qin (Qin Mugong) married his princess Nongyu to Xiao Shi, the master of the flute (*xiao*). Nongyu also played flute well. Their flutes sounded like the phoenix warbling. One night, the couple flew to heaven, followed by the phoenix. The Duke built the Monument of the Phoenix Lady (Fengnüci) in her honor.

[2] Ruan Dacheng's (1587–1646) *Yanzi jian* and Kong Shangren's (1648–1718) *Taohua shan.*

[3] *Luan*, a phoenix-like mythical bird, with a beautiful, enchanting voice.

[4] Yuming refers to Tang Xianzu (1550–1616); the collection of his four famous *chuanqi* plays is titled *Yumingtang simeng* (Four Dreams of the Yuming Hall).

[5] Tianchi refers to the famous dramatist Xu Wei (1521–1593), whose assumed name is "Tianchi shanren" (A Dweller of Tianchi Mount).

Done with painting eyebrows, you don a scholar's cap.
Yet, Penglai Isles are in a sea that looks shallow but turns deep.
Like Magu scratching an itching back with her claws,
Every note of the play makes our hearts throb.

Zhang Zao of the Suzhou Riverside

CAO RENHU'S COMMENTARY POEM

Chanting away the day by the green window,
Her ambition for the drama arena is not yet worn out.
Beating the coral bar into pieces,[1] she composes a new play.
It is filled with passion between the heroic lads and ladies.

The disciple of the Black Gowns[2] is a master of romance;
She wrote new lyrics to dispel her own frustrations.
From painting eyebrows to holding a scholar's brush,
She should prevail over the Land of Phoenix and Unicorn[3].

In chilly weather, her green sleeves fold over the writing desk.
She sheds pity for the stranded female talent.
Relying on only a few sheets of cloud paper,
She imagines the engaging pursuits of a young scholar.

A drowsy nap with drooping hairpins,
The dreamland bears elegant names.
The sky in springtime is perfectly fine,
When suddenly, a cry from an oriole startles her awake.

The happily wedded are all predestined;
Their former and next lives are in Heaven's hands.
Golden horses match golden companions,
Indulging like the immortals on a single pillow's dream.

---

[1] "Beating the coral bar into pieces" may mean striking the music bar while composing tunes. It may also imply that the playwright studied all the previous dramas in order to create a new one; as corals or coral net can refer to extensive collection of a certain category, especially in paintings.

[2] Black Gown (*wuyi*) normally refers to common, inferior people. But "the Black Gowns" here may imply the family of scholar officials, such as the background of Wang Yun.

[3] Refers to the male realm.

Like lightning and dust, one's fantasies vanish.
The flowers of illusions disappear upon awakening.
Do not take pains to distinguish illusion from reality,
When the butterflies transform in the spring wind.[4]

It is so easy to forget what I have learned all these years.
I sigh over the essay with my fate of the Nine Titles[5].
The green gown[6] has been constantly soaked by a man's tears;
One never expects the complaints from a boudoir to be stronger.

I have long besmirched Penglai for being a subordinate official.
I also wrote lyrics of spring dreams by the mirror.
Reading this newly composed drama doubles my life's regret.
This lady of moth brows, indeed, stirs a man's strong feelings.

Cao Renhu of Jiading

---

[4] A reference to Zhuangzi's Butterfly Dream.

[5] The Nine Titles (*jiuming*) refer to all ranks of officialdom. During the Zhou dynasty, there were nine official ranks, known as the Nine Titles.

[6] The green gown (*qingshan*) stands for menial officials. During the Tang dynasty, the eighth and the ninth low-ranking officials wore the green color (*qing*).

THE CHARACTERS

in the order of their appearance

PROLOGUE SPEAKER

WANG, Menglin (Dream Unicorn), also addressed as Ruiqing and referred as *Jieyuan*, *Zhuangyuan*

SHANCAI, a boy Buddhist at the service of the Bodhisattva Guanyin

LADY XIE, Mengfeng (Dream Phoenix), also called Qiongzhen (Genuine Jade), from Scene 18 onwards addressed as MISTRESS; WANG's wife

SPRING, LADY XIE's maid

FRAGRANCE, LADY XIE's maid

MASTER XIE, LADY XIE's father; an imperial official

MADAM XIE, LADY XIE's mother

MASTER WANG, Wenhan, style name Tunan; WANG's father; a court official

MADAM WANG, maiden name Yang; WANG's mother

BROTHER, WANG's elder brother

YAOQIN, also called Brother Zhou; WANG's butler

HEAD NUN, head of the Purple Bamboo Convent

NANNY ZHANG, wet nurse of LADY XIE

YANG, WANG's cousin

GAO, WANG's cousin

PIPA QIAN, a sixty-three-year-old prostitute

LADY HU, Menglian (Dream Lotus); WANG's concubine

MOTHER HU, maiden name Wu; LADY HU's mother

LADY HUANG, Menglan (Dream Orchid), also called Fangsu (Natural Fragrance), Ah Su; WANG's concubine

YARD, MASTER WANG's servant

MC, Master of Ceremonies, or wedding conductor

EMERALD CLOUD, a maid

SCARLET, purchased girl by WANG

SNOW, purchased girl by WANG

TANHUA, LADY XIE's young brother Yunlang; a *tanhua*

GRANDMA, WANG's grandmother; a widow

MAGU, a Daoist immortal

SERVANT(S), LITTLE NUN, MAID(S), MONK, IMPERIAL HERALDS, WET NURSE, HOUSEKEEPER, DOORMEN, COURTESANS

Act One

SCENE 1. Prologue[1]

PROLOGUE SPEAKER.[2]

[c1] Transcending peace within the four seas;
Tranquil harmony spreads in eight directions.
All enjoy the glory of success. For a moment,
An awakening eye opens from a drunken state.
Clearing manuscripts in a quiet studio,
I discard old writings and
Start with a new chapter:
The Son of the Wangs in the Capital and
The Daughter of the Xies in Wulin are wedded
Like a unicorn and a phoenix sharing the same dream.
Even happier, daughter of Hu in Lin'an and
Lady Huang of Wujun,[3] two talented girls,
Happen by fate to meet the dashing Scholar Wang.
Together they enjoy twenty years of honor and wealth.

One morning I suddenly awake,
Feeling lost in the vast mist of life.
Luckily Magu[4] comes to me and

---

[1] The first three scenes and Scene 24 were published in *Renditions*, no. 64 (Autumn 2005): 96–106.

[2] The prologue is traditionally given by an older male, who speaks in the voice of the author. According to the norms of Chinese drama, the male is always the first to come onstage. However, in *Fanhua meng*, Lady Wang herself appears onstage first. Tan Zhengbi therefore assumes that as a feminist assertion. For more, see Tan Zhengbi, *Zhongguo nüxing wenxue shi*, 3rd ed. (Tianjin: Baihua wenyi chubanshe, 2001), 356.

[3] Lin'an, present-day Hangzhou, was the temporary capital of the Southern Song dynasty. Wujun was in Suzhou. Both Hangzhou and Suzhou were areas well-known for their beautiful women.

[4] Magu, a goddess of clairvoyant power. Ge Hong (281–341) of the Jin dynasty records in his *Shenxian zhuan* (Anecdotes of Immortals) that Magu has witnessed the conversion of the Eastern Sea into mulberry fields three times since she became an immortal. Also see Scene 25, n. 6.

Strikes the morning bell.
I am finally awakened from my dream of glory.
With a long laugh,
I cast all my mad frustration into the Eastern Sea.[5]

A lost female knight-errant ventures into the land of illusions;
The beauty in a painting completes her unicorn-phoenix dream.
Lady Hu and Lady Huang are bound by their romantic fate;
Immortal Magu lets the dream of glory vanish at her fingertip.

Here comes Wang Menglin. (PROLOGUE SPEAKER *exits.*)

[5] The location of the Eastern Sea in Chinese legend is uncertain. It most likely refers to the Yellow Sea. Here it simply refers to any vast ocean to the east of China.

SCENE 2. A Lonely Sigh

WANG, *wearing a moon-white cloak, with her pale skirt tightened by a silk belt, enters.*

WANG.

[a1] **With a clear mind and strong bones**
A young lady's aspirations soar to the clouds.
She asks Heaven how to realize her ambition.
Let her pure brush emit a profusion of colors.
Let her precious sword strike a whirling wind.

(*Sighs.*)

Still she hates the arduous path to confront in life.

(*Sitting down.*)

[c2] Buried deep in the boudoir for a dozen years,
I can be neither an official nor an immortal.
Every reading rouses my admiration for Ban Chao[1];
Holding a wine cup, I chant the poems of Li Bai[2].
In spite of my soaring ambition,
I am not fated to be a Mulan[3] or a Chonggu[4].
Since I have no share in the Jade Court or the Golden Steed,[5]
I can only pour my fantasies into a dream.

---

1 Ban Chao (33–103), a famous military commander on the western frontier during the Han dynasty.

2 Li Bai (701–762), a most celebrated poet of the Tang dynasty.

3 Hua Mulan, a legendary girl who took her aged father's place and fought twelve years in male disguise, first appeared in "Mulan shi," a folk ballad of the Northern Wei dynasty.

4 Huang Chonggu, the daughter of a Tang commander, cross-dressed as a boy since childhood and was a soldier until she revealed her sexual identity at a marriage proposal. She remained single all her life but never had opportunity to succeed. In Xu Wei's (1521–1593) sixteenth-century drama *Nü zhuangyuan*, Huang Chonggu, in male guise, attains *zhuanyuan* status, becoming the number one scholar in the country.

5 Refers to Hanlin Academy (Hanlinyuan), the Imperial Academy, and a war general career.

I am from the Wang Family, a native of Chang'an. My family belongs to the distinguished clan in Guanxi with generations of scholars and officials. While alive, my grandfather was the imperial inspector of the Jiangxi province. Unfortunately his premature death left my grandmother alone. My father's name also appeared on the royal list of exam winners and he had assumed the office of *langguan*[6]. My mother, named Yang, is a virtuous lady from a famous family in the prestigeous area east of the Yangtze. She knows how to manage a house and has everything in order. My father had worked for the imperial court for half his life and yet, being completely incorrupt, he left office with two empty sleeves[7]. My parents have only two children, my elder brother and me. Although I never went to school, I have learned to read and write. Yet, simply because I was not born a male, I have been deprived of the opportunity to gain honor for my ancestral family. Wearing a skirt and hairpins, I have no way to become somebody and achieve fame.

The spring time is pleasant with
Willows beckoning and flowers blooming
Orioles singing and swallows chattering.
Yet I find no way to soothe my restless feelings.

[a2[i]] **Blooming flowers and charming willows**
Join the spring contest with charming smiles.
Singing orioles and chattering swallows
Surround the carved balustrades with their cheerful echos.

What a beautiful day! If I fail to find a subject for composing a poem, I am sure to be mocked by the spring.

(*She lifts the brush. On the point of writing, she puts it down with a sigh.*)

With merely a vermilion brush and some flimsy sheets,
How could I capture the full beauty of spring?

(*She plays her zither.*)

Attempting to express my sad sentiments,
I become too lethargic to pluck the chilly strings.

(*She picks up a book and reads.*)

[6] An assistant official.

[7] Empty pockets. The Chinese traditional gown has wide sleeves which can be used as pockets to hide money or other things.

"Such expanse of drifting ripples shimmer in clear weather.
The color of hills against a drizzling sky also creates wonder.
If West Lake is likened to the fair Lady Xi Shi[8],
Her beauty shines equally with or without cosmetic powder."

"The Ode to West Lake" is by Mr. Su[9]. (*She sighs.*)

In this life I'll probably never see its like;
Still I wish I could see it in my dreams.

(*She throws away the book with anger.*)

Alas! **Thinking of my fate has doubled my resentments.**
I suffer endless frustration over failing aspirations.

The more I read the more bored I become. I'd better unfold this scroll painting of a beauty that came from the Suzhou area to see whether it can cheer me up. (*She hangs the scroll up and looks at it, smiling.*) How wonderful! Look at her serene spirit and graceful manner as if Goddess Sunü[10] came to earth or a fairy flew into this world. If I were a man, I would definitely seek a lady like her to marry. Now I cannot help but make a wish. Perhaps my wish may be granted. Who knows? (*She burns incense and kowtows to the painting.*)

[a2[ii]] **With utmost sincerity,**
I plead for the presence of Yunying[11].

(*Looking up.*)

Oh, she looks alive with such dashing beauty;
Her lingering gaze seems fixed on me.

(*She cries out.*)

---

[8] Xi Shi was a famous beauty of the State of Yue in the late Spring and Autumn period. West Lake lies within the territory of this ancient kingdom.

[9] Su Shi (1037–1101) wrote two poems while he was drinking at West Lake. The weather was clear at first but later it rained. Thus the poet compares the lake to a beautiful lady with and without makeup.

[10] Sunü, a goddess of the Huangdi (Yellow Emperor) period, is associated with music and string instruments as well as with sexual practices in relation to immortality.

[11] Yunying, a fairy dwelling in a cave by a bridge over the Blue Stream in Lantian, Shaanxi province. According to the Tang-dynasty legend, Pei Hang met Yunying in the cave and they became an ideal couple. The Ming drama *Lanqiao ji* (The Romance of the Blue Bridge) is based on this legend.

My Beauty, my Beauty!
I am crying for you at the top of my voice.
I am calling you softly from my longing lips.
Why do you not take any pity on me?
Even for a talk, I can only be with you
In a vision beholding your lovely face.

I remember that last year in Handan I met Lady Huang from Wuxia and Lady Hu from Lin'an, both truly beautiful. Yet our chance meeting was all too brief, and we had to part after only a glance, never to meet again.

Separated by mountains and clouds,
I can only pine for them in my dreams.

(*She sighs.*) Although my father holds the position of an official and I lead a life of luxury, I was after all born a female. How can I become somebody in this world? (*She weeps.*)

Thinking of a womanly fate deepens my sadness.

(*Yawning.*)

Suddenly I feel overwhelmed with weariness.

Oh, I am so tired. I'd better take a little nap.

(WANG *drops her head on the desk.*)

SCENE 3. Falling into a Dream

SHANCAI (*dances on to the stage*).

Shancai, Shancai, he waits upon the Lotus Throne[1].

Today he is visiting the mundane world by a divine decree.

I am the Buddhist Boy Shancai. Obeying the decree of the Bodhisattva, I came to earth to help Lady Wang realize her dream. Now that I am here, please wait and watch me perform the transformation.

Music plays softly. SHANCAI *takes out a mirror and guides* WANG *to get up. He takes out a set of male clothes and cap and starts to dress* WANG. SHANCAI *flips his Buddhist duster over* WANG's *face and body. Then he sends* WANG *back to sleep by the desk.*

SHANCAI. Please listen, Wang. Following the Bodhisattva's command, I have transformed you from a woman to a man. From now on, you can have freedom in your scholarly career as well as in the nuptial chamber. I now take my leave of you.

To music offstage, SHANCAI *exits. Startled,* WANG *stands up.*

WANG (*calling*). Holy god, please turn back! Please wait for me to express my gratitude! Dear me, why has he disappeared in a wink? (*Looking up and down her own body, she is astonished.*) Good heavens! I have really become a man. How strange it is!

[a3[i]] **Strange indeed, indeed strange!**
What a shocking surprise:
My body and appearance have thus changed.

(*Looking into a mirror, she laughs.*)

Now indeed I have become a *xiucai*[2].
Now indeed I have become a *xiucai*.

---

[1] The seat of the Bodhisattva Guanyin.

[2] *Jinshi* (presented scholar) was a successful candidate in the national imperial examination during the Ming and Qing dynasties.

I was born a female to wear skirts and hairpins.
Now I don the scholar's gown and a cap.

I sway my body left and right, and have my cap and gown in perfect order. (*Adjusting his gown and cap, he is ready to leave.*)[3]

Stepping down the terrace,
I feel at liberty and at ease.
I let myself swank and swagger.

I cannot resist running to the front hall to inform my parents. (*He laughs.*) I am really so happy. (*Walking, he sings.*)

[a3[ii]] **I saw the Immortal Boy descend to my studio.**
I saw the Immortal Boy descend to my studio.
Then he stood on the clouds outside the balustrade.
In the blink of an eye, he returned to Heaven.

(*Smiling.*)

Smiles beam upon my face.
Smiles beam upon my face.
Finally I can seek the dream in my mind;
Be done with the debts of womankind.

I am going to tell my grandma and my father and mother. They will surely be surprised, but with joy! (*He hurries away, singing merrily.*)

Go to tell them in the front hall.
Go to tell them in the front hall.
They're sure to be delighted.
O'er this sight they'll all rejoice.

---

[3] Personal pronouns "he" or "his" will be used to refer to WANG from here onwards.

SCENE 4. Spring Embroidery

LADY XIE, *wearing a light-colored skirt and a water-green cloak, comes onstage with two maids,* SPRING *and* FRAGRANCE.

LADY XIE.

[a4] **Following the sun,**
Flower shadows climb up my green window.
Arising from the orchid boudoir,
I am greeted by the orioles singing from the eastern wall.

SPRING, FRAGRANCE.

Trying on her light silk dress today,
Our lady's beauty matches
Willows embracing the pond and
Flowers blooming along the terrace.

LADY XIE.

[c3] The east wind plays with screen shadows till dawn;
It spurs cherry-apple trees to a full bloom overnight.

SPRING.

Several singing birds perch on the trees;

FRAGRANCE.

How much do they know of adornment?

LADY XIE. I am Lady Xie. My name is Dream Phoenix (Mengfeng). My family calls me Genuine Jade (Qiongzhen). I am a native of Wulin. My father is an official of the Capital and works at the Hanlin Academy.[1] My mother, from the Jia Family, is the first wife. My younger brother, Yunlang, and I are their only children.

Today the spring weather is indeed charming. Maids, would you please gather the scissors and embroidery from my bed? I want to do needlework in the Welcome Pavilion.

SPRING, FRAGRANCE. Yes, Miss. (*Roll up the bamboo screen and place a table.*) Everything is ready now, Miss, if you please?

LADY XIE *starts embroidering, with a maid doing the same on each side.*

---

[1] See Scene 2, n. 5.

LADY XIE.

[a5[i]] **Light wind and serene clouds swing in the spring.**
Getting up early, I came to embroider in the pavilion.

FRAGRANCE. What flowers are these? So fragrant.

LADY XIE.

A gentle breeze wafts the scent of cherry-apple blossoms.

Orioles sing offstage.

LADY XIE (*listens intently*).

Listening to warbling orioles on the blooming boughs,
I cannot help laughing at those
who pine away in spring for no reason at all.

SPRING.

[a5[ii]] **Weeping willows sway and swallows fly back and forth.**
Flowers press heavy on balustrades, as days grow long.

FRAGRANCE (*turns aside*).

I stopped my needle and have no mind to
Embroider the mandarin ducks any more.

(*Stealing a glance at* LADY XIE.)

Born with such a beautiful noble face, how come
Her heart has never been stirred by the spring?

LADY XIE. Now our embroidery work is done. Why not take a walk down the terrace? (*She starts walking.*)

MASTER XIE *and* MADAM XIE *come onstage in casual clothes.*

LADY XIE.

[a5[iii]] **Taking a break, I slipped away from my Phoenix Boudoir**
to seek rare flowers.
With gentle steps, I wade through this famous garden
of fragrant plants.

(*She encounters* MASTER XIE *and* MADAM XIE.)

MASTER XIE, MADAM XIE. What are you doing here, our dear daughter?

LADY XIE. I am merely relaxing my legs during a break from my needlework.

MASTER XIE. Needlework is the mandated profession for a good lady.

Follow the model of Lady Su of the Jin
embroidering Palindrome;[2]

MADAM XIE.

Even the Weaving Maid Tiansun[3] fails
to catch up with her skills.

MASTER XIE, MADAM XIE.

Happiness is infinite when the husband and the wife
Lean upon each other like bones and flesh.

(*Turning to the maids.*) Spring and Fragrance, please take good care of your mistress. We are now leaving.

SPRING, FRAGRANCE. Sure, we will.

LADY XIE.

[a6] **Nothing to regret for each passing day;**
Joy extends in the simple studio of a lady.

ALL.

How can one ever appreciate enough
the pleasure of books and a zither
and fragrance from a scent burner?

[2] Su Hui, a woman poet of the Former Qin. She invented the palindromic verse and wove it in silk, known as the *Xuanji tu* (Xuanji Diagram).

[3] Tiansun refers to the weaving fairy in the heaven, from the folktale "Niulang Zhinü" (The Cowherd and the Weaving Maid).

SCENE 5. A Farewell

WANG *enters in a round-collared green scholar gown, silk belt, and boots.*

WANG.

[a7] **I won first place in the Autumn Examination.**
How can I ever fall behind with an ink brush?

(*He sits down.*)

My aspiration is steeled with years of perseverance.
My arduous reading can load five carts with books.
Today I've found my path to climb to the sky.
Who dare say that I am not a truly great man?

I am Wang Menglin. My style name is Ruiqing. After I was transformed into a male, I've been bent on studying. Last year, I luckily gained first place in the Autumn Examination. As I have longed for seeing the beautiful scenery of West Lake, I may as well take a break to visit it now. Of course, I need to have permission from my parents first. (*Calling offstage.*) Father and Mother, may I invite you to come over and talk to me?

Enter MASTER WANG *in a round-collared gown with gray beard and a black official gauze cap,* MADAM WANG *in full gown and the phoenix coronet, with* YAOQIN *in black top and pants and* BROTHER *in black beard.*

MASTER WANG.

[a8] **Happy atmosphere fills the entire Capital.**
All celebrate the success of great scholars.

WANG. I am happy to see you, Father and Mother.

MASTER WANG, MADAM WANG. We are happy to see you, too.

WANG (*seeing his brother*). Hello, Big Brother.

BROTHER. Hello, Young Brother.

All sit down.

MASTER WANG. What do you want to tell us, my dear son, since you called us over?

WANG. I want to talk to you about a trip. I've long admired the landscape of Wuyue and I want to go sightseeing there. Would you please allow me, my dear parents?

MADAM WANG. No, my dear Son. Those mountains and lakes are far away. You are still too young. How can I let you go?

MASTER WANG. My dear Mistress, although our son is still young, we should encourage him to go out and experience the world. What harm is there in allowing his sightseeing?

BROTHER. The views around West Lake are truly unique. My little brother should definitely go and have a look.

MASTER WANG. Well, when do you plan to leave, my son?

WANG. If father and mother allow me, I'll leave right away. Today is an auspicious day for traveling.

BROTHER. Young Brother, have you packed your things yet?

WANG. Oh yes. I already bade Butler Yaoqin to have them ready.

MASTER WANG. Son, you can go and say goodbye to your grandma now.

WANG *exits.*

MADAM WANG. Um, my Lord, our son is still a child. If you let him go out into the world by himself, he might play the fool and do harm to his academic progress. It's better not to let him go.

BROTHER. In my view, my brother has fixed his mind on fame and success. How can he ever behave like a dandy? In the days when Menglin was a lady buried in her boudoir, she was full of resentment and frustration. Today as a man, he can finally stand up with his brows arching high. Mother, please don't try to stop him from pursuing his happiness.

MASTER WANG. You're quite right, my son. Mistress, please don't worry too much.

WANG *enters again, followed by* YAOQIN *with the luggage.*

YAOQIN. Young Master, your luggage is ready.

WANG. Very well. Now it's time to say goodbye.

MASTER WANG, MADAM WANG. All right, no ceremony.

YAOQIN. Wait. I'll get a horse.

YAOQIN *exits.* WANG *starts his farewell rituals.*

WANG.

[a9] **Bidding goodbye to my folks, I'll roam along the Zhe River**
And roll in the dust of the faraway mountains.

MASTER WANG, MADAM WANG.

Son,
Don't get lost in the playful waves.
Return to the Capital as soon as you can.

BROTHER (*turns aside from his parents and sings to* WANG *alone*).

Dear Brother,
Although many pretty ladies are around here,
Please remember the old saying,
"The Southern Land produces great beauties."

WANG *nods.* YAOQIN *comes with a horse.*

YAOQIN. Young Master, it's time to set out.
WANG. Father and Mother, I am leaving now.
MASTER WANG, MADAM WANG. Please take care, Son.
WANG. Sure, I will. Big Brother, farewell now.
BROTHER. Be careful on the road.
WANG. Don't worry.
YAOQIN (*bows to* MASTER WANG, MADAM WANG, and BROTHER). Your humble servant is leaving.
MASTER WANG, MADAM WANG. Please take good care of our junior son.
YAOQIN. Yes, I will.

WANG *gets on the horse and exits with his servant to the left stage; others exit to the right.*

SCENE 6. Meeting at a Convent

HEAD NUN.

Bamboo groves surround the garden corridor.
The Convent, though in the city, looks rustic.
Clouds are blooming into large moon flowers.
Birds tiptoe on the branches rows upon rows.

I am the Head Nun of the Purple Bamboo Convent. Yesterday the butler of Master Xie Residence sent some embroidered banners here. He informed me that Lady Xie is coming to burn incense today. I must bid all my disciples to get ready. (*Calling offstage.*) Hail, Sister Nuns, please get ready. The daughter of the Xie Family will be here at any moment.

Reply offstage — "Yes!" Enter two servants.

SERVANTS. Is the Head Nun in?
HEAD NUN. Oh, yes. I am here.
SERVANTS. Lady Xie's sedan chair has arrived.
HEAD NUN. I am just waiting to welcome her.
SERVANTS. Please step down from the sedan, Miss.

LADY XIE, *in a light-colored skirt and a blue and green cloak, enters, accompanied by an old nurse and a young maid.*

LADY XIE.

[a10[i]] **The wind blows my fairy dress, sending fragrance into the air.**
Having left the embroidery pavilion, I arrived at the gate here.

(*Meeting the* HEAD NUN.)

HEAD NUN. Respect to you, Miss.
LADY XIE. Countless blessings, Head Nun.
HEAD NUN. Please forgive me for being late.
LADY XIE. No offence.
HEAD NUN. Miss, now please light your incense.

LADY XIE *strikes the bell and bows with a lit incense stick.*

HEAD NUN. Now the praying is over. Miss, please take tea in the Lotus Pavilion.
LADY XIE. Head Nun, after you.

Exit together; enter another two servants.

SERVANTS. Hello—, where is the Head Nun?
HEAD NUN (*rushes out*). Oh, I'm coming. Who are you?
SERVANTS. We are from Master Wang Residence. Our mistress wants to burn incense here. Her sedan has already parked at the gate.
HEAD NUN. Mistress, please step down from the sedan.

MADAM WANG, *wearing a white skirt and the phoenix crown, enters with two maids.*

MADAM WANG.
[a10[ii]] **In the deep shades of green bamboo and lofty pines,**
I come to feel the melody of solitude in a Zen woods.
HEAD NUN. I apologize. I didn't know that you were coming, Madam. Please forgive me for not being able to receive you at the front gate.
MADAM WANG. Don't worry.
HEAD NUN. Now please light your incense, Madam.
MADAM WANG (*bows with a lit incense stick*).
[a11[i]] **Modeling my respect to the clouds of mercy,**
The sandalwood burner exhales purple fragrance.
The wind, circling in the sky, brings near the sound of waves.

(*She looks at the banners unfolding above.*)

Who hung those banners? My, what wonderful needlework!
Looking at the dragon strokes and phoenix stitches,
I can't help feeling the orchid heart and beautiful mind of the embroiderer.
Its exquisite work can match the tapestry of the clouds.
Such a wondrous hand
Cannot be found even for a thousand taels of gold.
She is definitely a match for the Weaving Maid Tiansun.

Head Nun, where did you get this pair of banners?
HEAD NUN. Oh, they came from Master Xie Residence. Lady Xie had them hung here to repay a blessing she received from the Buddha.
MADAM WANG. Oh, I see. When did Lady Xie come?
HEAD NUN. Today. She is still here now. (*Calling offstage.*) Sister Nun, serve tea please.
LITTLE NUN (*carries tea in*). I am coming.
HEAD NUN (*stands up and serves the tea*). Please have some tea, Madam.
MADAM WANG. Thank you.
NANNY ZHANG (*comes in quietly and tugs at* LITTLE NUN's *sleeve*). Little Sister, please tell me. Who is that old lady?
LITTLE NUN. They say she is the wife of Master Wang, the mother of the new *jieyuan*[1] crowned at the examination last fall.
NANNY ZHANG. Oh yes. She is Madam Wang. Master Wang is an acquaintance of our master. Why shouldn't I say hello to her? (*Goes forward and kowtows.*) Are you Madam Wang? Please accept the kowtow of a humble old lady.
MADAM WANG (*pulls her up*). Oh, please don't.
HEAD NUN. This is Zhang, the wet nurse of the lady from the Xie Residence.
MADAM WANG. Oh, I see. You are Nanny Zhang for Lady Xie. Please sit down and have a chat.
NANNY ZHANG. Oh, how dare I? With your noble mistress sitting right here.
MADAM WANG. My pleasure. Just take a seat, Nurse.
NANNY ZHANG. All right. I will take one in the lower place then.
MADAM WANG. This pair of colorful banners came from your young lady's hand, I guess.
NANNY ZHANG. Yes, you are right.
MADAM WANG. Done by such a beautiful hand with such a noble heart. A rare masterpiece indeed. Quite unique in the world.
NANNY ZHANG. No bragging. If there is such a thing as an imperial examination for women, this Miss of ours will beat Lady Huang of Jinjiang[2] with her sensitive mind and colorful brush, not to mention her wondrous skills in drawing and embroidering.

[1] *Jieyuan* was the scholar who ranked first in the provincial imperial examination during the Ming and Qing dynasties.
[2] Refers to Huang Chonggu. See Scene 2, n. 4 for more.

MADAM WANG. How old is your young lady? Is she engaged yet?

NANNY ZHANG. Madam, please allow me to report to you.

[a11[ii]] **Like a jade hidden in the woods,**
Our Miss is in the prime of her life.
Having just passed eighteen years of spring,
She is waiting in her Phoenix Pavilion for a flute calling.
She writes as beautifully as Shaojun[3].
Her talent surpasses Daoyun[4].
Her beauty defeats Xizi, a Ming imperial consort.
Our Master and Mistress,
Worried that no man can ever match their daughter in talent and beauty,
They are desperately searching for her ideal mate.

MADAM WANG. May I know the name of the young lady?

NANNY ZHANG. She is called Dream Phoenix.

MADAM WANG (*laughs*). My second son happens to be called Dream Unicorn.

HEAD NUN (*laughs*). Phoenix and Unicorn are a perfect match.

NANNY ZHANG. May I ask how old your second son is? Is he engaged to anyone yet?

MADAM WANG. He is of the same age as your Miss. It is hard to find a lady to match him. So he has not yet accepted any engagement.

MAID (*enters*). Nanny Zhang, where are you?

NANNY ZHANG. I am here!

MAID. Our Miss is asking for her sedan to go home.

NANNY ZHANG. Yes. The sedan has been waiting for a long while now. Please ask Miss to come out.

MAID. Miss, please.

LADY XIE *enters*.

HEAD NUN (*greets* LADY XIE). Miss, sorry that I was unable to wait on you because of Madam Wang's visit here. Please forgive me.

---

[3] Possibly refers to Zhuo Wenjun, a woman of the Western Han who was good at verse and string music. During her widowhood, she eloped with Sima Xiangru (179–118 BC). Their romantic love has been a popular subject in fiction and drama, such as a Ming *zaju* named *Zhuo Wenjun siben Xiangru* (Zhuo Wenjun Elopes with Xiangru).

[4] Xie Daoyun (317–342), a woman poet of the Eastern Jin, known for her poetic line that likens snowflakes to willow catkins.

LADY XIE. Don't worry. I am leaving for home now.

HEAD NUN. I've prepared some humble food. Miss, would you mind staying a little longer?

LADY XIE. Thank you. But I have to go now.

NANNY ZHANG. Miss, Madam Wang is in the front hall. Would you please come and say hello to her?

MADAM WANG (*nodding*). Maid, send for my sedan.

MAID. At your service. (*Calling offstage.*) Mistress is asking for her sedan. Please get ready.

Reply offstage — "All right!"

NANNY ZHANG. Madam, our Miss is here to see you.

LADY XIE. Madam, countless blessings.

MADAM WANG (*surprised with joy*). Countless blessings to you too, Miss.

LADY XIE. I didn't know that you were here. I apologize for being remiss.

MADAM WANG. Oh no, please don't apologize. Thank you for seeing me.

WANG's SERVANTS. Madam, please get into sedan chair.

XIE's SERVANTS. Miss, please get into sedan chair.

MADAM WANG, LADY XIE (*turning to* HEAD NUN). Head Nun, thank you for all the trouble. We have to say goodbye now.

HEAD NUN. Please forgive me for any negligence.

MADAM WANG, LADY XIE. Don't worry.

LADY XIE. Madam, please!

MADAM WANG. Miss, please!

Each gets into sedan chair.

ALL.

[a6] **Praying at the Lotus Throne**
Brings near a romance of the Red Dust.

LADY XIE (*glancing at* MADAM WANG, *sings aside*).

Strange it is that we sowed
Feelings deep at first sight.

MADAM WANG (*glancing at* LADY XIE, *sings aside*).

My heart won't be at rest until I know
How to tie together Unicorn and Phoenix.

Exit in opposite directions.

SCENE 7. Seeking a Fair Lady

WANG (*wearing his previous* jieyuan *gown*).

[a12] **Passing time in a pleasure boat,**
As if I were rafting to a fairy isle.
The lake reflects like a crystal mirror.
Distant hills appear emerald green.
Under the lofty clouds,
The scenery looks exceptionally charming in the rain
And delicate in the sun.
Such beauty can never be captured by a painting.

(*Sits down.*) Since I came to Wulin, I have been dawdling on the lake. The day before yesterday I went downtown to visit my cousin Brother Yang. Unexpectedly, my aunt's son Brother Gao was also there. We chatted for the whole day. I did not go home until it was really late. Yesterday was the Duanyang Festival;[1] I watched the dragon boat race. (*Laughing to himself.*) Laughable indeed. Every day I go out on the pretense of sightseeing. Actually I am searching for a great beauty. Although I have met dozens of ladies, none of them can be called a beauty from nature. Thus I am disappointed and bored. Today, feeling too lazy to go anywhere, I may just stay in and read a book.

(*He gets on the high seat by the desk and starts reading.*)

[a13] **Tired of light music from the flutes,**
I collect my mind for the colorful brush.
Although the lake and hills are bewitching,
There are no ladies to match their beauty.

(*Sighs.*) I don't know how my career is going. Although my blue gown has been changed into a green one, who knows

When the scholar kerchief on my head
can be changed into a black gauze official cap?
So many worries on my mind.
Who can share them with me?

[1] Observed on the fifth day of the fifth lunar month, in memory of the great poet Qu Yuan (ca. 340–ca. 278 BC). Also known as the Dragon Boat Festival and Duanwu Festival.

YANG *in cap and belt and* GAO *in head kerchief and gown ride in on horses, followed by their servants.*

YANG, GAO.

[a10] **Swishing the whip, we rode over the carved bridge.**
The Zen Wood appears right in front.

SERVANTS. Masters, we've arrived at the Temple of Invisible Divinity.
YANG. Go up and report then.
SERVANT A. Hello —, is the Monk in?
MONK. I'm coming, coming. Where are you from?
SERVANT B. Is *Jieyuan* Wang in the temple?
MONK. Yes.
SERVANT B. Hurry and tell him that Master Yang and Master Gao from the city are paying him a visit.
MONK. Okay. (*Goes in.*) Brother Zhou —.
YAOQIN. What's up?
MONK. Master Yang and Master Gao are here for a visit.
YAOQIN. Very well. You may leave now.

Monk exits.

YAOQIN (*reports to* WANG). Master, Master Yang and Master Gao are here for a visit.
WANG. Please let them in.

YAOQIN *turns his back to invite the two masters. The two masters get off their horses. Their servants exit.*

YANG. Where's the young master?
YAOQIN. He is in the Purple Cloud Study.

All turn and walk. WANG *stands up and straightens his gown and head kerchief.*

WANG. Ah, come in, my Brothers. Forgive me for not receiving you at the gate.
YANG, GAO. We're happy to see you again.

All sit down. A little monk brings tea.

GAO. Cousin, why didn't you go out to enjoy yourself today?
WANG. Nothing really interesting, I am too bored to go.
YANG, GAO. Why?
WANG. Brothers, you don't know what I came here for. (*He sighs and sings.*)

[a14] **My first goal is to see the lake and visit my buddies.**
My second goal is to look for great ladies.
Who knows, there is no path to the Peach Spring[2].
No wonder Lazy Liu[3] has lost his heart in searching.

GAO. Oh, I see.
YANG (*giggles*). If dear brother wants to find a beautiful lady, there is one right here.
WANG. Where?
YANG. Well, her address, I forgot it at the moment. But Brother, don't worry. Let me think. (*He pulls* GAO *aside.*) Brother Gao, why don't we fool him somewhat for sport?
GAO. How?
YANG (*whispers to* GAO). So and so, um, how's this trick?
GAO. Hope it works.

YANG *and* GAO *turn to* WANG.

WANG. Please have a seat.
YANG. Sure.
WANG. Have you remembered her address yet?
YANG. Yes, I have it. But she is not a lady from a decent family.
WANG. I bet she is a courtesan type, isn't she?
YANG. You're right.
WANG (*laughs*). As long as her mind is sensitive and her face is charming, who cares about her nightly romance? Please tell me what is great about her?
YANG. What is great about her? Well. (*Sighs.*)

---

[2] Also known as the Peach Blossom Spring; referring to an utopia, arcadia, or a dreamland. The idea originated from Tao Yuanming's (365–427) "Taohuayuan ji" (Record of the Peach Blossom Spring).

[3] Refers to Liu Chen of the Eastern Han. Liu and Ruan Zhao met two fairies and stayed there for half a year. When they returned home, they found that seven generations of time had passed. They went back to look for the fairies but failed to find their traces, thus feeling lost.

[a15] **Her elegance dwarfs Su Xiao[4].**
Her talent weighs down Xue Tao[5].

WANG (*surprised with joy*). Really? I can't believe there's such beauty in this world!

YANG.

More surprising than that,
Her flirting skirt far surpasses that of Pan Jiamiao[6].

WANG (*moving his chair closer, asks*). What is her name?

YANG.

People all call her Beauty Pipa Qian.
The entire south strives to see her beauty.

WANG (*laughing*). On hearing this I can't help laughing out loud.

GAO *starts giggling.* YANG *checks him at once with a waving hand.*

YANG (*behind* WANG's *back*).

Even if he were the wise Lord Zhou[7],
He is sure to fall into my clever trap.

WANG (*calms down*). Have you ever seen this lady? Don't fool me.

YANG (*pretends to be serious*). What're you talking about? Would I fool my dear brother? I saw her with my own eyes. Talent plus beauty, perfect.

GAO (*adds with a smile*). I saw her once too. Truly beautiful.

WANG (*happily*). If so, may I know where the Beauty lives?

YANG. Inside the city by the Western Gate.

WANG. Well, thank you for the information. I'll pay her a visit tomorrow morning.

YANG, GAO. Dear me, it's already past noontime. We must be leaving now.

WANG. I've had some wine and food ready. May I invite my brothers to have a hearty drink by the flowers?

---

[4] Also known as Su Xiaoxiao, a famous courtesan of the Qiantang area in the Southern Qi.

[5] Xue Tao (770–831), a famous woman poet of the Tang dynasty.

[6] Possibly refers to the imperial concubine Pan of the Southern Qi. On his coronation day in 499, Dong Hunhou ordered her to walk on the gold lotus paved on the floor, saying "Lotus flowers bloom with her every step."

[7] Refers to Zhou Yu, a character in *Sanguo yanyi* (The Romance of Three Kingdoms). He was frequently tricked by Zhuge Liang in spite of his intelligence.

YANG, GAO. No, thank you. Cousin, you are a guest here yourself. How could we further impose upon you?
WANG. Don't talk like that, Brothers. Stay, if you take me as your little brother.
YANG. Well, obedience is the best sign of respect. I'll give a feast in return some other day.
WANG. Uh, formalities again?

All laugh.

WANG. Please!
YANG, GAO. Please!

Bowing to each other, all exit.

SCENE 8. A Foul Visit

PIPA QIAN, *in heavy makeup, wears a red blouse, a green skirt, a blue vest, and a pair of red shoes. Holding a kerchief in one hand and a fan in the other, she enters with a grimace.*

PIPA QIAN.

[a16] **I am the courtesan of all courtesans in Suzhou and Hangzhou,**
With my face caked with powder, head crowned with flowers,
Hair cropped three-inches long, and moth eyebrows quite bald,
Even a man with a heart of stone will melt at the sight of me.

(*Sits down.*) I am no other than the famous courtesan Pipa Qian of Hangzhou. I was born with such beauty that even the moon sees me and has to hide itself behind the clouds. However, it would not be an exaggeration to say that I am the Pigsy[1] reborn. My face is so pretty that even flowers have to shy away at the sight of my coming. Who cares about those who think I am worse than a cow demon incarnate!

Every day after putting on my makeup, I look into the mirror and find myself a great beauty. I then lean against the door simpering at the passersby. People call me a ghost. (*Laughing.*) Well, in spite of my beauty, young dandies no longer visit me. Such a waste of my good looks really vexes me. This morning I got up a bit too early. Now I am feeling tired. A little nap seems to be in order. Why not take it now?

PIPA QIAN *falls asleep.* WANG, *wearing a new scholar kerchief, a green gown with hand-painted flowers, and a bright red shirt, walks in buoyantly with a fan.*

---

[1] Pigsy (Zhu Bajie) is a comic pig character in the novel *Xiyou ji* (Journey to the West). Here it refers to Pipa Qian's ugly appearance.

WANG.

[a5i] **Leisurely I walk, straightening up my headgear and gown.**

(*Touching his heart with a smile.*)

A first time romantic tryst makes me nervously frown.
Last night I dreamed of Lady Du Weiniang[2].
Although I am used to be a pedantic scholar,
My heart is in turmoil for her just as the Suzhou Governor.

Thanks to my two cousins for the detailed information, I easily found my way in downtown. Slowly, I'm reaching my destination. This must be it. Oh, why is the gate still bolted tight? No carriages and horses are in sight. Perhaps I should knock and find out why.

(*Knocking at the door.*)

Hello —, is anybody there?

PIPA QIAN (*startled to a wake up, sings slowly*).

[a5ii] **Suddenly awakened from a love dream,**
My heart beats in ecstasy with passion.

(*Yawning.*)

Oh my dear,
Sitting up, a fair lady, I am all over perspiring.
Who is there at the door knocking and knocking?
Who is it?

WANG. Me. Please open the door.

PIPA QIAN (*listens and turns cheerful*).

Suddenly my ears caught a fresh voice.
He must be a dashing romantic prince.

Well, what a miracle! The guy knocking at the door is no ordinary customer. Let me open the door and have a look. (*Holds up her fan to cover her face.*) Young man, where are you from?

WANG *turns his back and sees* PIPA QIAN.

WANG (*surprised*). My dear, what a fat lady. She must be a herald for Beauty Pipa Qian. (*He bows to her.*) In admiration of Lady Pipa Qian, I came here especially to visit her.

---

[2] A courtesan of the Tang dynasty.

PIPA QIAN (*turns aside and laughs to herself*). Gracious me, I old Pipa Qian really have good luck, haven't I? I never expected that someone so young and handsome would bother to come and see me. Funny indeed. (*She turns to face* WANG.) It is an honor to have you. Please come in and take a seat.
WANG. Thank you.

PIPA QIAN *and* WANG *walk together.*

PIPA QIAN *(turns aside)*.
[a17[i]] **I am stealing a look at him from beneath my fan.**
Bless me,
What delicate bones, sober spirit, and smooth face.

(*Simpering.*)

The sight sends my soul fluttering.
Indeed,
A Red Skirt loves a Green Gown.

WANG (*looking around*).
A careful look, I found nothing tasteful
In the furnishing of this reception hall.
I begin to regret coming at all.

(*Deep in thinking.*)

I am pondering—

PIPA QIAN. My Prince, come with me to my upstairs boudoir. (*Pulling* WANG *up.*)
WANG.
Ah,
I could hardly imagine such a situation,
Utterly out of my expectation,
Utterly out of my expectation.

PIPA QIAN. Young Prince, take a seat please.
WANG. Wait a minute. This lady dresses gaudily. Why is she always covering her face with a fan? Why?
PIPA QIAN. Daughters, please serve tea.
WANG. May I ask in what role you serve Beauty Pipa Qian?
PIPA QIAN. What a ridiculous question! I *am* Beauty Pipa Qian. Who are you looking for?

WANG (*shocked, standing up*). If you are the Beauty, why don't you fold away your fan and let me see your graceful face?

PIPA QIAN *removes her fan and assumes a flirting but coy manner.*

PIPA QIAN. Please look at me now.

WANG *looks at* PIPA QIAN *and jumps with fright.*

WANG. Wow, what an ugly hag. Are you sure you are Beauty Pipa Qian?
PIPA QIAN. Sure, I am Pipa Qian.
WANG. Really?
PIPA QIAN. No mistake.
WANG (*stupefied, sighs*). Damn it. My brothers, Yang and Gao, fooled me.

(*Turns aside.*)

[a17ii] **At the sudden revelation of this flowery whore,**
I am scared to death.
My soul scatters and my sweat has wet the gown.
Strange indeed,
She is even uglier than a mountain demon or a wild ghost.

(*Stamping his feet.*)

I hate you, ensnaring Gao and Yang.
Why did you fool me into such a demon hunt?
Well, **it is also my own fault.**
Obsession with beauties made me lose my head.

A maid brings the tea. PIPA QIAN *serves it to* WANG.

PIPA QIAN. Young man, please don't lose your senses. Have some tea.

WANG *accepts it unwillingly.*

PIPA QIAN (*smiling*).
I feel very, very happy.
Seeing you today doubles my love feelings.

(*Laughing, she moves her body closer to him.*)

Please move your body closer.
Please move your body closer.

WANG (*chuckling, turns aside*). What should I say? Looking at her face, you can't help being scared. Seeing her stupid behavior, you really want to laugh. What should I do?
PIPA QIAN (*stroking* WANG's *shoulder*). Young man, why are you murmuring to yourself instead of talking to me? May I know where you are living and what your honorable name is?
WANG. I am named Wang, a native of the Western Capital.
PIPA QIAN. How old are you?
WANG. Eighteen. What is your great age, Mother?
PIPA QIAN (*shaking her hand in flurry*). Oh my, what language are you using? Watch your tongue please. You men come here as guests to visit us whores. You should address us politely as "Sister" or "Fair Lady." If you want to ask our age, you should use the term "youth" or "prime."
WANG (*bowing with clasped hands*). Thank you for your instruction. Fair Lady, may I ask, how old is your youth?
PIPA QIAN (*filled with joy*). I am forty-five years your senior, merely sixty-three years old now.
WANG (*laughs*). Still not old yet.
PIPA QIAN (*calls offstage*). Daughters, please serve wine.
WANG. The weather is hot. Please don't bother to get wine.
PIPA QIAN. Nonsense. How can we not warm some wine? Quick, please get the wine ready.

Daughters reply offstage and come out with wine.

PIPA QIAN. Prince, please drink.
WANG. I'm never good at drinking. Sister, help yourself please.
PIPA QIAN. Don't be so ceremonious. Drink a little, all right? (*She forces* WANG *to drink a cup and downs several cups herself, becoming drunk.*) Oh yeah, I'm getting drunk. Daughters, please prepare the summer bed. The prince and I are going to bed.
WANG (*panic*). Oh — ahhh. Don't be so romantic! I am leaving now.

About to go, he is pulled back by PIPA QIAN.

PIPA QIAN. Mister Wang, please don't make a mistake today. You and I are fated to meet here even though we live a thousand miles apart. Why do you have to pretend to be a stranger in front of me? (*She pulls* WANG *toward her again.*)

WANG (*looking worried*). Oh yes, thank you Mother for your kind love. Why do I shun it? But today my humble body is not feeling well. I have to leave now. How about my coming tomorrow to accompany you?
PIPA QIAN. Little Wang, please save your words to trick a two-year-old. How could you use them to fool me? I don't care about tomorrow or the day after tomorrow. Today I refuse to let you go!
WANG (*begs*). Mother-Sister, I promise you that I will come tomorrow. It is not a lie.
PIPA QIAN. Even if your promises make the sky shower flowers, I would simply see them as scattered clouds in the air.
WANG. Mother, please take pity on a young lad.
PIPA QIAN. Easier said than done. Daughters, please give a hand. Carry him over for me.
MAIDS. Yes, Mother.
WANG (*truly panicked*). Mother, Sisters, please let me go! Someone is coming!
PIPA QIAN (*looking behind her*). Who is coming?

WANG *throws* PIPA QIAN *to the ground and runs off.*

MAIDS. Ah ya, Mother has taken a bad fall. (*They help* PIPA QIAN *to get to her feet.*)
PIPA QIAN. Dear me, there's such audacity in this world. My anger is like a dagger piercing my heart. (*She screams.*) Wait and see how I catch him! (*She attempts to run after him. Two maids stop her.*)
MAIDS. Mother, the man has already run away. Too late to catch him now.
PIPA QIAN.

> Oh, I am stabbed to death by anger.
> To let go of such an unfeeling prince,
> You kill a love-filled Pipa Qian!

Exit all.

SCENE 9. Destined to Meet

YAOQIN (*enters laughing*). I am none other than the butler of *Jieyuan* Wang. Since I followed him all the way to the south, I have visited many scenic spots and have seen many good shows. What extraordinary fun I've had! My young master is really laughable. One day he goes out looking for a lovely lady. On another day, he looks everywhere for a great beauty. No wonder he was fooled by Master Yang and Master Gao into visiting the so-called Beauty Pipa Qian. That day the young master got up early. He put on the clothes of a dandy and went to visit the brothel in a cheerful mood. But after a few hours, he ran back crestfallen. No sooner had he stepped inside the door than he started scolding me and gave me a good beating under the pretext of my tardiness in receiving him. The following day he went alone downtown to settle accounts with Yang and Gao. He made havoc that day.

(*He laughs again.*)

Well, I was pretty much in the dark about what had happened. The other day I had no obligations. Behind the back of my young master, I went to see Pipa Qian.

(*Biting his fingers with a big shrug.*)

Oh my, even the Wuyan[1] reborn or the Momu[2] incarnate would not look that ugly. Look, what a monstrous face. How could my young master not feel insulted? Ever since the master got back from Pipa Qian, he has not felt well. He stays in the temple every day. But this morning after breakfast, he disappeared. I have asked all the monks and searched every corner of the temple, but I failed to find a trace of him. So I must get a horse and look for him by the lakeside.

(*He gets on the horse and exits in a loud charge.*)

---

[1] Wuyan is the name of a place during the Warring States period. Here it refers to a woman from Wuyan called Zhong Lichun. She was extremely ugly and remained single until she was forty. However, she was intelligent and presented herself to King Xuan of the Qi with her notions of virtue. She became the imperial concubine. But unfortunately, "Wuyan" becomes the equivalent of an ugly woman.

[2] Momu, a legendary woman of the Huangdi period, known for her ugliness.

LADY HU (*enters in a blue blouse and a white skirt*).

[a18] **The withering garden harbors so much sorrow;**
Shocking, blossom-laden boughs become bare and old.
My beauty after a sleep appears even lovelier.
Though I'm too languid to paint my eyebrows,

(*She sits down.*)

Living in a hut, I wear no silk and satin.
My slim waist sways with a face scanty of rouge.
What I loathe most is stitching in and out,
Sewing others' bridal garments year after year.

I am Dream Lotus from the Hu Family. I am a native of Lin'an. Unfortunately, my father died, leaving my gentle mother and me to support each other. We live in a desolate place and are mired in poverty. Who knows if good days will ever come? After getting up in the morning, I feel terribly bored. A walk outdoors will perhaps lift my spirits.

(*Taking a walk.*)

[a19i] **Sigh after sigh in the morning,**
I can feel my waist shrinking.
Looking at my skinny shadow,
I am shocked yet with a smile.

(*With tears.*)

My feelings are so tender;
Autumn moon and spring flowers,
Who can appreciate my hidden sorrows?
The prime of my life sneaks away right before my eyes.
The rosy color of my cheeks fades stealthily.

(*Sighs.*)

I fear, such emptiness and idle moments will
mercilessly rob me of my youth.

LADY HU *exits.* WANG *walks in slowly in a blue gown.*

WANG.

[a19ii] **Leaving the orchid boat, I stroll toward the western hills.**
Upon the still path, I see no traces of a soul.

Looking afar, withering willows and chilly clouds
compose an autumn lamentation.
I thread my way through the woods and cross the bridge.

(*The sound of a flute.* WANG *listens.*)

What lady is playing the jade flute?
Chasing the west wind, it unfolds such a sorrowful tune.

I got up this morning feeling desolate. So I am taking a stroll in the western hills. Look, the woods, still and deep, are filled with birds' singing and flowers' perfume. What a beautiful scene!

LADY HU *enters. She shies away seeing* WANG.

WANG (*turns aside*). Oh, there is such a beauty in this world. Doesn't she have the celestial bearing and unique charm that would topple a state? (*Stealing glances at her.*)

MOTHER HU (*enters*). Living alone without a neighbor, I can only listen to the chattering birds to pass my day.

Um, where's my daughter?

LADY HU. I am coming.

Seeing WANG, MOTHER HU *is surprised but happy.* LADY HU *exits with looking-back smiles.*

MOTHER HU. Oh, a young gentleman. Please come in.
WANG. I'm a stranger here. Dare I go in?
MOTHER HU. Never mind. Sir, please.
WANG. All right. Mother, after you.
MOTHER HU. Sir, please.
WANG (*steps in with a bow*). Mother, please accept my respect.
MOTHER HU. Countless blessings, Sir. Please take a seat.

Both sit down.

MOTHER HU. May I ask where you are from? What is your honorable name?
WANG. Mother, let me tell you in detail.

[a19[iii]] **In the old Locust Hall,**
The Wang Clan has a long list of honor.

MOTHER HU. Is your father still in service or retired?

WANG.

He is still serving at the court.

MOTHER HU. My! You're a nobleman then. My humble self should have paid you respect.

May I know how old you are now?

WANG.

Speaking of my age, two times nine.
A humble scholar merely won first place in Autumn Examination.

MOTHER HU. Oh, you are a *jieyuan*! Are you married yet?

WANG.

My vermilion gate still misses a virtuous Meng Guang[3].
On the wings of a phoenix, I still search in the mist.

MOTHER HU. Oh, I see. Why have you traveled such a long way to come to the Land of Wu?

WANG (*smiles*).

For seeing the beauty of the lake and hills,
I have made this special trip.

MOTHER HU. Just to see West Lake. What elegant taste you have!

WANG *laughs.*

MOTHER HU (*stands up and turns aside*). Hold on for a minute. I see that this young man speaks in a refined manner. He looks stylish and promising. Someday he will be rich and famous. Speaking of my daughter, Dream Lotus, she is already sixteen, and still not engaged. Even if she meets someone in the future, how could she ever find such a talented scholar? Why shouldn't I offer him my daughter who matches him well in talent and looks? Well, it makes sense. It really makes sense! (*She turns to face* WANG.)

WANG. Mother, please sit down.

MOTHER HU. You sit down, Prince.

WANG. May I know Mother's name?

---

[3] Meng Guang was a paragon wife of the Eastern Han dynasty. She and her husband Liang Hong lived a hermit life. Later in Suzhou, even though her husband was a hired farmhand, Meng Guang raised her rice bowl up to her brows before eating at every meal to show her respect for him.

MOTHER HU. My maiden name is Wu. My husband is named Hu. Unfortunately he died young, leaving my daughter and me behind. The girl you met at the front gate is my daughter, Dream Lotus.

WANG. Oh, that beautiful lady is your darling.

MOTHER HU. Thank you for your flattery. I have something in mind, but I wonder whether I should tell you.

WANG. Certainly, Mother. Speak about whatever it is on your mind.

MOTHER HU. Although my daughter grew up in a poor family, she knows a bit about books and ink. If you do not mind her plain looks and humble background, she'll be happy to clean house for you.

WANG. Thank you Mother for your kindness, but ... (*He stops in hesitation.*)

MOTHER HU (*laughs*). Prince, you don't have to hesitate. I know what you mean. Coming from a humble background, how could my daughter dare occupy the position of the mistress of the house? She will be happy if she could just be married to you.

WANG (*bows with joy*). Mother, you really know how to read a man's mind. In that case, your daughter may feel being slighted.

MOTHER HU. Certainly not.

WANG. Coming here, I forgot to bring any engagement gifts. What shall I do?

MOTHER HU. As the old saying goes, "A thread makes the marriage." There is no need for anything expensive.

WANG. Since you say so. (*Taking off two jade pendants from his belt.*) I have a pair of jade pendants in my silk belt. I would like to give them to your daughter as an engagement gift.

MOTHER HU (*taking them over*). Thank you. (*She steps out and calls offstage.*) Daughter, where are you?

LADY HU. I'm here.

MOTHER HU. Well, my Daughter, have you heard what we have been talking about?

LADY HU. Yes, I have.

MOTHER HU. What do you think of it?

LADY HU (*smiles*). What can I think of it? But how could you so easily give me to someone as a concubine?

MOTHER HU. My dear Daughter, you are wrong this time. I'm your mother. How can I not be concerned about your lifelong happiness? But this prince is

[a19[iv]] **Handsome and high-spirited,**
He stands above all in his dashing manners.
One can never overestimate his future fame and wealth.
His father, **a minister serves at court.**

A family with generations of officials and scholars
Will never let down your life expectations.

(*She takes out the jade pendants.*)

Daughter, this is his engagement gift. Do you accept it?
LADY HU (*taking it over, she turns aside*).

On hearing all this, I feel as happy as I am scared.

(*She looks at the jade pendants.*)

Looking at this Lantian[4] jade,
Gazing at its brilliance,
I feel that my marital luck has fallen from the sky.

(*She exits.*)

MOTHER HU (*brings tea over and serves*). Prince, please have some tea.
WANG. Thank you, Mother.

YAOQIN *enters on horseback, with his whip held high.*

YAOQIN.

[a20] **Following the traces, I am searching high and low.**
With a cracking whip, my horse races like the wind blow.
Around the lake and hills I have looked every corner;
But still nowhere can I find my dear master.

Strange indeed, the whole morning has passed. I still can't find a trace of him. Now I've come to the western hills. There is still no sign of him. I'll try calling him aloud. Master! Master!

(WANG *listens;* YAOQIN *calls again.*)

YAOQIN. Master! Where are you?
WANG. Yaoqin, I am here.
MOTHER HU. Hmm, whom are you addressing, Prince?
WANG. My servant is here looking for me.
MOTHER HU. Oh, I see. (*She goes out and greets* YAOQIN.) Please come here.
YAOQIN (*enters and sees* WANG). Oh my, I have been looking for you everywhere. You're right here.

---

[4] A county in Shaanxi province famous for jade. It also refers to the mountain, to the east of Lantian, producing jade.

WANG. I was taking a walk and by chance arrived here. This mother kindly invited me for tea. So I am late in returning.

YAOQIN (*bows*). Old Mother, please accept my respect.

MOTHER HU. No ceremony, Young Brother.

YAOQIN. Already noon has passed. Shall we leave, Master?

WANG. Yes. I must be leaving now.

MOTHER HU. Please take your time. When you become famous and rich someday, please don't forget us.

WANG. Mother, please don't worry. I am not an ungrateful man. In the coming year, when I've finished my competition at the Spring Examination, I will definitely send someone over to get your daughter. (*Bowing a goodbye.*)

Meeting like duckweeds on the water,
Our feelings are deeper than the water.
A single word of promise
I take as weighty as a thousand taels of gold.

MOTHER HU.

When the apricot tree blossoms in the coming spring,
We'll lean against our gate waiting for your good news.

WANG (*getting on the horse, holds both his hands over his heart*). Mother, please go in.

Exit in opposite directions.

SCENE 10. Autumn Pounding[1]

LADY HUANG (*enters in a blue blouse and a pale skirt*).

[a21] **In a lamenting autumn night,**
The sky is blue like water;
The moon appears an ice wheel.

The moon appears an ice wheel.
The jade dews are forming inaudibly.
A golden breeze is stroking my face gently.

I am Dream Orchid from the Huang Family, a native of Suzhou. Unfortunately, my kind mother died years ago. My strict father brought me up. Although born in a poor family, I have cultivated a taste in letters and ink. I've turned away all those uncultured suitors. I have sworn to myself that if I fail to find a talented scholar in my life, I would shave my hair and become a nun rather than marry! (*Sighs.*) This is:

Nobody knows my heart's secret lamentations.
I can only share them with the lofty bright moon.

I had some clothes soaked in starch during the day. Why not give them a pounding in such bright moonlight?

(*Taking out the washing, and starts pounding with a rod.*)

[a22[i]] **Stealthily quiet,**
A desolate yard.
Utterly lonely,
My shadow, the only companion.
Cruelly sorrowful,
Crickets shriek by the terrace.

[1] Chinese women used to wash clothes by soaking them first, then pounding them on a stone slab that was called *zhen*. Washing clothes by pounding them on a slab in autumn is called *qiuzhen*. Autumn pounding often coveys a sense of desolation. However, the rhythmical pounding, more a simulacrum of sexual activity than source of seduction, may also have sexual implications in classical poetry.

Coldly piercing,
Geese honk into the horizon.
A long long night,
A sleepless lady feels thus depressed.

(*With tears.*)

My heart is broken with the pounding sound.
Despite the bright moon and a gentle breeze,
I have no hope of falling into a sweet dream.

WANG (*recites a poem offstage*).

Tonight the moon shines to the apex of my expectation.
Who knows who still dwells in the autumn lamentation?

LADY HUANG (*listening*).

Oh, **in the small hours of the morning,**
Who is chanting a poem from the neighboring yard?
Doubling my doubt,
What scholar is sitting thus late into night?

WANG (*enters in a moon-white gown*).

[a22[ii]] **Shimmering green is the moonlight in the yard.**
Melodious is the pounding of a washing rod.
Scattering are the sounds of the autumn and cries of the geese.
Lonely is the guest by the cold lamp in a desolate inn.

As soon as I became engaged to Lady Hu, I left for the Land of Wu. Tonight I am staying over in its garden-like riverside. Suddenly the pounding of a washing rod broke the stillness of the night. Too bad, the wall blocks my view. Otherwise, I could see the washerwoman.

(*Looking around.*)

Oh, there's a weeping willow tree by the wall. Why not climb up and have a look?

(*Climbing up.*)

If I press the branch low enough,
My lithe body can easily swing over the wall.

(*Catching sight of* LADY HUANG *from the tree, he is stunned.*)

Alas, **what a city-fallen bewitching beauty.**[2] More like
A flying fairy descended from the Ninth Heaven.
A fantastic luck!
Meeting two fairies in this Peach Blossom Spring quest.
What a joy!
Even an iron heart will melt in passion.

Well, wait a minute. The feminine charms of this lady are just as enchanting as those of Lady Hu. Meeting such a great lady on such a romantic moonlit night, how could I possibly let this opportunity slip between my fingers? Wait and see how I jump over this wall.

(*Shaking his head.*) Oh, no. Only a rapist or a robber would break into another's yard at midnight. If I get caught, where should I hide my face?

(*Watching the lady again, he laughs.*)

Sorry, I can't care that much any more. Brave it and jump! (*He jumps over.*)

LADY HUANG. My goodness, someone has jumped over the wall. Brother and father are sleeping. What shall I do? I'd better go up and call them for help.

She starts walking; WANG *blocks her way hurriedly and bows to her.*

WANG. My Fair Lady, please don't be scared. Don't make much ado. I am not an evil man. Fair Lady, please look at me. Have you ever seen a robber dressed up so neatly in a scholar's gown?

LADY HUANG (*looking him up and down, turns aside*). Oh, he is actually a delicate scholar. But I must question him. Since he is a man of letters, how could he be so irresponsible for his behavior? (*She turns back.*) Why did you jump over the wall at midnight?

WANG. Fair Lady, please allow me to explain. (*Bowing.*)

[a23[i]] **I bow humbly to report to the Jade Fairy.**

(*Turns aside.*)

[2] As early as recorded in the *Hanshu* (Book of Han), a unique beautiful woman has been associated with the expression of "city-fallen" or "state-fallen." It has two connotations: (1) a woman's beauty is such that it brings danger to the existing power; (2) a woman has caught the eye of the whole city or nation for her unique beauty.

About to tell the truth, I feel an infinite shame.
By stealing a flower, I have indeed demeaned myself.

(*Turns back.*)

Fair Lady, please listen to me.
I was not born a crazy man.
Forgive me for being still young.

LADY HUANG. Since you are from a Confucian family, don't you think you have besmirched Confucianism with such behavior?

WANG.

I did not intend to soil my scholar cap.
It is your bewitching beauty that seduced me.

LADY HUANG. What nonsense are you talking about?

WANG (*with shame*).

I am **not used to shady behavior.**
It's only because
The Blue Bridge[3] **is within my reach.**
How could I **be blind to our destiny?**
I am **sorry for what I've done. But**
How could one bridle such enflamed passion?

(*Bows.*)

Miss, I beg for your sympathy.

LADY HUANG. Since you are a young scholar, how can I make a fuss over this matter? May I know where you live, what your honorable name is, and why you came here?

WANG. My name is Wang Menglin, style-named Ruiqing. Following my father, I am living in the Capital of Yan[4]. I came here for a casual visit. Tonight I suddenly heard the pounding of a washing rod. A moment of audacity spurred me to steal a look at you. Your beauty sent me into ecstasy. Please forgive me. (*Bowing.*) I'll be very grateful to you for your magnanimity.

LADY HUANG (*bows in return*). Well, don't mention it. Sir, you are free to leave now.

WANG. What? How could I just leave like this? My Fair Lady, what is your name and how old are you?

---

[3] The Blue Bridge stands for a rendezvous for lovers. It refers to a bridge over the Blue Stream in Lantian, Shaanxi province. Also see Scene 2, n. 11.

[4] Refers to Beijing.

LADY HUANG. I am humble Dream Orchid from the Huang Family. I'm seventeen years old.

WANG. Oh, I'm just a year older than you. May I know whether you have any parents?

LADY HUANG. Well, my mother died young. I only have a father living with me.

WANG. Have you accepted a dowry yet?

LADY HUANG (*bashfully lowers her head*). Not yet.

WANG (*with joy*). Oh, how wonderful! What a lucky wall I jumped over. My Fair Lady, may I have the audacity to tell you something?

LADY HUANG. Please, Sir?

WANG. Sister, with your fairylike appearance, you are indeed a great beauty. I have been ashamed of my vulgarity and empty talent. If you can accept me as I am and are willing to yield to a concubine position, I would definitely treasure you in a house of gold.

LADY HUANG. You are an immortal in the Jade Hall whereas I am a rustic lass from the wild fields. Today our accidental meeting is like nothing but duckweeds drifting together. Please forget it. I feel embarrassed by my poverty for fear that it will bring insult to your vermilion gate.

WANG (*laughs*). My Fair Lady, you are being far too modest. Since you don't mind my proposal, I have a jade hairpin with me and would like to give it to you as an engagement gift.

(*He takes out the hairpin and gives it to her.*)

LADY HUANG (*accepts the hairpin*). Thank you for your love. But I have a father who is very strict with me. I dare not make such a decision by myself.

WANG. Don't worry, Sister. Soon I'll send someone over to ask your father for your hand in marriage.

LADY HUANG. I have something else on my mind.

WANG. Speak your mind, please.

LADY HUANG. I am afraid that someday when you become rich and famous, flanked with Jade Hairpins, where will my place be in your house?

WANG. Dear Fair Lady, you are worrying too much now. I am not an ingrate, am I? If you do not trust me, under the moon and stars, I will swear an oath to end your doubts.

(*He bows to Heaven.*)

Heaven is above:
If I, Wang Menglin, ever forget Lady Huang,
I should be punished by Heaven and Earth.

LADY HUANG. My dear Fiancé, your deep feelings have filled me with infinite gratitude.

[a23ii] **Pray to Heaven with utmost sincerity.**

Here and now we tie the love of our three lives.[5]

WANG (*watching her, smiles*).

Goddess Chang'e[6] **is our only witness tonight.**

LADY HUANG. My future Husband, please accept a bow from your humble wife.

WANG *stands up facing her and returns the bow.*

LADY HUANG.

His tender love despite my plain looks
Makes me even more self-conscious.

(*She turns aside.*)

Accepting a secret engagement on a moonlit night,
I fear that I stepped over the bounds of proper behavior.

WANG (*turns aside*).

Who says Sima[7] **is daring and romantic?**
Look at me, ha ha ha…
I take the willow boughs along with cherries by hand.

LADY HUANG (*steals a glance at him*).

From a mere glance,
I see his willowy body and buoyant manners.

WANG (*attempting to approach her with intimacy, steps back*).

I want to
Hold her hand and lean on her slim shoulder;
A sudden shyness holds back my eager steps.

LADY HUANG.

Why have **rosy clouds spread over his cheeks?**

---

[5] A Buddhist expression, referring to one's former life, present life, and future life. It is generally used to mean one's whole life.

[6] In a Chinese legend, Chang'e ate the elixir stolen from her husband and flew to the moon. She is known as the Solitary Fairy of the Moon.

[7] Refers to Sima Xiangru, famous for his romantic love with Zhuo Wenjun. Also see Scene 6, n. 3.

WANG (*looking into the sky*). Um, the moon is setting in the west. I'm afraid I have to leave now.
LADY HUANG. How are you going to leave?
WANG (*laughs*). Since I came from beyond the wall, I have to climb back over it, I guess. But there's no tree on this side. What shall I do?
LADY HUANG (*thinking it over*). Oh, yes. There's an old locust tree behind the house. You can climb it and jump over the wall.
WANG. A great idea!
LADY HUANG. Follow me, my Lord. (*Taking* WANG, *she walks in a circle.*) Here it is.
WANG. Dear Wife, please take care. I'm leaving now.

(*Climbing up on the wall.*)

[a6] **Hurriedly I am leaving even though I desire to stay.**
LADY HUANG. My Lord, when can we see each other again?

(*Weeping.*)

My silent tears stream down the blocking east wall.
WANG. Dear Little Wife, please take care. We will meet someday. Please don't worry!
Don't let your longing ruin your pretty looks.

Exit in opposite directions.

SCENE 11. A Chrysanthemum Banquet

MASTER WANG (*enters, in long black beard, with his servant* YARD).

[a24] **The Clan of the Locust Hall enjoys generations of honor;**
Winners are listed in the Imperial Edict over and over again.
Now it is my son's turn to serve the court with his brush.
How dare he not live up to the privileged standard?

The Eastern Region stresses compositions.
The Western Capital grades them with high criteria.
Now if my son could rise with great success,
All would contend in admiring our phoenix.

I am Wang Wenhan. My style name is Tunan. I am serving as an imperial minister. My son Menglin has already won first place in the Autumn Examination. Recently, my Colleague Xie's daughter became engaged to him. If in the coming spring, my son can succeed in the South Palace, we can hold the wedding and the celebration of his court success together. Today is the Double Ninth Festival[1]. I have asked the servants to prepare a banquet. Mistress and I will have a festive celebration. Yard!

YARD. Yes, Lord.

MASTER WANG. Is the banquet ready yet?

YARD. Yes, it's ready.

MASTER WANG. Please have the banquet set in the garden and invite my wife to come to the banquet.

YARD *turns to invite* MADAM WANG. *She enters in evening dress with two maids.*

MADAM WANG.

[a4] **The jade tree in front of the hall has been long awaiting.**
Moments of pondering are followed by endless worrying.

(*She greets* MASTER WANG.)

Countless blessings, my Lord.

[1] Observed on the ninth day of the ninth lunar month. It used to be customary for people to climb hills on this day. It is often associated with the bloom of chrysanthemums.

MASTER WANG. Please accept my bow, Madam.

Both sit down.

MASTER WANG. Today is the Double Ninth Festival. I have a banquet laid out in the western garden so that you can enjoy the beauty of chrysanthemums.
MADAM WANG. Thank you, my Lord. It's a pleasure to accompany you on this occasion.

Walking together.

MASTER WANG.
The Imperial City is surrounded by the green hills far and near.
For a better view of the festival, one climbs to the North Tower.
MADAM WANG.
The mums around the pavilion appear dewy after the rain.
The frost over the garden is like pear blossoms in the Fall.
MASTER WANG. Look, Madam. What an autumn view we have in the garden!
MADAM WANG. Pretty indeed!
MASTER WANG. Please serve wine.
SERVANTS (*coming with wine*).
[a25[i]] **In time of peace,**
Amid a festival,
Our eyes are filled with autumn splendor as in a painting.
MASTER WANG. Madam, shall we stand by the balustrade and have a better view?

Both get up. MASTER WANG *straightens his cap with a laugh.*

MASTER WANG.
Press down my black gauze cap
to prevent my thin hair from being blown away.
Lean against the balustrade so as
to enjoy the autumn grandeur.
MADAM WANG (*sighs*).
Suddenly I think of my son far away.
Who knows where he is drifting today?
To the wind I cast a helpless sigh.

MASTER WANG.

Madam,
Why did you turn joy into a mood so sad,
with your two eyebrows knit too tight?

Madam, why do you look so unhappy?

MADAM WANG. I really have no complaint. The only thing that worries me is our son who has not yet returned after such a long absence.

MASTER WANG. I've already dispatched someone to get him. He will be back in a couple of days. There is nothing to worry about, Madam.

[a25ii] **Do not worry.**
Do not look sad.
Your little dragon horse will be in the Capital in no time.

MADAM WANG. He is still a child, without a mind of his own. I'm afraid that he would be seduced by willows and flowers and forget about his career.

MASTER WANG (*laughs*). You used to pick on me like this all the time. Do you really think your son will follow in my footsteps?

How could he ever lose his rainbow aspiration
For the love of those floating willow catkins?

MADAM WANG. Something else is bothering me as well.

Although Menglin has changed into a male body,
He still keeps the tender and delicate traits of a lady.

MASTER WANG. The more you think, the more worried you will become.

MADAM WANG.

My Lord,
I fear that our son has fallen ill in a country inn,
Groaning somewhere under the autumn wind.

MASTER WANG (*nods*). That is a problem. (*Sighs.*) My son (*Getting up.*)

[a26] **Have you packed your luggage and raised your whip?**
Please gallop back to dispel your mother's worries.

(*To* MADAM WANG.)

Madam, **why need to bother about him at all?**
Relax your worried face.
Don't sink into anxiety.
Your son will arrive here in no time.
Your worries will vanish with a cheerful joy.

MASTER WANG, MADAM WANG (*raising their hands high*).

Pray to the Blue Heaven,
Please bless and protect our son!

MADAM WANG. That little wretch of mine has been gone too long. He must have been indulging himself in pleasures. I wonder how he will cope with the forthcoming Spring Examination.

[a27] **What worries me,**
What worries me is his negelect of study
and his willful dissipation.
If so, how can he match the Phoenix of the Jade Pavilion?

MASTER WANG.
Who doesn't praise,
Who doesn't praise our son's handsome looks?
Isn't he worthy of the name of a good bridegroom?

MASTER WANG, MADAM WANG (*chorus*).
An ideal marriage is difficult to find on earth;
A heavenly match is rare in this human world.
What a lucky thing,
Family Wang and Family Xie have been tied by a red string.

SERVANT (*enters*). Lord, all the gentry in town have been gathering for a banquet. They have already invited you twice.

MASTER WANG. All right. Please have my sedan ready.

Servants reply offstage.

MASTER WANG. Madam, I am sorry that I'm unable to accompany you any further.

MADAM WANG. Lord, leave as you please.

MASTER WANG *exits with two servants.*

MADAM WANG. Maids, please go in with me.

Exit together.

SCENE 12. On the Road

WANG, *wearing a scholar head kerchief and a green gown tightened with belt, enters on a horse.* YAOQIN *follows, carrying the luggage on a shoulder pole.*

WANG.

[a28] **The autumn wind blowing,**
The traveler worrying,
My eyes look far into the horizon.
Behold the long ridge,
A sight of withering grass;
Chase the remaining evening glow,
A clatter of galloping horse hooves.

(*Looking backward, he sighs.*)

Recalling the dreary journey,
A lonely soul has wondered thus long,
Leaving the worried parents gaze
at dawn and dusk for my return.

(*Cracking the whip.*)

Racing toward the Imperial City,
I hate the endless monotony of mountains and rivers.

(*The sound of flute offstage.*)

Suddenly I hear a distant flute;

(*Looking around.*)

Nothing but the siren of an outgoing ship.

(*Holding up the horse, he calls.*) Yaoqin!

YAOQIN. Yes, Young Master.

WANG. I'm tired. Let us stop here.

YAOQIN. As you wish. (*He gets off the horse and sits on the ground.*) Young Master, while you are resting, I will let the horse graze a bit. (*Exits with the horse.*)

WANG (*recites*).

[c4] Dropping my whip at dusk,
I have traveled miles upon miles of grass.
Braving the frosty wind,
I recall the dream-like West Lake.
Distant hills, dotting the horizon here and there,
Seem to break my heart with sorrows of nostalgia.
Withering willows and husky raven cries,
A shred of vanishing sun wraps me in this alien land.

It's been several months since I left the Capital. Worried about my parents, I am hurrying back to Mount Yan[1]. During my trip to Lin'an, I became engaged to Lady Hu. Then, while visiting the Land of Wu, I climbed over the wall on impulse to meet Lady Huang. A moment of unrestrained passion under the moon made me promise to marry her. I am obliged to send a matchmaker to her father later and find her a place in my house. (*Laughs.*) Thinking it over, I've really overdone it. In terms of looks, Lady Huang is plain compared to Lady Hu. However, since she is already engaged to me, I'll take her anyway.

(*Yawning.*) Ahhh —, the more I rest the more tired I feel. I'd better take a walk.

(*He stands up, straightening his gown and looks up at the sky.*)

Oh, how time flies when I am resting. The sun is now setting to the west.

[a29] **Faint smoke floats over the distant trees;**
The moment of sunset arrives again.
Cold clouds and withering willows
Watch water fall like a flying stream.
Seeing seagulls gather on the sandy beach,
Listening to the piercing cries of the geese,
Wrinkles helplessly furrow my brow.

(*Sighs.*) Gazing into such an autumn sight, I am overwhelmed with reflections upon life.

Lamenting the autumn,
I shrink thinner than the petals of a yellow mum.

(*Sighs.*) Recalling my romance by the lake and hills, I can't help feeling a regret.

---

[1] Refers to Beijing.

Longing for the ladies by the lake and hills,
I have no more mind for success and thrills.

YAOQIN (*enters with the horse*). Young Master, it's already sunset. Let's continue our journey.

WANG. Very well. Bring me the horse.

YAOQIN. Yes, Master. (*He brings the horse over.*) Young Master, please mount the horse.

WANG *mounts the horse.*

WANG.

By the stream, west to the bridge, zigzags a narrow path.
Which inn tonight shall the clattering hooves enter?
Where's the autumn splendor for passing a boring day?
Frosty leaves are ruddier than spring flowers.

Act Two

SCENE 13. Reporting Success

MASTER XIE, *wearing a red gown and a black gauze cap, enters with* MADAM XIE *wearing a gown and a phoenix coronet.*

MASTER XIE.

[a30] **Auspicious clouds gather over Imperial Capital.**
Stars of letters get together in the spring garden.

MADAM XIE.

Our son is still too young.
Let us first share the news of success from our son-in-law.

(*Meeting* MASTER XIE.)

Good morning, my Lord.

MASTER XIE. Good morning, Mistress.

MADAM XIE. Today the Imperial Edict will be announced. I don't know whether our son-in-law is on the list or not.

MASTER XIE. I've read his papers for all three examinations. His are by no means inferior to the others!

MADAM XIE. If he succeeded, the good news should have been reported by now.

MASTER XIE. That's true.

A swarm of imperial heralds enter, beating gongs.

IMPERIAL HERALDS.

[a17[i]] **A clattering of the gongs**
Brings about miles of spring grandeur.
With cheers of joy,
The imperial heralds march straight into the gate.

SERVANTS. What are you doing here?

IMPERIAL HERALDS. We've come to carry the good news. The son-in-law of your court won the title of the first place *zhuangyuan*. We would like to see your Lord for a reward.

SERVANTS. Please wait here.

Servants report to MASTER XIE.

MASTER XIE. All of you, please come in.
IMPERIAL HERALDS (*enter, bowing*). Lord, congratulations! Your son-in-law won first place. We came here to tell you the good news.
MASTER XIE. Really? He got it, did he?
ALL. Yes, he did. There cannot be any mistake. Look at this official list.

Taking out the list, MASTER XIE *looks it over.*

ALL.

Lord, **a great success slips nobody's eye.**
The first place winner will enjoy praise nationwide.
The four seas are astonished by the leap of this Gold Turtle[1]**.**
With luck coming from years of fortune, the young man
Vanquished all the Spring Candidates by a single hand.
How extraordinary!
How extraordinary!

MASTER XIE. Servants, please take those messengers to feast in the reception hall and then send them away with their reward.
SERVANTS. Yes, Lord.

MADAM XIE *exits with the servants and enters again.*

MADAM XIE. Lord, you are happy indeed!
MASTER XIE. Mistress, you're happy too, aren't you?
MASTER XIE, MADAM XIE.

[a17[ii]] **Joy upon joy everywhere,**
The young Wang is indeed a handsome man.
Being matched with our daughter,
This marriage of talent and beauty will create the best of life.
Let us celebrate our dragon son-in-law with happy laughter.
Let us greet our sun phoenix with wedding music.

---

[1] During the Tang and Song dynasties, there were Gold Turtles placed on the court steps. A scholar of the Hanlin Academy would stand on the steps between the Gold Turtles when seeing the emperor. Today the phrase "standing between the Gold Turtles" is suggestive of winning the first place in the national imperial examination.

Grand is the ceremony, as if viewing red apricots
on a marching stallion along a celestial street.
Our phoenix's nest is finally established.
Our phoenix's nest is finally established.

(*Exit.*)

SCENE 14. Murmurs over the Strings

WANG (*enters in a gauze cap and a moon-white gown*).

[a7] **Although my humble name is in the Imperial Edict,**
There are still a few things that trouble my mind.

(*He sits down.*)

Who is playing the jade flute in the dark?
The wind penetrates the bamboo screens
and the moon shrouds the yard.
How can I resolve the entanglement of love
from a thousand miles away?
My dream by the green window last night
seems to indicate an answer.

Since my return to the Capital, I have been lucky to win first place in the Spring Examination. Before I came back, my parents had already arranged my engagement to the daughter of Master Xie. We have not yet consummated the marriage. People say that she is a lady of talent and beauty. I'm not really sure. But my own engagement to Lady Huang and Lady Hu is certain. Yet I don't know when we will meet again. I had promised them that I would send for them as soon as I got to the Capital. Now I want to bring them here, but I'm afraid that my parents will be angry with me. (*Sighs.*) What shall I do?

WANG *is deep in thought.* YAOQIN *comes with tea.*

YAOQIN.
Other chambers are filled with music and song;
Our studio appears too quiet in the pale moon.

Master, please have some tea.
WANG. Put it there. May I ask where the Elder Master is?
YAOQIN. He is listening to opera in the Flower Pavilion.

WANG *nods.*

SERVANT (*enters*). By the order of our master, I've come to invite *zhuangyuan*.

Master, your brother has arranged a banquet in the Flower Pavilion. He asked me to invite you. Master, please go and enjoy the music and the moon.

WANG. Please tell your master that I'm not feeling well and cannot attend the banquet.

SERVANT. Yes sir. (*Exits.*)

YAOQIN. The moon is bright like daylight. Since Master does not have the peace of mind for opera, why not play something on the lute?

WANG. Not a bad idea.

YAOQIN *sets up the string instrument.*

WANG. You may leave now. I'll call you if I need anything.

YAOQIN. Yes, Master.

He exits. WANG *starts playing.*

WANG.

[a31] **The sky is clean as if newly washed by rain.**
Night clouds are light and fragrance subtle.
Plucking strings under the moon is all for self-expression.
Gentle music from the lute and pipe,
Wafted by a breeze beyond the wall,
Sounds as if fairies hum from the Toad Palace[1].
How many beautiful nights like this can one encounter in life?
If happy moments can be found here and now in this world,
Who still desires for the Abode of the West Queen Mother[2]?

(*Shaking his sleeves, he stands up and walks.*)

[a32[i]] **Standing up, I walk to the front terrace.**
Strolling back and forth,
I wandered among the flowers and bamboos.
Thinking of my jade-like beauties far away,

[1] The moon.

[2] West Queen Mother (Xiwangmu) can also be translated as Queen Mother of the West. Her abode stands for heavenly paradise. Originating from Chinese mythology, she is regarded as the highest female authority in Heaven.

Who can drop a message for us from the clouds?[3]

(*Sighs.*)

My heart is divided in two places.
When can I join them in our reunion?

(*Clasping his hands behind him, he staggers.*)

No way out, I feel lost.
I'm tortured with fears of getting caught
by a self-concocted romance.

(*He sits down, facing the moon in dull silence.*)

BROTHER (*enters in a state of drunken reverie*).
[c5] The jade cups are filled with shimmering agate light.
The pavilion is fraught with the fragrance
of flowers in the still night.
Languid dancing and singing seem to freeze
upon the silky bamboo screens.
Drunken ladies collapse in bed against the east breeze.
(*Seeing* WANG, *he calls.*) Brother!

WANG *seems not to hear but sighs alone.*

BROTHER (*turns aside*). Seeing Ruiqing sigh to the moon, I know there must be a reason. Let me ask him. (*Approaching* WANG, *he shouts into his ear.*) Brother!
WANG (*startled to a jump*). Oh, Big Brother is here.
BROTHER (*laughs*). I've been here for quite a while.

Bowing to each other.

BROTHER. Young Brother, I sent someone to invite you to a moon party. Why didn't you come?

---

[3] The two lines "Thinking of my jade-like beauties far away,/ Who can drop a message for us from the clouds?" are from the play *Zichai ji* (Purple Hairpin) by Tang Xianzu (1550–1616). Instead of unconscious borrowing, Wang Yun seemed to deliberately declare the influence of Tang's play. Play-lovers of Wang Yun's time certainly knew those famous lines from Tang's play well. Also see Scene 22, n. 3.

WANG. Thank you for the kind invitation, Brother. I was unable to because I have not been feeling well.

BROTHER. I saw you sigh to the moon a moment ago. What is bothering you? Why don't you bare your heart to your own brother?

WANG. Nothing, really.

BROTHER.

Brother,

[a32[ii]] **A long sigh cast to the wind reveals your discontent.**
I, a stupid brother of yours, can hardly diagnose the cause of
your heart's ailment.
With your name on the Imperial Edict,
you have realized your dream of fame.
A red string is already tied, securing you
a hundred years of domestic bliss.
All the frustrations of your past have been wiped away.
What is still worrying you today?

WANG *sighs again.*

BROTHER. Young Brother, why do you hold your tongue tight? (*Moving his seat closer to* WANG, *he laughs.*)

Don't try to hide it from me, Young Brother.
You and I are linked in blood like branches of one tree.

WANG. It's already late into the night. Let us go in and talk heart-to-heart by the lamplight. (*Calling aloud offstage.*) Yaoqin, please serve tea.

WANG *and* BROTHER *sit down facing each other.* YAOQIN *brings the tea.*

WANG. Yaoqin, you can go to bed now. Please shut the door behind you.

YAOQIN. Great. That is exactly what I want. (*Closing the door, exits.*)

BROTHER. I've never asked Young Brother before. But did you meet someone during your sightseeing in the south?

WANG (*chuckles*). Meet someone? Yes, but it was ridiculous. I was fooled by our cousin of the Yang Family. He tricked me into visiting the so-called great Beauty Pipa Qian and turned me into a laughingstock. While idle yesterday, I jotted down the incident. Here it is, if you want to read it.

Passes the manuscript. BROTHER *reads and laughs.*

BROTHER. Congratulations, Brother! From such a passionate scene, I gather you were missing her a moment ago, weren't you?

WANG (*laughs aloud*). Ridiculous! Now I'd better confess to you what is in my heart.

[a11^{i}] **During a melancholy journey along the Wuling Stream,**
I, like the Dumb Liu, got lost twice in love.
Though meeting like duckweeds drifting together,
The affections still linger.
Flowers and willow boughs have registered
our wondrous encounter and romantic fate.

(*He turns aside with a sigh.*)

Ladies of my heart, are you able to sleep yet?
How could you know that I am pining for you and
My fragile body struggling to carry the weight of my gown?

BROTHER. Brother, from what you say, I sense that you have met a great beauty.

WANG. You are right. When I was in Lin'an, abiding in the Temple of Invisible Divinity, a casual walk to the western hills led me to a fair lady from the Hu Family called Dream Lotus.

BROTHER. Oh, I see. How old is she? Is she pretty?

WANG. Sixteen years old. Perfect in talent and beauty. No sooner did I see her that I took off the twin jade pendants from my belt and presented them to her as my engagement gift.

BROTHER. A true beauty is hard to find. It was smart of you to ask for her hand at once.

WANG. Afterwards I toured Suzhou for fun. On a moonlit night, the pounding of a washing rod seduced me into meeting a lady from the Huang Family named Natural Fragrance. Overwhelmed by her charm, I gave her my jade hairpin as an engagement gift.

BROTHER. How could you meet another one? You're blessed by fortune, eh? But when compared, which lady is superior in talent and appearance?

WANG. To be impartial, I think Lady Hu is superior to Lady Huang.

BROTHER (*chuckles*). Young Brother, you seem to be a bit too careless. If you meet Lady Liu from the east of the river, what are you going to do? You are young after all and have not seen the world.

WANG (*laughs*). If you want to know the way down the hill, you must ask the one who has tumbled there before.

Both laughing.

WANG. Big Brother, I promised each of them that when I won the Spring Examination, I would seek her for a marital reunion. Now I want to send someone for them. But I am afraid that our parents would blame me. That is why I look so worried.
BROTHER. What's to be done then?
WANG (*pretends to be ashamed and smiles apologetically*). How can you be my Big Brother if you don't know what to do?
BROTHER (*puts on a comic smile*). What can I do about it?!

WANG *stands up, bowing to him.*

WANG. Big Brother, please take pity on your Young Brother.

(*Sighs.*)

[a11[ii]] **For the sake of the two ladies in Suzhou and Hangzhou**
I've racked my brain for months in a row.
Today, **I have to beg you for help.**
Please speak to our parents for me.

(*A pleading smile.*)

If you lend me a hand today,
I will be indebted to you for life.

(*Bowing.*)

I will pay you back someday.
BROTHER. What are you going to pay me?
WANG (*smiles*).
Well,
I shall choose two pretty maidens and
have them trained in dancing and singing.
Then I'll present them to you as a gift to
wait on you with golden wine cups.
BROTHER (*laughing aloud*). Brother, don't worry. You can leave everything to your Big Brother. But please remember what you have promised me today.
WANG. Of course.

The night watch sounds four times.

WANG. Oh, we've lost ourselves in talking. Listen, the night watch is striking the fourth hour. We must go to bed now.

BROTHER. You're right. (*He gets up.*)

When the studio falls silent without a soul,
The moon will double its brightness in solitude.

WANG.

A heart-to-heart talk between two brothers
Slipped unknowingly deep into the night.

Big Brother, good night.

BROTHER. Good night, Young Brother.

Both exit.

SCENE 15. Moving to the Capital

MADAM WANG, *wearing a bluish green top and a pale skirt with a silk waistband, enters with a maid.*

MADAM WANG.

Born a pearl on the palm of a well-known family,
I became the life companion of a Confucian scholar
and have waited on his widowed mother.
Thanks to my happy marriage, my son's success and
My husband's honor has brought me uttermost joy.

My maiden name is Yang. It has been quite a few years since I followed my courtier husband to the Capital. I'm happy that my mother-in-law is healthy and that my two sons are filial. Owing to the luck brought about by our ancestors, my son Menglin has already established his name and position. Having chosen an auspicious day for his wedding, I feel somewhat relieved. However, the other day the first-born told me that when Dream Unicorn was down in the south, he became engaged to two ladies. As he is too timid to fetch them over without my knowledge, he has troubled his brother to tell me. Well, since the two ladies are already engaged to our son, how can we abandon them? So I dispatched my housekeeper, Yard, and his wet nurse to get them. Several days have passed. Why have they not arrived yet?

YARD. Mistress, please accept your old servant's bow.

MADAM WANG. Oh, you are back. Have the two ladies arrived?

YARD. Yes, both have arrived. I first went to Lin'an, looking for Hu. When I went to Lady Hu's house and announced my intention, her mother was overjoyed. Unable to leave each other, the mother and the daughter came together. Then I went to Suzhou and met Old Man Huang. I explained why I had come and gave him the dowry. But he was unwilling to tag along, so Lady Huang came here by herself. Upon our arrival last night, it was too late to get into the city. Now the two ladies' sedans are parked right at the gate. However, Lady Hu's mother is still waiting in the inn, as she dares not to come without your permission.

MADAM WANG. Please send the ladies' sedans in. Then go and get Mother Hu.

YARD. Yes, Madam. (*Calling offstage.*) Carry the sedans in, please!

Reply offstage — "Very well." YARD *exits.*

MADAM WANG. Maid, please go out to welcome them.

Maid exits with "yes" and then brings in the two ladies who are wearing green blouses and white skirts, followed by wet nurse.

LADY HUANG.

[a18] **Leaving behind my hometown, my heart still lingers there.**
Looking back, I can no longer catch sight of my dear father.

WET NURSE. Please accept my bow.

MADAM WANG. All right. Get up now.

WET NURSE. Ladies, this is the Mistress of the House. Come and meet her.

LADY HUANG, LADY HU. Mistress, please allow your humble maids to bow to you.

MADAM WANG (*looking at them with joy*). All right.

LADY HUANG, LADY HU.

[a9^{i}] **With bashful cheeks and mincing steps,**

(*Bowing.*)

We stoop to bow at the seat of our Mistress.
Growing up in the rustic fields, we're not used to rituals.
Please forgive us for still being young and ignorant.
We shall seek your instructions morning and night.

MADAM WANG.

[a9^{ii}] **With charming faces and willowy limbs, the two are**
Delicate and fresh like twin lotus flowers on the same stalk.

Which one is Lady Huang?

LADY HUANG. Your humble maid is here.

MADAM WANG. Her tongue is gentle like a newly born oriole.

(*She turns to* LADY HU.)

So you are Lady Hu.

(*Laughing happily.*)

Wonderful!

Slim and delicate like a flying swallow[1],

---

[1] It may also allude to the famous imperial concubine Zhao Feiyan (The Flying Swallow Zhao).

No wonder my son loves you.
Even I feel stirred with compassion.

I wish that you two Orchid Sisters[2] be good companions in the days to come.

WANG *enters in his moon-white gown and black gauze cap.*

WANG.

[a9iii] **When the court service was over, the sun has moved west.**
I tidy up my gown to salute my mother in the front hall.

(*Seeing the two ladies, he retreats hurriedly.*)

Alas! **All of a sudden, I saw two ladies.**
The sight threw me hastily back.

Oh, what a strange scene!

(*Wiping his eyes with his sleeves, he looks again.*)

Is this an encounter in the woods or under the moon?
How could those two be standing right in our Grand Hall?

(*Walking back and forth, he steals glances at the two ladies.*)

LADY HU (*surprised to discover* WANG, *she turns aside*).

[a9iv] **I see a young man standing outside the balustrade.**
What a charming youth in a black cap with a snowy face.

(*Wiping her eyes, she looks more closely.*)

Oh dear, **this is my old Lord Liu.**

(*Quickly averts her sight.*)

A sudden sight of him fills me with vast bashfulness.

LADY HUANG (*catches sight of* WANG).

Oh, **I'm destined to marry you and wait on you in bed.**
Thank Heaven for having fulfilled my dream.

MADAM WANG (*discovers* WANG *standing outside but asks deliberately*). Hey, who is sneaking looks at us from behind the curtain? What an audacious man!

---

[2] *Langui* means sisters of Golden Orchid. The term "Golden Orchid" came from *Yi jing* (The Book of Changes): "If the two are of one heart, their sharpness can cut gold; if their words are from the same heart, their fragrance smells of orchids."

Ducking from her sight, WANG *exits;* MADAM WANG *roars with laughter. All laugh.*

MADAM WANG. Though a man serving at court, he still behaves like a child.

Maid, now you can take the two ladies to Grandma. Please also tell the servants to tidy up the rear mansion of the Delicate Spring and have the two ladies settle there with Maid Chunying at their service.

MAID. Yes, Madam.

LADY HUANG.

Floating like a cloud, the sailing boat carried us to the splendid Capital.

LADY HU.

We settle down here as if entering the Abode of the West Queen Mother.

MADAM WANG.

Since I have two beauties from the Southern Land,
I no longer need to admire the virtuous Lady Mo Chou[3].

[3] An ancient girl from the City of Stone, good at singing and dancing. It also refers to Mo Chou of Luoyang, a virtuous lady who married into the Family of Lu at the age of fifteen and bore a son at sixteen. The two references are often mixed.

SCENE 16. A Wedding

MASTER WANG *enters in a black gauze cap and a red gown, with* MADAM WANG *in her red gown and phoenix coronet.*

MASTER WANG.

[a24] **The happy atmosphere fills the mansion;**
Music and songs echo through the halls.

MADAM WANG.

The male and female phoenix are finally joined in wedlock.
The beautiful lady matches our handsome son, as we wished.

MASTER WANG. Hello, Madam.

MADAM WANG. Hello, my Lord.

MASTER WANG. Today is the day of our son's wedding. The bridal sedan will arrive at any moment. Why don't you invite Grandma to come to the wedding?

MADAM WANG. I just went over to invite Grandma. But she said that being a widow, it is not suitable for her to be present at the wedding. I'll tell the newly wedded couple to pay her their respects tomorrow.

MASTER WANG. Well, it is her grandchildren's wedding. Who minds her presence?

Wedding music rises offstage; servant rushes in.

SERVANT. Report to my Lord. The bridal sedan has arrived.

MASTER WANG. Ask the Master of Ceremonies to start the wedding.

Servant shouts the Lord's order. A crowd enters with the sound of drums and pipes. They perform according to the wedding rituals. MC *signs above* WANG, *the bridegroom, who is wearing an auspicious wedding gown with red ribbons and a silk flower slanting across his chest. Then* MC *signs above* LADY XIE, *the bride, who is wearing a wedding gown and a phoenix coronet. With her face veiled, she is supported by two bridemaids.*

MC (*after conducting the ceremony, announces*). The wedding is concluded. (*Exits.*)

ALL (*chorus*).

[a33] **The beautiful jade grows in Lantian.**
A good marriage promises a hundred years of bliss.
A great joy to the wedded phoenix couple.
One is a great scholar of the Jade Hall;
The other is a great beauty in the Golden House.
The twin stars compose the harmony of heaven;
The beautiful couple weaves happiness on earth.
The golden peacock unfolds its tail on the wedding banquet;
The lucky stars are twinkling above the grand celebration.

MASTER WANG, MADAM WANG. Hold the painted candles ahead and lead the newly weds to their nuptial chamber.

ALL (*turn and start to parade*).

[a34] **Silver candles glisten,**
Silver candles glisten,
Showing the way to the Garden of Penglai[1]**.**

Golden screens shine,
Golden screens shine,
Reflecting the cheers of the banquet.

A hundred years of love,
A hundred years of love,
What a sight!
What a sight!
Watch the rainbow gowns dazzling at the grand feast.

(*After sending the wedded couple to their nuptial chamber, all turn back.*)

[a35] **The groom is talented**
The bride is charming,
What a well-matched fair couple.
From now on,
The pair can spend their life in happy dancing.

(*All exit. The drumbeat sound of the night watch is heard.*)

---

[1] Penglai is the dwelling place for the immortals. It often stands for ideal place, paradise, and utopia.

WANG.

[a36[i]] **Having just finished the wedding banquet,**
The watchtower sounds its first beat for the night.

(*Getting up, he bolts the door.*)

Quietly I've closed the vermilion gate.

(*Looking at the back of* LADY XIE.)

She hides her bashful face, sitting silently by the lamp.

(*He sighs.*)

I suddenly think of my two engaged beauties.
The strings of my heart are pulled toward them.
Now the wedded phoenix is in the nuptial abode;
The other two lie alone on their pillows by dim light.

(*He sits in silence. The night watch strikes the second hour.*)

LADY XIE.

[a25] **The silver holder shines as time drips away.**
All my shame is hidden behind a small fan.

A long sigh from WANG.

LADY XIE.

He is casting sighs long and short.
It is indeed hard for me to understand.
Perhaps he married me not of his own accord.
Perhaps he has some other ladies on his mind.
Why does he look so restless and upset?

WANG (*smiles apologetically*). It is my fault. A precious lady is sitting right before me. At least I should go and have a look. Isn't it ridiculous of me to worry over the other two ladies on my wedding night?

(*He gets up and trims the candle. Taking a look at* LADY XIE, *he is surprised with joy.*)

(*Turns aside*). Oh my, I must have met a fairy tonight.

(*With a big smile, he wipes his eyes.*)

My, amazing!

[a36ii] **Against the emerald cloud tiara,**
Her face resembles a flower,
As if a jade fairy descended from the sky.

(*Casting forward his ample sleeves.*)

Heaven rewards the efforts of a dashing scholar of Hanlin
And blesses him with a fairy from the moon.
Following Zhang Chang[2] to paint a lady's eyebrows
And becoming the twin birds flying together[3]
Is much better than being a tiger
crouching on the top list of the Imperial Edict.

WANG *laughs aloud and* LADY XIE *looks puzzled.*

WANG.

It is hard to have such good fate and timely luck.

(*Shakes his body with his hands raised in jubilation.*)

May I ask the twin stars of the Milky Way
whether you envy us tonight?

The sound of the third night hour.

WANG. Oh, the watchtower has already announced the third hour. (*He approaches* LADY XIE.) Miss, it's already deep into the night. Shall we go to bed?

LADY XIE *does not move.* WANG *laughs.*

WANG. My dear Miss, please.
[a37] **Lift your head and relax your knitted brows.**
Can you remove the blocking fan?

(*Taking away the fan from* LADY XIE.)

---

[2] Zhang Chang, an imperial official of the Han, became famous because of painting his wife's eyebrows. A classical tale of spousal love.

[3] Wang Yun uses the term "yu fei," which refers to two birds, wing to wing, flying together, signifying ideal love relationship.

Alas,
Flipping away the veiling clouds, I see the true beauty of the moon fairy.

(*Bowing to her.*)

Miss, look,
The laurel shadows slant across the window.
It must be midnight now.

WANG *exits, with one hand holding a candle and the other supporting* LADY XIE.

SCENE 17. Spring Lament

LADY HUANG *wears a blue blouse, moon-white vest, and a white skirt with silk waistband. She walks slowly onto the stage.*

LADY HUANG.

[a38[i]] **In the Pear Blossom Chamber locked by dense poplars,**
I arose with an aching slender waist.
A face with makeup invites more self-pity.
With endless longing and ailments,
A fair lady is pining away.
Alone, I lean against the balustrade,
My vision threads its way across the fragrant grass.
A heart of passion edges toward its breaking point.

(*She sits down, reciting.*)

[c6] Scattered apricot petals dancing in the spring breeze,
A day of splendor is right before my eyes.
The east wind caressing the grass into a drunken slumber,
The pavilions sink in the solitude of the Fasting Days.

Flipping away the tousled fringe hair,
Folding hands into ample sleeves,
I lean over the balustrade,
Watching two ducks in playful fight.
I'm too languid to get on the swing,
For a ride in a twinkling dream of spring.

I am Huang, the Dream Orchid. After I was engaged to Wang, the Number One Scholar, he has kept his promise and brought me to the Capital, along with Sister Hu. How time flies! In the blink of an eye, another spring has arrived. (*Sighs.*) Although I have been hidden in this treasure pavilion, I still feel the pinch of a female's suffering fate. Sister Hu is still young for passion. She is sleeping too much in spring. After putting on my morning makeup, I stand alone in this pavilion, finding it ever more difficult to fritter away my time. I am thus overwhelmed by sorrows and frustration.

(*With tears, she sings.*)

[a39] **Lonely, lonely the tears splatter over my face of a peach flower.**
Slowly, slowly I shun my eyes from the round mirror.
Parrots by the eaves are chirping my secret love.
Purple swallows alight by my window
to share my spring lament.
Sitting by the vanity, my sadness so wells up that
I have no strength left for combing my hair.
The oriole's alarming call disturbs the peace of my mind;
Yet I am too listless to raise a lady's fan to chase it away.

Oh, Sister Hu has come out.

LADY HU (*enters slowly*).

[a38[ii]] **Who has awakened a spring lady from her sweet dream?**

Orioles sing offstage.

LADY HU.

The orioles on the willows are cheerfully singing.
Like the spring hill that hates to be redundant,
I have become too thin to fill my garment,
With gold bracelets slipping off my tiny wrists.
But who pities such a delicate beauty?

(*Folding up the screen.*)

With self-love, I fold up the bamboo screen.

(*Seeing* LADY HUANG, *smiles.*)

LADY HUANG (*smiles back*). Dear Young Sister, your morning toilet presents your beauty exceptionally well today.

Look at those curled clouds of hair. For whom are you toiling over your looks?

LADY HU (*laughs*). Elder Sister, my love for beauty is innate. I toil over it for nobody but myself.

LADY HUANG. Young Sister, you and I are both lonely in our boudoir, clinging to each other like a skeleton clings to its own shadow. Who could know that even a Charming Prince from the Jade Palace can also be an ungrateful man? (*With tears in her eyes.*)

LADY HU. Elder Sister, please open your mind and console yourself.

LADY HUANG. I am not really a complaining type. But he is over there enjoying the spousal happiness of a talented man with a beautiful lady, while you and I are jailed in such an empty boudoir day and night. The chamber net is splendid, yet the phoenix inside is thus lonely. In such bright springtime, how could I not help feeling unhappy? (*Sighs.*)

LADY HU. Elder Sister, now you've again dragged yourself into the common lot. Serving in the gold palace and waiting on the jade banquets are routines of those common wives. How can they match me in my happiness playing a flute under the moon or plucking a flower for a poem?

LADY HUANG. Virtuous Sister, your view is indeed elegant and noble. But a woman's beauty easily fades. One can't help feeling resentful.

LADY HU. Follow your fate and do not worry. Look at us now. Madam Wang has treated us with magnanimity. We wear satins and eat delicious food. Even my mother has been well taken care of. I am content with what I have. Nothing really bothers me. Our Lord is still newly wedded; his heart has no room for us. However, since he unleashed his passion on us in the past, how could he easily abandon us? Elder Sister, please be cheerful. We can't let the beauty of spring slip between our fingers. Shall we take a walk in the garden?

LADY HUANG. Yes. Please come, Sister.

They stroll together.

LADY HUANG.

[a40] **Idle daytime is hard to fill.**
With swaying skirts over mincing steps,
Two ladies roam among the flower bushes.

LADY HUANG, LADY HU (*chorus*).

Shoulder to shoulder, we stand by the Jade Pavilion.
We hold our breath for fear of disturbing the birds beneath.
Clear ripples upon the calm lake
Reflect two lady images: one full of self-pity and
The other loves music and the flute.
An idle dawn is succeeded by an idle dusk.
May I ask Heaven,
Whose yard has been truly adorned by the charm of spring?

LADY HUANG.

[a41] **I sigh over the suffering fate of a woman.**

LADY HU.

It is no use to wallow in complaints and frustrations.

(*Leaning over the desk.*)

Yet, my frail body is so easily tired.
Holding up the brush, I turn too spiritless to write.

LADY HUANG.

Casting my sigh to the wind,
Leaning over the balustrade,
I still cannot release my hard feelings.
I can do nothing but gaze at the blossoms with a feigned smile.

Oh, I feel pretty tired now. Shall we go back home?

LADY HU. Yes. Elder Sister, please.

[a42] **Stamping on the green moss,**
A fragrant heart gets exhausted.
Looking into the fading clouds and light breeze,
One feels the approach of the noon.

LADY HUANG (*turns aside*).

Lingering into the dusk, one has to
Sleep lonely in the embroidered quilt by the burning incense.

In a garden of varied flowers, the sun moves slowly;

LADY HU.

An endless day is visited by nobody but warbling orioles.

LADY HUANG.

Sitting alone for long hours breeds feelings of frustration;

LADY HU.

Better go and inscribe poems outside the Cherry-Apple Mansion.

Exit together.

SCENE 18. The Female Union

MADAM WANG, *wearing a pale skirt and a satin frock, enters with a maid.*

MADAM WANG.

[a43i] **I'm pleased that my daughter-in-law**
sings the same tune along with me.
An ultimate joy a parent can feel and see.

A year has passed since my son had his wedding. I am glad that my daughter-in-law is matchless not only in talent and beauty but also in virtues. However, I am concerned with Dream Orchid and Natural Fragrance. How can they tolerate living in the back quarters for so long? It has been hard for me to mention the two ladies when the newlyweds are enjoying their honeymoon year. But it seems to me that the lady from the Xie Family is not really the jealous type. Today I'll bring the matter to light when she comes. I'll feel much better when I rid my mind of it.

LADY XIE, *now* MISTRESS, *enters with a maid.*

MISTRESS.

[a43ii] **I was spoiled with willfulness as a girl.**
Now learning to behave as a wife,
I feel embarrassingly awkward.

(*She greets* MADAM WANG.) Countless blessings, Mother-in-law.

MADAM WANG. Please have a seat, Daughter-in-law.

MISTRESS *sits down.*

MADAM WANG. I want to have a word with you, but I'm wondering whether you are willing to listen?

MISTRESS. Mother-in-law, please speak your mind.

MADAM WANG. It is about your husband before he was married.

[a44i] **During a leisure tour down to the south,**
He came across two beauties by chance.

MISTRESS. Who were they?

MADAM WANG.

The willowy Lady Hu lived in Hangzhou and
The charming Lady Huang dwelled at Suzhou.
My son seemed to be attached to them
With a passion of three lives.
With a passion of three lives,
He became engaged to both stars without hesitation.

MISTRESS. What sort of families are those two ladies from?

MADAM WANG.

They are both pearls nurtured in decent families.

MISTRESS. Where are they now?

MADAM WANG.

They are living in the back quarters.
Now your husband's fortune entirely depends on you,
hoping that you clear his path like the east wind,
so that he can
place two flowers by the happy Golden Hairpin.

MISTRESS (*getting up, turns aside*).

[a44ii] **Upon hearing the news, I thought to myself**
Surprised with joy, I found that my tiny heart
could swallow back my jealousy.
I, a jade lady in a red skirt, have thus been mistreated
by a so-called Charming Prince.

(*With a frown.*)

Lord, Lord,
You are such a conceited fool.
Your conceitedness leads to your mistrust of me.
What a bully. When the time comes, I would definitely
Create a painful scene to torture you.

Um, I'd better take the opportunity to appraise the beauty of those two ladies.

If truly beautiful as said, I would take them in as sisters and
Console the sweethearts before the stars or under the moon.

(*She turns back.*) Mother-in-law, since the two ladies are here, may I ask you to send them over to meet me?

MADAM WANG. I was just about to call them. (*She turns to a maid.*) Emerald Cloud, please bring the two ladies here to meet the mistress quickly.

The maid exits and comes back with the two ladies.

LADY HUANG, LADY HU.

[a45[i]] **A long, long corridor leads to a splendid courtyard**
As if blessed by a different spring.
Slowly, slowly the lotus feet
Zigzag along the path beneath the floating skirts.

A parrot cries offstage — "Joy to sisters!"

LADY HUANG, LADY HU.

A secret joy
Arises upon the message of a teasing parrot.
A suppressed giggle mixed with shyness
Makes me fidget with my green blouse.

EMERALD CLOUD. The ladies are here.

MADAM WANG (*facing* LADY HUANG *and* LADY HU, *points at* MISTRESS). Come here please, ladies. This is your mistress. Come and pay respect to her.

LADY HUANG, LADY HU. Mistress, please accept our bow.

MISTRESS. There is no need to kneel down.

LADY HUANG *and* LADY HU *bow to her.*

MADAM WANG.

Daughter-in-law,
I have placed the twin Pink Powders[1] in your charge.
From now on it is your duty to teach them feminine virtues.

(*Turns to the two ladies.*) Take heed, ladies. You must

Obey and serve your mistress submissively.
Serve her submissively.

MISTRESS (*beholding the two ladies with a happy smile*). You are truly as beautiful as they say.

[a45[ii]] **High above the common stalks,**
Two lotus flowers shoot out the water.

In ancient times, a beauty is compared to a jade pendant of an exquisite fan. Lady Hu resembles it.

[1] Pink Powder (*hongfen*) stands for woman or prostitute.

Charming indeed, she can beat courtesan Xiangjun[2]
with her delicate features.

LADY HUANG, LADY HU (*looking at* MISTRESS, *turn aside*).
Taken by surprise,
The angelic beauty of our mistress is beyond rivalry.
What a shame,
We attempted to compete with her for her husband.

MISTRESS (*turns aside*). Scholar Wang, Scholar Wang, you are indeed a lucky man. Such beautiful ladies, having one is enough. But Lord, you insist on having them in twins and pairs.
What a man! With the lucky star of romance,
He took over two states by one surprise.
His greed is so unthinkable;
His greed is so unthinkable.

MADAM WANG. Daughter-in-law, when are you going to introduce them to your husband?

MISTRESS. Today is not good. Wait till I choose an auspicious day. I need to have their chambers ready and everything properly arranged before their reunion.

MADAM WANG (*nods with happiness*). Good idea. (*Getting up, she turns aside.*) Thanks to Heaven, my daughter-in-law reveals no jealousy at all. Instead, she beams with a happy smile. A virtuous lady at such a young age with such a generous heart is hard to find. Hard to find, indeed. (*Turns back.*) Okay, now two ladies return to your back quarters. Daughter-in-law, you can go and get things prepared.

MISTRESS. All right.

All exit.

---

[2] Refers to Li Xiangjun, who appears as the female protagonist in Kong Shangren's famous play *Taohua shan*.

SCENE 19. Double Happiness

MISTRESS, *wearing her phoenix coronet and a red blouse with a pale skirt, comes onstage.*

MISTRESS.

[a46] **A Devil of Letters is indeed unpredictable.**
His tricks form a treacherous noose.
I feel angry but want to mock him,
for his ridiculous behavior.
I'd better put on a show to fool him.

(*She sits down.*) A year has passed since I was married to my Lord. I thought we were of one heart, sharing the same life music. Who would think that he had been engaged to two girls even before me? Were I not informed by mother-in-law, how could I ever get an inkling of his secret life? Luckily, these two girls are pretty and have good manners. Their gentle figures are indeed lovely. However, I can't resist blaming my Lord for his haughtiness. He should have told me honestly about his past. Why did he deliberately deceive me for so long? Not even a hint. I am tempted to let him meet with the two girls. But, if so, he may think it easy to slight me. Well, I will hide these pieces of engagement jade. Wait and see how I play with him when he comes back from the court.

MISTRESS *exits.* WANG *enters in his gauze cap and red gown, with two court guards.*

WANG.

[a5^{i}] **Peaches of longevity are drunk with infinite spring beauty.**
My brush is rejuvenated in the Lake of Phoenix.
Looking high into the lofty clouds,
I, a humble scholar, finally climbed to the court.
Now father and son are serving the Emperor together.

Arriving home, WANG *gets off his horse. The guards exit. Two servants enter.*

WANG (*sits down*).

With the singing of roosters at dawn,
I went to serve the morning court.
Flowers greeted my sword with pretty petals and
Glistening dewdrops upon them are just vanishing.
Heaven never let down a man of strong will.
Now natural fragrance has dyed my official gown.

SERVANT A (*brings up the tea*). Master, you are off court duty quite early today.

WANG. Yes. Not much to do at court today. Servant, beat the calling board.

SERVANT B *answers and beats the board. Housekeeper comes in.*

HOUSEKEEPER. Oh, Lord has come home. Mistress, please greet the Lord.

MISTRESS *enters, sitting with her back to* WANG. *He goes to greet her.*

WANG. Good morning, Mistress.

She ignores him. Surprised, WANG *turns aside.*

WANG. Why, how strange? Mistress used to greet me with her smiles every day when I was off work. How come today she does not even look at me? There must be a reason. Let me figure it out. (*He turns back.*) Hi, Mistress. You sit there wordless, with a sullen face. If there is something that makes you unhappy, please tell me.

She still ignores him.

WANG. Mistress, your silence will drive your humble husband mad.

[a5ii] **With anger frozen on your knitted eyebrows,**

(*He turns aside, laughing.*)

Gee, **your varied beauties take more ink to capture.**

(*He turns back.*)

Mistress,
don't blame me for trying to dig out the root of your anger.

(*Patting her shoulder playfully.*)

My dear Miss, for what after all?
I wish you could bare your breast to me.

MISTRESS (*throws her ample sleeves and gets up*).
Phew,
Your cheeky words have doubled my unhappiness.

(*She turns her back to* WANG.)

WANG (*turns aside*). Oh my, it looks like I am the root of her anger. (*Thinking hard.*) But I've done nothing wrong. (*He turns back.*) Mistress, it seems to me that somebody has offended you. Am I right? (*Pleading with his clasped hands.*) I really can't figure out whom or what is to blame. I beg you, Mistress, please speak.

MISTRESS. You think harder then.

WANG. What should I think? Oh, you mean that I am to blame, don't you?

She gives him a cold shoulder.

WANG (*hurrying with a bow*). Mistress, if I have done anything to offend you, please tell me where I have been wrong so that I can apologize to you.

MISTRESS. You want the truth? It's not that hard for me to tell you.

WANG (*hastening with another bow*). Yes, please tell me, Mistress.

MISTRESS.

[a5iii] **The heart of a dandy is thus crooked.**
Even before you gained success and fame, you thought of
Having two beauties locked in a bronze tower[1].

WANG (*astonished*). Oh no, please. Wha... wha... what are you talking about? Please think it over before you speak. Don't wrong an innocent man.

MISTRESS. Where could you duck your head? (*She takes out two pieces of jade.*) Look, where are these from?

WANG (*taking a look, turns aside*). Dear me, these are the engagement hairpin and pendants that I gave to the two girls. How could they be in the hands of the mistress! (*Sighs.*) Since my secret is betrayed, I have to confess. (*Stamping his feet.*) Well, I can't hide my shame any more. (*Bowing to* MISTRESS.) Since Mistress already knows the truth, your humble husband dare not argue any more. It was all my fault. I beg your forgiveness. (*Pleading with successive bows.*)

---

[1] It alludes to Cao Cao, who built a famous pavilion with a giant bronze bird on its roof by the end of the Han dynasty (ca. AD 211). Also known as the Bronze Bird Pavilion (*Tongquetai*). The two beauties refer to Elder Qiao (Da Qiao) and Young Qiao (Xiao Qiao), the two beautiful daughters of Lord Qiao of the Three Kingdoms period.

MISTRESS (*scoffs*).

As the Number One Scholar, you have high status.
I'm merely a humble woman at the mercy of a marriage.

WANG (*laughs*). Mistress, don't stretch the topic too far. Today my only wish is to win your mercy. I wish your virtue and magnanimity would allow the two girls to stay.

MISTRESS. To be honest, your request is utterly out of the question.

WANG. I am alone to blame. I accept the responsibility. But really the two girls are innocent, having nothing to do with it. I beg your pity for them.

MISTRESS (*in a rage*). What a shameless man, trying to fool me with your cheeky face. Think you can get away with it? No way.

WANG (*bows again humbly*). Please don't be angry, Mistress. I don't want them any more. You may keep them by your side as your waiting maids.

MISTRESS. I have my own maids to wait on me. Who needs your care?

WANG (*looking worried, turns aside*). What's to be done? (*Sighs.*) There's no way out. Now I can do nothing but kneel down.

He steps forward to kneel before her when MISTRESS *shuns him with laughter.*

MISTRESS. What shame! What shame! For the sake of two girls, you would kneel down to beg. How ridiculous!

WANG (*laughs, bowing*). My sweet Mistress, please be more virtuous. Don't follow the path of a common wife.

MISTRESS. I was born the way I am. Why should I change my nature just for you?

WANG (*sighs*). All right, if you can't tolerate the girls...

MISTRESS. What can you do if it's not all right?

WANG (*turns aside*). Sigh, it is easy to see through millions of things. But it is too difficult to anticipate a woman's mind. Who would have guessed this wife of mine, a rare beauty in the world, is but an incarnation of jealousy? It seems utterly impossible to change her mind now. Well, how can I, for the sake of two concubines, bring harm to our spousal love? Oh, my two fair ladies, sorry I have to betray you now.

Don't blame me for ingratitude and shallow feelings.
Blame that cursed fate of yours.

(*Sighs.*) Losing two concubines is okay. But I can't bear Mistress's cold shoulder for long. I'd better make another apology to pacify her anger. (*Turns back.*) Mistress, since you don't need them as your maids, tomorrow I'll find two men and marry them off. Please don't be angry with me any more.

MISTRESS (*with a cold smile*). Don't try to fool me with your sweet words. I'm not an idiot.
WANG (*laughs*). Mistress, you know my character, don't you? My words are my bond. I never tell a lie.
MISTRESS. Don't regret then.
WANG. Of course not.
MISTRESS. All right. I forgive you this time.
WANG. Thank you, Mistress, for your forgiveness.
MISTRESS. All right. My dear Lord, please take a seat.

Both sit down. MISTRESS *calls out.*

MISTRESS. Maid, serve tea please.

Old maid brings up the tea.

MISTRESS. Lord, I see that you are still being deceitful.
WANG (*laughs*). Don't exaggerate, my dear Mistress. I can swear by my heart to Heaven.
MISTRESS. Are you sure that you will not cause any more trouble?
WANG. Yes, I have completely removed such things from my mind.
MISTRESS. That is what a decent man should do! (*Turning aside to give an order to old maid.*) Please hurry up! Call the two ladies to come to meet their Lord.
OLD MAID. Yes, Mistress.

She exits, then enters with LADY HUANG *and* LADY HU.

LADY HUANG, LADY HU.

[a43] **Adjust my cloud coronet to**
Reveal a flower-surpassing beauty.

MISTRESS (*gets up*). Please follow me. (*She leads the two ladies in.*) Lord, here are your two old flames. Do you still recognize them? (WANG *stands up, surprised with joy.*)
WANG.

[a47[i]] **They look like the two beauties I knew in the past.**

(*Wiping his eyes, he looks again.*)

Wiping my eyes, I gaze at the ladies again
I doubt whether they are real beings or my hallucinations.
Mistress, **please explain this coincidence.**

MISTRESS. What need is there to explain? A moment ago you talked about marrying them off. I've had their dowries ready, simply waiting for their right man.

WANG (*looks puzzled*). If so, why let them come to meet me?

MISTRESS. Dear Lord, you shared romantic love with them in the past. How can they spare a farewell to you on their nuptial departure today?

WANG (*looking dazed*). But, but, but how can we find two families right now to marry them off? It takes time to locate the right men. Mistress, you're being a little too rushed.

MISTRESS. Well, if it's too difficult to find two families, one family is okay. Let them be married to just one man, then.

WANG (*jumps*). Even one man, can we find him so quickly?

MISTRESS (*giggles*). Lord, you aren't trying hard enough. If the matter is placed in my hands, I guarantee to find one right away.

WANG. You're joking, aren't you? How could you, a woman who never steps beyond the house, find someone eligible for them?

MISTRESS. I've found one right here. Lord, open your eyes and see if you don't believe me.

WANG (*more perplexed*). Oh, where? Where is he?

MISTRESS. As far as beyond the horizon, as near as right before my eyes.

WANG (*pondering*). Horizon or before your eyes? Mistress, it must be me then.

MISTRESS. Me? If it were not you?

WANG (*guffaws*). Mistress, Mistress, you are really killing me with your deceitful little game.

> **I already place the green willows in your charge.**
> **How dare I entertain that pretty dream of jade?**

MISTRESS. Now you can give your heart rest.

WANG.

> **No. My heart is still jumping.**

MISTRESS. For what?

WANG.

> **For fear of committing another mistake by haste,**
> **For fear of adding billows to the raging sea.**

MISTRESS. Now it's your turn to be over worried.

WANG (*chuckles*). I don't wish for any extra worry. But as the old saying goes, "An action without enough deliberation leads to inevitable regret."

MISTRESS. But you can be free of worries this time. Absolutely no change on my side.

WANG. Thank you respectfully.

MISTRESS. Two ladies, please come and meet your Lord.
LADY HUANG, LADY HU. Yes, Mistress. Lord, please accept our kowtow.
WANG. All right.

WANG *stands aside and the two ladies kowtow to him.*

MISTRESS (*watching him intensely*). Lord, my Lord, you are such a lucky man.

[a47ii] **Climbing a laurel tree,**
You jumped on the head of the Gold Turtle alone.
Today, **to enjoy the springtime,**
You'll marry two beauties as your concubines.
Heaven has so favored you that
All joys are brought under your green window.

WANG (*beholding the two ladies in delightful smiles*).

It pays **to be bent on knees for honor and success; but**
My black gauze cap after all bows down
before my beloved ladies.

MISTRESS.

Lord, Lord,
Don't get lost in happiness.
Watch me,
A bitter wife of sour jealousy.

WANG, *feeling embarrassed, bows to her with more apologies.*

MISTRESS. Maids, set up a celebration banquet in the Hundred-Flower Pavilion for our Lord.
MAIDS. Yes, Mistress.
MISTRESS. Lord, please!
WANG. Mistress, after you.
WANG, MISTRESS (*chorus*).

[a6] **Romance creates the best in human life.**
Who can ever copy our happy love?
We've won the first beacon of splendor in our land.

(*Both exit.*)

SCENE 20. A Fair Consultation

WANG (*enters in a water-green gown and a red jacket, with head kerchief*).

[a48] **Flower petals scatter and orioles age;**
In a wink of an eye spring wastes away.
What a sleepy day, with the gentle touch of a mellowing breeze.
Thirsty for wine, I think of the Yangtze.
Mad with poetry, I want to roar.
What a desire for a twin green lotus
to share my heart and aspiration.

(*He sits down.*) Back then, a stroke of passion led me to an engagement with two ladies. Now with a virtuous wife and two charming concubines, I should be satisfied with my life. It is indeed the luck of a lifetime to have a wife who harbors no jealousy.

A year ago, I made a promise to my brother that I would buy him two beautiful girls after I completed my nuptial reunion with the two engaged ladies. Months ago, I found two pretty girls, Scarlet and Snow, and asked my two concubines to take care of their singing and dancing lessons. I placed the two girls in separate quarters.

Quite some time has passed. I don't know how the girls are getting on. As I'm not busy today, I may as well go and ask my concubines, Dream Lotus and Natural Fragrance. If the two girls are well-trained by now, I can talk it over with my wife and present them to my brother right way. (*He gets up and walks.*)

[a49[i]] **Lotus leaves float like coins on the pond.**
Emerald bamboos encircle the windows.
What a joy to be idle during a fine day.
One views garden beauty without haste.

Oh! Look at those lovely pomegranate blossoms in full bloom. Why shouldn't I get a couple to please my concubines?

(*Folding up his sleeves, he picks up two, placing them on his fan.*)

With a plain fan holding two ruby flowers,
I'll decorate with my own hand
the hair of my dear concubines.

I'll cheer my ladies to bloom like peach flowers.
Having such pleasure, who still needs
the Twelve Golden Hairpins[1] of a decadent palace?

He exits. Enter LADY HUANG *and* LADY HU.

LADY HUANG, LADY HU.
[a49ii] **Clear and idle is a fine day,**
Gently stroked by a southern breeze.
Getting up from the bamboo mat,
The red pillow prints on my cheeks slowly fade.
LADY HUANG (*flips through a book by the desk*).
I read in leisure the tales of famous ladies and orchid clubs.
LADY HU (*playing a flute*).
I play the flute like an angel with a happy grin.

(*Leaning against* LADY HUANG.)

And I lean against a fragrant shoulder.
LADY HUANG (*pushes away* LADY HU *playfully*).
Ah ya! **To whom do you exhibit your feminine charm?**

Orioles sing offstage.

LADY HUANG, LADY HU.
Listen to the orioles along the eaves.
Their singing weaves around the blooming boughs.
LADY HUANG (*sits down*). Young Sister, you and I are patronized by a kind mistress and our Lord is such a man of tender care. We are indeed the lucky ones among the female sex.
LADY HU. True.

WANG *enters stealthily.*

WANG (*with a sudden laugh*). You two ladies are having fun, aren't you?

---

[1] "Golden Hairpins" generally refers to ladies. The expression "Twelve Golden Hairpins" (*Shi'er jinchai*) was used in Cao Xueqin's (1715–1763) *Honglou meng*, representing the twelve significant women in the novel. Cao's novel started circulation in handwritten copies in 1760s.

LADY HUANG, LADY HU. Oh, Lord. You are here. (*Bowing.*) Countless blessings to our Lord.

WANG. No ceremony. What have you been doing here?

LADY HUANG, LADY HU. Tired with embroidering, we took a little nap. But the singing birds awakened us. We were just chatting.

WANG. Although enjoying such tranquil pleasure, you two may still feel a bit lonely. So I came over to add some fun.

LADY HUANG, LADY HU (*laughing*). Please have a seat, Lord.

WANG. You sit down, too.

LADY HUANG, LADY HU. Dare we sit down in the presence of our Lord?

WANG. Nonsense. Just sit down. (*Pulling the two ladies to their seats.*) On my way I saw the pomegranate flowers bloom so lovely that I picked up two to double your beauty. (*Inserting the flowers in their hair, he looks them up and down.*) Oh my, with these two red flowers, your faces are bright with the shining of your cloud hair. The beauty is really overwhelming. I can't help but improvise two verses for you.

LADY HU *grinds the ink and holds the paper while* LADY HUANG *waves the fan.*

WANG (*writes as he recites aloud*).

[c7] Languidly embroidered by the solitude window,
She fell into a slumber.
Upon awakening, the Golden Hairpin slanted.
I decorated her cloud hair happily with a blooming flower.
Thus the charm of my sweetheart has been enhanced.

With a delicate fan, she waves the air.
Her beauty blends with fragrant flair.
The orchid scent wafts like a filmy veil.
The beauty of its green petals is rare and a thrill.

(*He adds the tune title and dedication.*)

Tune. Pusa man
To Lady Huang, the Dream Orchid

(*Recites and writes again.*)

[c8] Slim and supple, she resembles a swallow.
Flowers are jealous of her glamour.

Willows admire her airy manner.
Startled by the singing orioles,
Her wakening annoyance seduces a love tender
As tender can be.

A red cloud adorns her hair.
Bees are flirting.
Butterflies are flirting.
Beautiful enough to be drunk with spring.
Worthy to live for it.
Worthy to die for it.

Tune. Yijian mei
To Lady Hu, the Dream Lotus

LADY HUANG, LADY HU (*reading the verses with joy*). Thank you, Lord!
WANG. Don't mention it.

All sit down.

WANG. The other day, I entrusted Scarlet and Snow to you two for lessons of singing and dancing. May I ask how they are doing now?
LADY HUANG, LADY HU. Your humble concubines are just about to report to you. The two girls are quite smart. They've already mastered the skills.
LADY HU. May I ask my Lord, what is your intention for the two girls?
WANG (*laughs*). I do what I want. Mind your own business.
LADY HU. Lord, you're getting a bit greedy, aren't you?
WANG (*guffaws*). Now you two ladies have learned to drink vinegar, haven't you?
LADY HUANG, LADY HU (*laugh*). Since we cannot do anything to stop you, we'll add our weight to Mistress's side.
WANG (*pointing to the two*). Well, well, well, tomorrow I'll put you two in the hands of Mistress. I'll no longer care for you.
LADY HU. Fine. Living with Mistress, what can we possibly lack?
WANG. Hey, Fragrance, please go and send for Mistress.
LADY HUANG. All right.

LADY HUANG *exits.* LADY HU, *on the point of leaving, is pulled back by* WANG.

WANG. You can't go. Stay here and keep me company.

LADY HU *stands there, smiling.*

WANG. Get me a cup of tea.
LADY HU. Yes.

She serves tea and WANG *drinks.*

WANG. Where has your mother been living these days? How come I never run across her?
LADY HU. By the order of Mistress, she is staying in Grandma's quarters as her companion.
WANG (*nods*). A good arrangement.
LADY HUANG. Mistress is coming.
WANG (*gets up immediately*). Where is she?
LADY HUANG (*giggles*). She will be here in a minute.
WANG (*giving a pat on her shoulder*). It is you, a mischievous lady, who scared me. What kept you away for so long? Where is Mistress?
LADY HUANG. When I went over, Mistress was playing zither in the pavilion over the water. I dared not disturb her until she finished her tune.
MISTRESS (*enters in a moon-white cape over her light-colored skirt*).

To pass the idle day, I picked up the writing brush.
To play with the breeze, I plucked at the strings.

LADY HUANG (*announcing*). Mistress is here!
WANG (*tidying his gown, bows*). Greetings, Mistress.
MISTRESS. Countless blessings to my Lord.
LADY HU. Countless blessings to Mistress.
MISTRESS. Thank you, pretty ladies.

WANG *and* MISTRESS *sit down.*

MISTRESS. My Lord, would you like to talk to me?
WANG. Yes. As the day seems to be boringly long, I invited you to come for a chat. I also have something on my mind to share with you.
MISTRESS. What is this about?
WANG. Well, it's about the two girls I purchased the other day.
MISTRESS. I was on the point of asking. Lord, what is your intention for them?

WANG. Mistress, you are always so smart. How could you fail to guess my intention?

MISTRESS. How could your humble wife guess what's on your mind? Please speak out.

WANG. All right. But please don't get angry with me.

MISTRESS. How dare I get angry with my Lord?

WANG (*smiling with a bow*). May I beg Mistress to choose an auspicious date so that I can fulfill my heart's desire?

MISTRESS. You said you bought the girls as a gift for somebody. How come you changed your mind?

WANG (*laughs*). Mistress, you're simply being too honest. I was merely joking. How could you take it so seriously?

MISTRESS (*putting on a long face*). Lord, you are quite wrong.

WANG (*waving his fan, with a feigned smile*). What's wrong with me?

MISTRESS. Today you are no longer what you used to be. You should behave with respect and dignity.

[a49[iii]] You, **soar all the way up to the ninth sky and**
Finally have climbed to the imperial court.
You should **develop yourself on the path of classical ethics**
And abandon the passions of the moon.

WANG (*laughing aloud*). What jarring advice to my ear! Why should this official gauze cap restrict my freedom? I must

Seize the hour and seize the day, with the wealth in hand,
Purchasing all the Twenty-four Bridges of the Wu City[2]

MISTRESS.

Indeed a shallow debauchee.
You've **already kept two concubines in your golden cage.**

WANG (*pointing to his two concubines*). As long as my Mistress is not jealous, why can't I have a long list of Golden Hairpins?

MISTRESS (*heaving a sigh*).

Even if your wife does not care,
You may become a laughingstock in the street.

WANG. Who cares about street gossips, as long as Mistress is tolerant?

MISTRESS. Sorry. It is impossible for me to be tolerant!

---

[2] Wu City (Wucheng) refers to Guangling in Jiangdu county of Jiangsu province. During the Southern Dynasties, the city became ruined after the failure of a rebellion led by Liu Dan. It was supposed to have twenty-four bridges for sightseeing.

WANG (*sneering*). Other men have Twelve Golden Hairpins at home, I merely wish for three or four starlets. Even so, you can't put up with it. Ridiculous, indeed ridiculous!

MISTRESS. If you are such a crazy, greedy man, what can I do? Do what you want.

LADY HUANG, LADY HU. Mistress, you must exercise your power. How could you let our Lord take such liberties? It is utterly lawless.

MISTRESS. Well, I must, then.

WANG (*mocking*). I see why you two ladies behave so mischievously. You've been spoiled by Mistress.

Dear Mistress, please think it over. With such manipulating power, how could your husband not feel intimidated?

MISTRESS (*with a sneer*). Lord, do you still remember your previous lesson?

WANG. Aaaah, terrible. Your coldness that day still chills my back.

All laugh.

WANG. Well, I'd better tell you the truth.

MISTRESS. Please.

WANG.

[a49[iv]] **I purchased two beauties with shimmering pearls;**
Yet nobody knows my secret intention.

MISTRESS. What intention?

WANG.

One day in the past
I made a casual promise to my brother.

MISTRESS. What promise?

WANG. I promised him that I would buy him two beautiful concubines if he helped me with my nuptial reunion with my two engaged ladies. Now the time has come. I want to inform you first, and then report it to our parents and set a date to present the gift of the two girls to my brother.

MISTRESS. Oh, I see. But why did you go to such lengths to fool me?

WANG. Sorry for letting you suffer through such an unpleasant drama.

All three ladies laugh heartily.

WANG.

Nobody knew that
The wedding gown is sewn for another man.

All believed that
I would keep Emerald and Black Jade for myself.
Now, my Wives,
Please have all the gold and jade jewelries ready.
To brighten
The two girls' wedding gowns and headdress.

MISTRESS. This kind of dowry? No problem. I'll take care of it right away.

WANG. Great. Don't spare any money.

MISTRESS. What a fair consultation we've had today in the tranquil mansion.

LADY HUANG, LADY HU. It resembles the steam drifting over noon tea by a playful wind.

Exit all.

SCENE 21. A Gift of Two Concubines

YAOQIN *enters in blue attire and a cap.*

YAOQIN.

Having served in his studio for years,
I finally saw my Master win the title of *zhuangyuan*.
I am now contented with my food and attire.
Yet my marital fate is still hanging in the air.

I am no other than Uncle Yaoqin. Years ago I started serving our Young Master, grinding ink and washing inkwells, sweeping the yard and burning incense. I took all sorts of hardships to help him gain fame and wealth. (*He laughs.*) Though a humble valet, I now wear bright garments and eat delicious food. People around all call me the Second Master. I enjoy my life without complaint. (*Frowning.*) But I still sleep alone.

How could I put up with such loneliness for the rest of my life? This morning Young Master bade me to have a banquet set up and to invite his brother over for a gift of concubines. I thought to myself if Young Master could give other men gifts of girls in pairs, why couldn't he give me just one for a wife out of human compassion? A bit of anger moves me. I must speak to Young Master when he comes out. Why not?

WANG (*appears in a splendid gown, waving a fan*).

A past promise made in a jest.
A gift of two beauties will be presented today.

Yaoqin, do you have the banquet ready?

YAOQIN. Yes, Master. It's been ready for a long time now.

WANG. Please send for the Elder Master.

YAOQIN. I've already sent. (*Kneeling down.*) Master, may your humble servant say something today?

WANG. Speak your mind.

YAOQIN. Thank you, Master.

(*Kowtowing.*)

[a50] **I've been overjoyed with Master's success**
in fame and wedlock.
But I have sighed over my own wretched fate.

(*He kowtows again.*)

I beg for your pity, Master.

WANG. Pity you for what?

YAOQIN.

Please bless me with a nice maid for a wife.

WANG (*laughing aloud*). What a nuisance! Beg for a wife yourself?

YAOQIN. All men are the same. Why should I be an exception?

WANG. Don't worry. I've already talked the matter over with Mistress.

YAOQIN (*surprised, joyfully*). Oh, what did you talk about?

WANG.

[a51] **I've already tied the red string for you**
By selecting a fair maid behind the golden screen.

YAOQIN. Which maid?

WANG. It is Spring, the personal maid of Mistress.

YAOQIN (*beaming with happiness, kowtows*). Thank you, Master.

WANG. But…

YAOQIN. But what?

WANG.

You're a bit too dumb for the maid.

YAOQIN. That does not matter.

Remember an old saying thus said,
"A talented wife always accompanies a stupid man in bed."

WANG (*laughs*). All right. Today is an auspicious day. Let us complete your wedding then.

YAOQIN (*kowtows*). Your humble servant kowtows to Master for your heavenly blessing.

WANG. Go and get dressed. You don't need to wait any more.

With a happy reply, YAOQIN *swaggers out with joyful laughter.*

SERVANT (*enters*). Elder Master has arrived.

WANG. Please let him in.

WANG *makes a gesture of invitation and then a gesture of welcome, as* BROTHER *comes onstage in a splendid gown.*

WANG. Hello, Big Brother.

BROTHER. Hello, Young Brother.

Bowing to each other while they take seats. Servant brings in the tea.

BROTHER. Young Brother. Why did you invite me here?
WANG. Big Brother, do you still remember the time when

[a52] **I plucked at the strings expressing my sadness**
over my two engaged ladies?

(*Holding up two hands in a bow of gratitude.*)

I feel indebted to you for your help
in fulfilling my heart's desire.
Today I have a grand banquet set in your honor.

BROTHER. Oh yes. You are holding the banquet to show your gratitude.
WANG (*smiling*).

Not only holding a banquet,
There's something more significant.

BROTHER (*simpering*). What can be more significant?
WANG. A word of promise made by the lamp that night. Your little brother has never forgotten it. Now two beauties have been selected and are ready to give you bed service.
BROTHER. Is it true?
WANG. How could I fool my Big Brother?
BROTHER (*bows*). Thank you, Young Brother.
WANG. Don't mention it. (*To* SERVANT.) Send for wine served in my own studio, please.
SERVANT. Yes, Sir.

WANG *and* BROTHER *walk about onstage. Two servants bring wine in.*

WANG. Yard, beat the calling board and ask Housekeeper to bring in the two girls.

Calling and response offstage.

WANG. All of you may leave now. No service is needed here.

Servants exit.

WANG. Have a drink, Big Brother.
BROTHER. You, too.

SCARLET *and* SNOW *enter in gowns of splendor, followed by housekeeper and a maid.*

SCARLET, SNOW.

[a53] **At the beckon of a call,**
We move our lotus feet toward the hall.
Joy in our hearts,
We float one after the other along the balustrade.

(*Seeing* BROTHER, *they quickly retreat.*)

Oh dear,
Raising our heads, we see a man.
With quick steps, we hasten back.

SERVANT. Why don't you go in?

SCARLET, SNOW.

It is a banquet for honorable guests.
How dare we show our faces?

HOUSEKEEPER. Look, that one is our Elder Master.

Servants and maids make faces, laughing.

SCARLET, SNOW.

Rituals at the grand ceremony we've heard of before.
Are we sent here in splendid gowns
to wait on such a grand banquet?

WANG. Why are they still not here yet? Let me go and have a look. (*Looking out.*) Hey, why don't you come in?

[a54] **Why are you still standing beside the lake balustrade?**
Two beauties by the hillside are so hesitant to come.

MAID. Two sisters say that they dare not go in for fear of being seen by the elder master.

WANG (*with loud laughter*).Crazy, aren't they?

Who ever heard Wu'e was afraid of being seen by King Xiang?[1]

---

[1] Wu'e refers to Goddess of Gorge Wu (Wushan shennü) by the Yangtze River and also stands for a beautiful lady. In a Yuan play, King Xiang of State Chu was said to be madly in love with the unfortunate Wu'e.

SCARLET, SNOW (*surprised, turn aside*).

What does he mean?

BROTHER *steals out, glancing at the two ladies.* WANG *catches him and laughs.* BROTHER *hurries back to his seat, with a fan to hide his embarrassment.*

WANG.

The ladies are slowly tidying their hairpins;
The man steals glances at their flower-like faces.

SCARLET, SNOW.

Who knows what we should do?

BROTHER.

Neither sitting nor standing, how restless a man is in waiting.

WANG (*puts on a stern face*). Two ladies, please come here. Some months ago I purchased you two, but not really for myself. However, you still belong to the Wang Family. From now on, you will be favorite concubines of my Big Brother. Please wait on him with tender care.

SCARLET, SNOW (*shocked, turning aside*).

[a55] **Like lightning, the news split my heart in halves.**
In silence, I wallow in self-pity.
Leaving the east chamber and entering the west,
Who knows what suffering or happiness lies ahead?

(*With tears.*)

Sigh upon sigh,
Flying petals of the same fate are
Dangling in the cyclone.

WANG. Sister Scarlet and Sister Snow, please don't feel sad. Elder Master is a family man, with tender feelings. Serving him is actually better than staying in my house.

Don't always think that a woman's fate has to be suffering.

Please come in with me.

MAID. Two sisters have arrived.

BROTHER (*anxiously*). Where are they?

WANG. Here they are.

BROTHER *looks at them, feeling shy. All laugh.*

WANG. Two ladies, please come to kowtow before your Lord.
BROTHER (*modestly*). Oh, no. No need.

Two ladies kowtow to him. BROTHER *attempts to pull them up, but stops with embarrassment.* WANG *laughs, patting* BROTHER's *back with his fan.*

WANG. Big Brother, please behave yourself. Watch your manners.

In a panic, BROTHER *fingers his beard with an awkward smile.*

WANG (*laughing aloud*).

[a15] **Laughable is the silly Big Brother.**
Crazy is the Young Brother.
Each has fulfilled his dream of desire.

Big Brother, today I present you with these two beauties. Please take good care of them and don't let them fall behind your other wives.

These two flowers are cast to your love.
Never let the Pink Powder weep behind an autumn fan.

BROTHER.

Young Brother, **don't waste your time in worries.**
How could I, a knight of romance,
behave like a rustic bumpkin?

WANG. Brother, you can take your two concubines home now.
SCARLET, SNOW. We have not yet said goodbye to Mistress.
BROTHER. Oh, yes.
WANG. All right. Maids, please lead them in.

Two maids exit with SCARLET *and* SNOW.

SERVANT (*enters*). Report to Master, the band and the Master of Ceremonies are ready. You are invited to witness the wedding.
BROTHER. Well, who is marrying today?
WANG. Yaoqin.
BROTHER. Who is the bride? No one told me.
WANG. It is Spring, the maid of your sister-in-law.
BROTHER. Oh, I see. I would like to go and have a look.
WANG. Brother, you are invited.

They turn around onstage. A band of drummers and bugle players start the wedding music. Conducted by MC, YAOQIN *in a brand new groom's gown and* SPRING *in bridal clothing and veil kowtow to Heaven and Earth.*

MC. The wedding is over.
WANG. Let us take the bride and bridegroom to their nuptial chamber.

The band exits. WANG *and* BROTHER *walk around back. Maid and housekeeper lead* SCARLET *and* SNOW *in.*

SCARLET, SNOW.
Step by step, we're departing from the fragrant boudoir.
With regret, we are leaving our dear Mistress.

WANG. Well, you are back now. Servants, please light the lantern and send Elder Master home with his new wives. (*Servants reply.*) Big Brother, I'll have my humble dowries sent over tomorrow.
BROTHER (*bowing*). I hope that does not cause you too much trouble.
WANG. No, not at all.

Maids come in with gauze lanterns.

WANG. Brother, please. (*Turning to* SCARLET *and* SNOW.) Please wait on your Lord with tender love. Goodbye now.
SCARLET, SNOW. Master, please accept our farewell bow.
WANG. No more bows, since you are my sisters-in-law now.
SCARLET, SNOW. Master, accept our bow, please!

[a56] **Dwelling in your mansion for over a year,**
We have been blessed with your tender care.

(*Turning aside.*)

Although we've never waited on you at banquet or in bed,
We have been enlivened like an abandoned lute for new music.

(*With tears.*)

Our Mistress is generous enough to fulfill her virtues;
Yet we are not fated to sacrifice our chaste for your sake.

BROTHER. I am leaving now. I'll come back tomorrow with thanks.

WANG. See you tomorrow.

[a57] **Spare no gold, I have them trained in music and dance.**
A gift of two fair ladies should rejuvenate a gentleman.

BROTHER (*with happy laughter*).

From now on, I'll be
Flanked by my beautiful ladies, drinking day in and day out.

SCENE 22. Spring Reverie

YAOQIN, *wearing black beard, enters in blue garment with phoenix belt.*

YAOQIN. I am the humble Butler Yaoqin. In past years, I have really enjoyed my life, with sufficient food and clothing, as well as harmony between husband and wife. Yesterday, Young Master bade me to have the garden cleaned and a banquet set up for a spring party. So I'll call the servants and work with them. (*Calling offstage.*) Fellow Brothers, where are you?
SERVANTS (*enter*). Lucky is the man to be waited on; unlucky is the dog that waits on others. (*Seeing* YAOQIN.) Hail, Old Zhou, how come you've got up already, instead of being with your wife in bed?
YAOQIN. Ridiculous, ridiculous. I am not that type of guy, am I?
SERVANTS (*guffaw*). Audacious rascal, you've never missed a day in doing that, have you? Why are you singing a different tune today?
YAOQIN (*laughs*). No more jokes. Remember what Young Master bade us yesterday. Have you carried out his order yet?
SERVANTS. Mind your own business. We have everything neatly done.
YAOQIN (*holding up his coupled hands*). Many thanks to you all. Your diligence sets a lazy man free.

The servants make all sorts of funny gestures and faces.

SERVANT B. Is today's banquet for the family or for guests?
YAOQIN. No outside guests are invited. It is a gathering of our Grand Mistress, Master and Madam, Young Master and Mistress. They have only invited Master and Madam Xie and their son, now a *tanhua*[1].
SERVANTS. Oh, a family party.
YAOQIN. Still pretty early. Let us sit here and rest for a while before serving them.
SERVANTS. A great idea.

All sit on the ground.

---

[1] *Tanhua* was the *jinshi* who ranked third in the national imperial examination during the Ming and Qing dynasties.

SERVANT A. Hey, that son of the Xie Family is really special, wearing an official cap at such a young age.
SERVANT C. No wonder. Young Master became *zhuangyuan* at the age of nineteen. Now Prince Xie won the third place *tanhua*. Such gifted men are hard to find.
YAOQIN (*twirling his beard*). Eh, speaking of the past sounds like an old tale. Back then, Young Master and I were both lads. Now we are husbands with long beards.

All make faces, laughing.

SERVANT A (*pointing to other servants*). They are latecomers who did not witness Young Master's wedding. At that time, Tanhua, coming to see his sister being married off, was merely four years old. Counting on the fingers, fourteen or fifteen years have passed.

YAOQIN *nods.*

SERVANT B. Young Master definitely has a lucky star for his career. Not quite thirty-six yet, he is already the minister of the imperial personnel affairs.
SERVANT C. What is really amazing is that Father, Son, Father-in-law, and Son-in-law are all serving at the Golden Terrace.
SERVANT B. However, Young Master's elder brother doesn't like being an official.
SERVANT C. Why not?
SERVANT A. Well, since our Young Master is already a minister, he may as well just enjoy life.
SERVANT B. Young Master has brought so much wealth to the Wang Family, not to say his brother, and that even his butler Old Zhou has more than enough to spend.
DOORMAN (*enters*). Hey, you guys are really having a good time.
ALL. What's the news?
DOORMAN. Master Xie and his son Tanhua have arrived.
ALL (*rising quickly*). All right, we'll report to our Master.
YAOQIN. Masters, please come in.

BROTHER *wearing a satin cloak with head kerchief leads the way. Enter* MASTER WANG, *in an official dragon gown with gauze cap, and* WANG, *dark beard, in a moon-white gown.*

MASTER WANG.

Spring shines upon the great mansion.

WANG, BROTHER.

Auspicious air fills up the Capital.

YAOQIN (*announcing*). Master Xie has arrived.

MASTER WANG. Please open the central gate.

Servants open the gate. Music begins offstage. MASTER XIE *in a sky-blue dragon gown and* TANHUA *in a bright red gown enter with servants.*

MASTER WANG. Thank you for coming to our humble dwelling. Forgive me for not coming out to greet you.

MASTER XIE. Master Wang, thank you for inviting us. Forgive me for being a bit late and keeping you waiting.

MASTER WANG. You are welcome. Please take a seat.

MASTER XIE. After you, please.

Bowing to one another, all sit down.

MASTER WANG. Serve tea, please.

Two servants bring tea.

MASTER WANG. Yesterday I saw the garden decorated with the colors of spring looking exceptionally pretty. So I have a banquet arranged for our two families. Why is our Madam-in-law not coming?

MASTER XIE. How dare my humble wife dally at your invitation? We father and son came first, and she will be here in a minute.

MASTER WANG. Great. Shall we go out to the garden now?

MASTER XIE. Yes, please.

Walking together.

MASTER XIE. My, the garden looks wonderful.

SERVANT. The banquet is ready.

MASTER WANG. Please serve drinks.

Soft music rises. MASTER WANG *is pouring wine for* MASTER XIE.

MASTER XIE (*trying to stop him with a hand*). Master Wang, we two are of the same age. And also we are in-laws. Let us discard the old rituals.

MASTER WANG. What are you talking about, my old friend? Please, let me serve you one cup to show my respect.

MASTER XIE. If so, you're treating me as a stranger, aren't you?

MASTER WANG. All right, all right. I'll obey you. (*Turning to* WANG.) Son, you serve the wine, then.

WANG. Yes. Here is the wine!

YAOQIN *and servants pass him the cups.* WANG *serves a cup each to* MASTER XIE, MASTER WANG, *and* TANHUA. TANHUA *serves wine to* WANG *and* BROTHER *in turn. All bow and sit down.*

SERVANTS (*kneeling down*). Start toasting.

HOSTS, GUESTS (*standing up, chorus*).

[a13[i]] **A gentle breeze in a sunny day**
Brings infinite spring beauty to our City of Phoenix.
The garden splendor fills our eyes with
embroidered lucky clouds.
Why admire the Jade Palace for the Immortals
Since we've found the Land of Penglai in this world?

MASTER WANG. Servants, use the large cups, please.

YAOQIN *and* SERVANT B *pass large cups of wine around.* MASTER WANG *takes one to serve* MASTER XIE.

MASTER WANG. Cheers, In-law.

MASTER XIE. Cheers.

Both drain their cups.

MASTER WANG, MASTER XIE.

Cup after cup,
Today we'll drink to our heart's content.

MASTER WANG. Servants.

SERVANTS. Yes, Master.

MASTER WANG. Hurry up. Go and set up a private banquet in the Welcome

Spring Pavilion. Master Xie and I will enjoy our drinks over there. Please call the Disciples of the Pear Garden[2] to perform for us.

Servants exit with a "yes."

MASTER WANG (*turning to* MASTER XIE). Well, my age-sake brother, let others have fun here. Shall we go to that small pavilion and have a heart-to-heart chat over the wine?
MASTER XIE. You are speaking my mind.

They rise up. All others at the table bow goodbye to them.

MASTER WANG. This way please.
MASTER XIE. After you.

Bowing to each other, they start leaving.

WANG. Servants, has Madam Xie arrived yet?
YAOQIN. Yes. She has been here for a while.
WANG (*turning to* BROTHER *and* TANHUA). Brother and Brother-in-law, let us take off our cloaks.
BROTHER, TANHUA. Certainly, why not?

Taking off their cloaks with the help of the servants, they sit down.

WANG. Yaoqin, please ask the courtesans to come and entertain us.
YAOQIN (*calling offstage*). Courtesans, please enter.

Four girls come onstage.

COURTESANS.
    Dancing fades like floating willow boughs.
    Singing ends with whirling peach petals under the fans.

(*Kowtowing.*)

Please accept our kowtow.

---

[2] Refer to play performers. See Introduction, n. 30.

WANG. Please get up. Sing a good song to accompany our drinking.
COURTESANS. Yes, Lord.
WANG. Serve wine in large cups.

YAOQIN *and a servant start serving.*

WANG. Brother-in-law, cheers!
TANHUA. Cheers!
BROTHER. Young Brother, cheers!
TANHUA. Cheers, Big Brother!

All drink up.

COURTESANS (*chorus*).
[a33] **A calling for fairies came from among the flowers.**
They've roamed the garden paths with their songs.
Spring is on the swing of its prime.
Peach and plum blossoms seem capable of speech.
A gentle velvet carpets the tender emerald lawn.
Sleeping willows stroke the painted eaves.
Spring floods the land;
Yet nobody seems to have noticed it.
Only orioles cheer and
Swallows applaud with their scissoring tails.
TANHUA. Oh, beautiful singing lingers in the ceiling.

Courtesans start serving wine.

WANG, BROTHER, TANHUA (*chorus*).
[a58^{i}] **Music of the flutes wafts far in the air,**
Like filaments weaving around the beams.
Being so aroused, flowers beyond the balustrade
Nod to the rhythms and orioles sing to their tunes.
WANG (*gets up and passes the wine*).
Ah, I hold up the red wine cup
And toast to Brother and Brother-in-law.
When you drink, you must drink like mad.
Get lost in the land of drunkenness.
Hey, girls, please sing another song.

COURTESANS. All right.
TANHUA. Big Brother-in-law, people say you have talent at the flute. But I've never had a chance to hear you. Would you please play a tune to the girls' singing?
BROTHER (*smiling modestly*). With my crude skills, how dare I perform before you?
TANHUA (*laughing*). Don't be so modest.
WANG. Yaoqin, please bring my purple flute here.

YAOQIN *gets the flute and hands it over to* BROTHER.

BROTHER. All right. I'll do it. But please don't laugh at me.
TANHUA. How dare I?

BROTHER *plays the flute while courtesans sing to it.*

COURTESANS.

[a11] **Stealing a glance at the bright shining sky,**
I still find the traces of morning clouds and evening rain.
A single flower weighs down the charm of the spring yard.
Its fragrant heart, adorned with layers of red petals,
Blooms to the oriole-warbling flute, like a floating cloud.
The spring fingers, out of a fragrant sleeve,
Pluck and insert it in the cloud hair.[3]

WANG, TANHUA (*applauds with cheers*). Bravo, the flute air is deep and nostalgic and the singing is graceful and stirring. Both are without equal!
BROTHER. Don't make fun of me.
WANG. Wine, please.

YAOQIN *pours wine.*

WANG (*turns to* TANHUA). Little Brother, please drink a cup for me.

---

[3] This stanza and its tune are taken from *Zichai ji*, Scene 16. This borrowing could be justified by the singing of courtesans as a performance. Also see Scene 14, n. 3.

TANHUA. All right. But may I borrow this flower to honor Buddha?[4] Big Brother, you drink this cup for me please.
BROTHER. Two brothers, please drink a cup with me.
WANG, TANHUA. Of course, of course.

All drain their cups.

WANG. Hurry up, serve more wine.

Servants pour more wine and the three brothers drain the cups again, roaring with laughter.

ALL THREE. Today's party is really fun.
WANG. Servants, please move the table to the Cloud Pavilion. We'll enjoy the peach blossoms there. Courtesans, please lead the way with music.

COURTESANS. Yes, Lord.
WANG. Brother-in-law, please.
BROTHER, TANHUA. Please!

Music arises. Bowing to each other, all exit. LADY HUANG *in a pinkish purple flower dress and* LADY HU *in a water-green flower dress, each holding a fan, enter with* MAID A.

LADY HUANG, LADY HU.
[a13[ii]] **Shoulder to shoulder, we stroll in the garden.**
Hand in hand, we step on the tender grass.
A fragrant breeze gently pushes us forward.
LADY HU (*tidying her hair*).
A thorny raspberry has caught my phoenix hairpin.

Orioles sing offstage.

[4] A common saying used in a situation when one takes advantage of the present given to him/her and offers it to someone else.

LADY HUANG, LADY HU.

Orioles are warbling on the spring treetops.
Blooming boughs display their charm in proud smiles.

LADY HU. Hush, What a beautiful pair of butterflies!

Each lady tries to catch a butterfly with her fan.

LADY HUANG, LADY HU.

Two fans are waving fast,
Startling the pair to flee apart.

MAID A. Ladies, please go over there and enjoy the swing.
LADY HU. Sister, would you please go with me?
LADY HUANG. Certainly.
Cheerful giggles arise from red apricot blossoms.
LADY HU.
Flying angels, swing in the shadowy willows.
Maid, please come with us.
MAID A. With pleasure.

Holding hands, the two ladies exit with MAID A. GRANDMA *in incense-color frock,* MADAM XIE *in sky-blue frock,* MADAM WANG *in red-blue frock, and* MISTRESS WANG *in moon-white frock, all wearing phoenix coronets, enter with two maids.*

COURTESANS (*chorus*).

[a58ii] **Spring penetrates the garden;**
All become fresh at the visitation of Goddess Green.
A banquet is in full swing beneath the blooming trees,
Amid the melodious flute beyond the willows.
Yes, cheeks are flush like drunken apricots.
The gentle breeze brings about
the first wave of warmth to the earth.
Over the fragrant grass and the red bridge,
We thread our way through the Pear Blossom Orchard.

MAID B. Look, Mistress, two ladies are high on the swing over there. Beautiful! How beautiful!
MADAM WANG. It looks really bewitching.

My finger points to the flying angels beyond the clouds.

MAID A (*kneels down*). Report to Grandma and Mistress. The ladies are waiting in the Evening Cloud Pavilion by the swing. They invite all of you to come and enjoy the beauty of the cherry-apple blossoms. (*Gets up.*)
GRANDMA. Oh, I see. Since they invite us out of respect, let us go and enjoy the scene.
MADAM WANG. This way please, Grandma.
GRANDMA (*turning to* MADAM XIE). Please.
MADAM XIE (*pointing to* GRANDMA). After you, Mother-in-law.
MADAM XIE, MADAM WANG.

Like climbing a stair, one gets lost in the bamboo groves.

GRANDMA, MISTRESS.

Seeking a path in the flowers, a bird knows best.

All exit. MASTER XIE *follows* MASTER WANG *to the stage, each waving a fan.*

MASTER WANG.

[a58iii] **In drunkenness, I discarded my imperial gown.**
Before the flowers, my official pretense is gone.

MASTER XIE (*staggering in drunkenness*).

Slanting the cap, I chant a mad verse.
The true self is still in the rut of love romance.

The four courtesans enter with WANG, BROTHER, *and* TANHUA.

WANG, BROTHER, TANHUA (*chorus*).

Yes, spring nectar flows from the strings and flute.
Beautiful courtesans lead the way.
The Golden Crow[5] is flying to the west;
Bright rosy clouds shine above us.
With a long laughter cast to the spring wind,
We've lost ourselves in the drunken peaches.

WANG. Oh, my Father and Father-in-law are both here.

All tidy their clothing and bow.

[5] The sun.

MASTER XIE. It's getting late. I must be leaving now.
MASTER WANG. Come on. Forget about time. What an opportunity for us two old buddies to share our thoughts! How could you leave at the climax of our excitement?
MASTER XIE (*laughs*). All right. With your kind insistence, I may indulge myself. Let us drink to the daybreak.
MASTER WANG. A great idea. Servants —
SERVANTS. Yes, Master.
MASTER WANG. Please set up another table on the Watching Immortals Pavilion.
SERVANTS. Yes, Master.
MASTER WANG. And courtesans all come to wait on us.
COURTESANS. Yes.

MASTER WANG and MASTER XIE *walk around, followed by* WANG, BROTHER, *and* TANHUA.

MASTER XIE.
[a58[iv]] **Under the moon and among the flowers,**
I am roaming in drunkenness with my bosom friend.
Master Wang, I, your humble brother,
Having squandered half of my life in verse and wine,

(*Flipping his cap like a drunkard.*)

Now I have no way out but to endure this official gauze cap.
MASTER WANG. During the years when I was young, I wallowed in the court of courtesans, being quite a dandy. Now I am tied to the official path. (*Twirling his beard with mirth.*) I don't feel that I have much time left in my life. Look, my beard has already turned gray.
MASTER XIE. Speaking of a meaningful life,
Ah, If I could become a rustic drunkard and enjoy nature,
I would plant five willow trees by the cottage gate.[6]
Such a life is better than a golden sash
attached to an official seal.

[6] Refers to the type of life Tao Yuanming lived. See also Scene 7, n. 2.

MASTER WANG. We have a long night to chat. Take your time and don't forget the Green Bamboo Leaves[7] in your cup.
MASTER XIE. Oh, yes, yes. Tonight we two

(*Singing with* WANG.)

Must drink and drink till roosters sing at dawn.
Then we can go and bow together
at the imperial morning court.

[7] A famous Chinese wine "Zhuyeqing."

SCENE 23. Recalling the Past

A screen hangs above the table onstage to facilitate a change of costumes. WANG, *wearing a gauze cap and a moon-blue gown, walks slowly onto the stage.*

WANG.

[a19[i]] **No matter what led to years of wedded bliss,**
I no longer recall the heady romances in my life.
No matter how my colorful brush shines with talent,
It cannot reverse the evolving course of Heaven.
Pacing back and forth,
My steps are laden with depression.

A cuckoo calls offstage.

WANG.

Listening to the hastening cuckoo in the treetop,
My heart is disturbed by every single calling.

(*Slumps in chair.*)

[c9] Sitting alone in the studio, I become dazed
Even before I attempt to figure out my fate.
I can hardly grasp events of the past.
Deeply puzzled,
My new doubts reinforce old uncertainties.

If one's destiny is pre-arranged,
why does one still need to seek a good omen?
The past and the future are too misty to see.
Has the Lord of Creation ever appreciated talent in this world?

I awoke with bad feelings this morning. What a restless, boring day!

(*Lethargic, moving lazily with hands clasped behind.*)

[a19[ii]] **Walking around, I ponder the things of the past.**

(*Yawns.*)

My body and soul seem to be shattered by a sudden strike.
My thoughts are suspended in mid-air.
My eyes are gazing blankly into the sky.
Fantasies as well as reality have attacked my heart by surprise.

(*Covers his heart with a hand.*)

Oh, how my heartstrings waver between holding and breaking.
Recalling my true self back then,
[a59[i]] I was
A lady in skirts and hairpins hidden away in the boudoir.
Now I have
Donned an official cap and serve at court.

(*Points to the pen.*)

Such
A small brush
Could have only served to
Release frustrations of a person's heart.
Dared I hope that it would
Wipe out a thousand-strong army and safeguard the state?

(*Shakes his wide sleeves vigorously.*)

Suffice it that
One wins the gold badge of recognition and imperial favor;
Why did I
Seek glory in titles and high office?

(*Mired in deep thought.*)

All of a sudden, I seem to realize that
These twenty years of riches and glory
Are nothing
But a daydream of Handan.[1]

---

[1] Refers to Handan Dream (Handan meng) or Golden Millet Dream (Huangliang meng). In the story "Zhenzhong ji" (The Dream inside a Pillow), a young man called Lu Sheng was taking a nap in an inn in Handan while the innkeeper was cooking millet. In his dream, Lu enjoyed all fame and wealth of this world. When he woke up, everything was gone but the millet was not yet well cooked. This dream, suggesting emptiness and the transitory nature of human glory, leads Lu to Daoist transcendence.

Exhausted, WANG *leans over the desk and falls asleep.* LADY XIE, *wearing a moon-white dress, with* LADY HUANG *and* LADY HU *in flowery cloaks, comes on to the stage.*

LADY XIE.

[a59ii] **Attracted by the trilling of the orioles,**
We went out of the Emerald Mansion.
Stepping in the springtime sunshine,
We have arrived at our Lord's studio.

LADY HU.

Ah, why is **the vermilion gate still quietly shut?**

LADY HUANG.

Perhaps **our Lord, loathing to see spring fade away,**
has kept his curtain down.

The three ladies come in and look at WANG.

LADY XIE. Why is our Lord sleeping alone in the studio with his gown and cap in such disarray?

Why does he
lean over the desk, looking utterly exhausted and drained?

(*With tears.*)

How painful to see our romantic dream expire this morning.

LADY HU *blocks* WANG *with a screen and takes off* WANG's *official gown, cap, and beard.* WANG *is restored to her female gender with blouse and hairpins as worn in Scene 2.* WANG *seems to be in a swoon.* LADY XIE *and* LADY HUANG *support her to her original position.*

LADY XIE. Oh dear, my Lord!

All the ladies look heartbroken.

LADY XIE.

Today **our twenty years of love comes to an end.**

THREE LADIES (*crying*).

Oh, our dear Scholar Wang!
What pain you will suffer to be self-locked in layers of regret.

The three ladies exit; WANG *remains.*

SCENE 24. Coming out of the Dream

WANG (*suddenly gets up and calls aloud*). Please come back, my dear wife. Please hold your steps, my dear concubines. (*Looking around,* WANG *is astonished.*) My, how strange it is! Well, what place is this? I was in my studio a moment ago. How could I be brought to this place? (WANG *looks herself up and down.*) Dear me, where are my gown, cap, and beard? Why have they disappeared? Strange indeed! What has happened? (*Thinking hard, she lets out a sudden cry.*) Oh no! I understand! I must have just woken up. My life of a glorious career was nothing but a grandiose dream.

(*She collapses to the ground and sings slowly.*)

[a60] **Dazed by a dream,**
My mind was upside down.
With a sudden awakening,
My body and soul have been shaken.
I try to capture the laughter of vanity
from that fading dreamland,
Only to find the stealthy mutability of the universe.

(*She gets up with a sigh.*)

Oh, pity for my twenty years' devotion to love. Now it is all gone with the wind.

(*Weeping.*)

[a61] **I feel pain for the flowers in the hairpin.**
I sigh over the moon scooped from the water.
I pity the dream of my next life that has
Vanished before I even had a chance to realize.
The more I think
The more frustrated I become.
My butterfly wings are drifting in the mist of regret.

(*With copious tears.*)

I have abandoned the wife who models herself
after the virtuous Meng Guang[1].

[1] See Scene 9, n. 3.

I have discarded the two concubines who wait on me in bed.
Gazing into the distance, I am unable to
see any signs of my lost kin.
The lofty sky and distant earth seem to
strike me like lightning.
The shadows of garden flowers swaying before the curtains
Only spur me into a greater rage, for they rightly symbolize
The fleeting nature of my glorious life in a vanished dream.

(*Wiping her eyes with a sleeve, she scrutinizes the painting.*)

(*With surprise.*) Ah! How come the beauty in the painting is exactly my wife, Lady Xie? (*Beating the desk with her fist, she cries.*) Oh, my dear wife!

[a62] **Like the glory in my dream,**
Our fated love vanishes.
The souls of my ladies, wafted by the wind,
Have gone to the Heavenly Altar.
In this world of Red Dust,
Who still remembers the old Blue Bridge?
After you flew away like a cranc,
It will be all in vain to look for your traces.
Do you still remember our tender feelings in that dream?
Back then you were my true love of the Golden Orchid[2]
Who understood the music of my heartstrings.
Now you have turned into the withered flower
and the vanishing dew.
Your betrayal has made the cuckoo cry in the setting sun.
This pain is enough to kill me!
This resentment is enough to kill me!
I have been reduced to a skeleton shadow
of heart-wrenching lamentation.

Thinking of Lady Hu and Lady Huang, how did they become my concubines through so-called destiny? (*Sings sadly.*)

[a63] **In the dream, we played gentle flute under the moon.**
I even hid your tender beauty in my golden chamber.
Upon waking up, you become utter strangers to me.

---

[2] The "Golden Orchid" here stands for the deep friendship between sworn sisters. Also see Scene 15, n. 2.

In the dream, our souls were intertwined,
Like red flowers around a green tree.
Upon waking up, my solitary shadow is my only companion.

(*Pounding the books on the desk bitterly.*) Ah! I have been trapped by these books. (*Throwing away the inkwell and brush.*)

[a64] **With bitter regret,**
I discard my books and throw away my brush.

(*With tears.*)

I could not command an army like Ban Chao in real life.
I could only stand between the Gold Turtles[3] in vain dreams.
Thinking back upon my vanity,
My tears rush like torrents.

(*A sigh.*) Today, even if I confess my dream of glory, who can really believe me? I'd better keep the dream to myself. (*Sighs again.*) Oh, my Heaven! Now that my dream of glory has turned into an empty romance, how can I suffer through the endless days and nights of boredom any more? (*She sighs in tears.*)

[a65] **Why should I be disillusioned from a daydream?**
Why should I agonize over those renewed frustrations?
I simply cannot forget those twenty years of glory.
How can my indignation vanish from the vast human world and the expanse of Heaven?

Oh my dear wife! Oh my two dear concubines!

[a66] **Thinking about our fated love,**
My sorrows rise like the tide;
Recalling our amorous moments,
My regret is cast far and wide.

Now although the painting still betrays the lovely face of my Lady Xie, it will be impossible to return the jade bracelet and pendants to those moon souls of the night.

My dear solitary Fairy of the Moon,
When can you descend from the clouds again
Just to shed your pity over my single-hearted foolishness that has been scattered to the wind?

[3] See Scene 13, n. 1.

[a67] I admire Chunyu[4] but her abode excludes me.
I envy Lu Sheng[5] who turns into a monk.
Yet how can I find their traces in the din of this world of dust?
How could I, a lost soul after a dream of fantasized glory,
Extricate myself from earthly ties
And enter the Land of the Immortals?
It is impossible to recover a bygone dream.
Who cares to sweep away the sorrows of a dreamer?
Today my plight contrasts with the east wind.
The setting sun mirrors the dying rosy clouds.

(*Sobbing.*)

With tears on my dress and the soul-stirring fragrance of the grass,
I will recapture the splendor of this dream of glory and
Turn it into a manuscript of mad passion, which will last until
Heaven becomes a wasteland and Earth meets its doomsday.

(*Exits.*)

[4] Chunyu could mean the ancient Chunyu Capital, which symbolizes a man's success in imperial examinations and the court. It could also refer to the paragon daughter Chunyu Tiying, who offered herself to be a court servant in order to exempt her father Chunyu Yi from his punishment.

[5] Disillusioned from the Golden Millet Dream, Lu Sheng abandoned the world of red dust (*hongchen*) and turned into an immortal.

SCENE 25. Becoming an Immortal

MAGU *wears an immortal crown and a cloud-pattern gown, holding a celestial duster. Two fairies, each in a green dress and phoenix coronet, hold their banners high to guide the way.*

ALL.

[a68] **Wandering freely above the sea**
Celestial wind fills our ample sleeves.
Reaching the apex of the Immortal Gate
One no longer desires anything from the world.
A free spirit befriends no one but
the bright moon and the pure wind.

MAGU (*recites*).

[c5[i]] Dingdong dingdong, clatter the rings and jade pendants.
The true priestess used to be a lady named Wang.
Seeing through the world from inside a kettle,[1]
She discarded all fame and wealth of the earth.

I am Magu, dwelling on the Island of Penglai, ranking high among the immortals. Now a Lady Wang on the earth has lost herself in inexpressible sorrows caused by a passionate dream. I will go down and drop her a hint of disillusionment. Then I will guide her to my Gate of the Immortals. Fairy Maids, please help me get changed.

Two maids respond and start waiting on her. Amid gentle music, MAGU *takes off her crown and dresses herself like a paddy-field peasant.*

MAGU (*holding her duster*). Fairy Maids, you two stay behind. I prefer to visit the Red Dust all by myself this time.

Exit the maids.

---

[1] The world inside a kettle is an ideal Daoist vision of life. Famous poet Li Bai wrote, "There is another world of sun and moon inside the kettle." Hugong, the Man of Kettle, refers to an immortal.

MAGU.

[a12] **With a roaring sound,**
I descend from the Celestial Palace.
Riding on a gust of wind,
I clear my path to the earth with my duster.
Beyond the clouds the celestial dwelling is utterly still.
The laurel in the moon is most serene.
Yet, to pacify the crying of cranes and phoenix on earth,
I have to leave my Land of Solitude for a moment.

MAGU *floats down from above.* WANG *enters, wearing a green dress with a green head kerchief, looking miserably sick.*

WANG.

[a38] **Despite my worries and anxiety,**
There is no way for me to trace the bygone dream.
It is even harder to understand its causes.
My sickness doubles with the advance of the autumn.
My books turn blank, no longer able to
anchor my spirit and soul.

(*The cries of the wild geese bring* WANG *to tears.*)

Wild geese are screaming sadly beyond the horizon;
Yet every single cry seems to wring away
the substance of my remaining life.

(WANG *sits down, sprawling over the desk.*)

(*Chants.*)

[c5ii] My heart breaks not merely for lamenting the autumn.
My sleepless nights have been laden with
Lingering relish for the adventures in my dream.
Here and now I cannot see my sweethearts,
Merely a moon tumbling down from the Western Pavilion.

Ever since I had a dream of splendor in the spring, I have been chasing its traces day and night. No appetite and endless insomnia. Sickly, I'm pining away. Now it's already mid-autumn, the falling scene drives my sadness to intolerance.

(*A sigh with tears.*) Oh, Heaven, why let me be thus tortured between life and death? (*Wailing again.*)

Isn't my sorrow like a pitiful murmur in a corner of an everlasting night?
Who could have the peace of mind to enjoy the bright moon in the sky?

(*Falling into a slumber over the desk.*)

MAGU *enters.*

MAGU.

[a69] **Leaving behind the palaces of jade and gold,**
Looking back to the Celestial Pavilion,
I see it being shrouded by colorful clouds and drifting air.
I alone strode into the blue sky, overlooking the vast sea.
For three times I have lived through the dusty world.
Who knows why I could see through
the fate of the universe from within a jade kettle?
I shed pity over human vicissitudes.
Who can give up struggling for wealth and fame
in that savage world?
If one is determined to seek self-salvation,
One must ride over the fate of the frail phoenix.
One morning taking off from the verdant land,
You will soar on the wings of a yellow crane
And arrive in Penglai at sunset.

MAGU *exits;* WANG *gets up slowly from her seat.*

WANG.

[a15] **Overhead, flying geese snatch away my heart.**
Poundings of a washing rod startled me out of reverie.
In bleary loneliness,
I blend my sorrow with the shrilling of crickets by the steps.
Languidly, I wander to and fro under the moon
like a lost soul.

(*The sound of a flute offstage.*)

Surprisingly, who is playing a flute against the wind?

(*A long sigh to the moon.*)

In such solitary moonlight, overwhelming thoughts pour from my head and rhyme like verse. I'd better jot them down.

(*She gets to her seat and starts writing.*)

[c10] Scratching my head, I complain to Heaven.
The vast void sends back no response.
Why should you abuse your power in
Creating chaos and letting the female be born handicapped?
Can't you explain the deep-rooted resentment of a woman,
Whose fate has been scattered like Pink Powder?
Can't you appreciate the sorrows of
talented ladies through the centuries?
Heaven and Earth, may I ask
Who can sharpen the fine sword of the heart?
Please cut off my sorrows and frustrations!

Ten thousand things in the world need impartial judgment.
Wise people should be contented with their destiny.
Yet I sigh over the fate of Heyang[2] whose eyebrows turned gray.
I admire Hermit Marquis if he could have retired
at the sign of backache.[3]
How could a perverted dream ever bring happiness to a person!
How could a book of madness ever reverse
the verdict set by Heaven?
Pondering and pondering,
I finally tear at my gown and curse the vanity in my fantasy.

(*Throwing down the brush with a long sigh, she stands up in profound sadness.*)

---

[2] Refers to Pan Yue (247–300), poet and also imperial magistrate to Heyang. He worked so hard that his hair turned prematurely gray. Yet he was executed by the emperor in AD 300. Heyang, an ancient county, now Meng county in Henan province. It underwent several radical changes in history, becoming an important town in the suburbs of Luoyang.

[3] Refers to Shen Yue (441–513), a busy official who always wished that he were a Daoist hermit, thus gaining the name "Hermit Marquis."

I attempt to leave this world,
Yet Heaven is pathless and too high above.
Failing to play an immortal celestial pipe
on the top of Mount Gouling[4],
I can only inscribe my poems on bookmarkers.

MAGU *steals in, standing above* WANG's *desk.*

MAGU.
I no longer remember how many years have passed
since I abandoned the Red Dust.

(*Pricking up her ears,* WANG *listens in astonishment.*)

Again and again, I witnessed the reversal
between sea and mulberry fields.
Whoever can see through the dream of human life
can find the ladder leading to Heaven.

WANG. My god, this verse can't come out of the mouth of an ordinary being. Who is she? (*Lifting her head,* WANG *sees* MAGU, *greatly surprised.*) Dear me, a goddess stands on a rosy cloud. She must have been stirred by my sorrow and come to my rescue. Let me hurry to greet her. An opportunity like this should not slip away.

(*Tidying up her gown and head kerchief, she kneels on the floor, shouting.*)

Immortal, Immortal!

I am a foolish lady on earth. May I know which immortal has descended here? I plead with you to stay for a while. I beg your pity for a disciple like me, beset with the fantasies of a dream. Please clear my head with your wise guidance.

MAGU (*laughs*). What a crazy woman!

[a14 + a70][5]

I thought you had climbed up to the Forbidden City.

---

[4] A mountain in Yanshi county of Henan province. According to a Daoist legendary tale, Immortal Wang Ziqiao promised to meet Huan Liang on Gouling on the seventh day of the seventh lunar month.

[5] Here the playwright used *Yan er luo* plus *De sheng ling*. One aria plus another is a type of composition in *qu* (drama) or *sanqu* (poetry).

Why do you suddenly **cast away your black gauze cap and**
Turn to salute a mountain dweller?
Where are your **two graceful concubines behind the golden screen?**
Why have you lost your virtuous wife, an ideal mate?

WANG (*covering her tears with a sleeve*). All this is the nonsense of a dream. Immortal, please don't mention it any more.

Now I want to have you as my true master. I want to be released from the sufferings of this world. (*Thus saying,* WANG *kowtows to* MAGU.)

MAGU.

Ayah, since you have **attempted so hard in serving the imperial court with your brush,**
Why bother to **ascend to the Celestial Capital through tortuous paths?**

WANG. Please reveal me your true identity, your Immortal Majesty.

MAGU.

This human has asked which immortal I am.
Does an immortal need to conceal her identity?
I have not set my foot on the Red Dust for a long time.
Neither do I care whether my name is known. However,
I once whipped Cai Jing during the Reign of Han Huan[6]**.**

WANG. Oh, I see. You are Immortal Magu. Great Immortal,

(*With hands clasped in a gesture of pleading, she sings in great sorrow.*)

[a71] **I sincerely seek a magic cure.**
I also desire immortality.
A dream upon the pillow has cast me to a wandering soul.
Why should I have such a passion for that fantasy?
Why such a passion for that fantasy?

MAGU. Nothing needs to be explained. It is all caused by your resentment against your fate of being a woman. Your daily sorrows and frustrations, distilled by a mind of wild imagination, have produced such a world of fantasy.

---

[6] It is said that during the reign of Emperor Huan in the Eastern Han (147–167), Immortal Wang Yuan summoned the presence of Magu in the house of Cai Jing. When Cai Jing saw Magu, a beautiful lady of eighteen with slender fingers like a bird's claws, he said, "When my back is really itchy, how wonderful if I could have her claws to scratch it."

WANG. What a pity if I have to abandon the achievements I have gained in half of my life and the love I have pursued with my entire life!

MAGU. Please open your eyes to honors and wealth in this world. No matter how solid they look, they are merely passing phantoms, like galloping horses in the drifting clouds. Who can possess them forever? Isn't it rather pointless to speak of the fame and wealth created by an illusion or fantasy?

WANG. But may I humbly ask, Master, where those fantasized figures come and go?

MAGU. They are all created by human obsession. They survive in the dream and vanish when you awake. They have no other source or destiny.

WANG (*looks stupefied, and then gains a sudden insight*). Now I understand. Twenty years of splendid love and success come from nothing but a possessive desire. There is no reason that one should live or die for it. I feel really ashamed. (*She kowtows to* MAGU.) I have finally seen through my stubborn foolishness and been released from my greed for wealth and fame. Immortal, please take me as your disciple.

MAGU. Are you awakened yet?

WANG. Yes. I am awakened.

MAGU.

[a72] Ah, **in my view, all honor and disgrace in this world**
can be traced back to a dreamer.
If you fail to break away from the spell of greed,
anger, love, obsession, life, and death,
You will keep wallowing in the pits of fame and wealth.
Wallowing in the pits of fame and wealth,
How could you be like me, free from worries and desires?

WANG. Please accept me as your disciple.

(*Standing up and straightening her gown, she kowtows.*)

[a50] **A word from the Immortal**
Wakes me up from my delusion and dream.
Being enlightened, I've gained my rebirth today.
Your disciple is
Determined to follow you to the celestial
Land of the Immortals.

(*She kowtows again.*)

Master, please take sympathy on me for my sincerity.
Let me ascend to the void with you.

MAGU (*smiles*). Now it is still too early. It takes time for you to shed your greedy desires and purge your mind from the dust. When you have regained the original nature and truly enlightened your mind, I'll certainly guide you to the Land of the Immortals.
WANG (*wiping off her tears, kowtows again*). Many thanks to my respectful Master.

Two fairy maids enter quietly, flanking MAGU *with their banners.*

MAGU. Look, the moon has declined and the Milky Way shifted its direction. Already deep into the night, I must be leaving now.

[a73] **Clouds like twin wings of hair come to greet me.**
Clouds like twin wings of hair come to greet me.
I ride on the blue bird, flying to my celestial dwelling.

WANG. Is my Immortal Master really leaving now?
MAGU.

Why do I lean against the lucky clouds but hesitate to leave?

WANG *is weeping.*

MAGU.

Don't cry any more.
Some day your light body will fly up to accompany me.

WANG (*holding up her clasped hands*).

Thank you for freeing me from the land of illusions, Master.
I am awed by your presence and your departure.
Like a morning bell waking me up
from the clutch of a nightmare,
My mind is suddenly kindled by your holy care.
I have indeed resolved to purify my body and soul.

MAGU. As long as your heart is sincere and your will strong, I'll guide you in becoming an immortal.

Gentle music arises. MAGU *exits with the two fairies.*

WANG (*laughing aloud*). I can't believe it! I really met an immortal tonight.

[a74] **A spring dream fell upon me from nowhere;**
I squandered the passion of my future, present, and past.
Discarding it as a fantasy of madness, I came to realize:

A woman as well as a man needs
A wakening return from a life gone astray.

(*Exit.*)

....

Shadows of flowers and palm leaves
reflect upon the window screen;[7]
Inside the boudoir dwells Daoyun, a talented woman.
Her interest lies nowhere but in the books;
The song of splendor is woven into her dream.
A hundred years of passion are a mere illusion;
Her pursuit of the Three Islands is just the beginning.
The melodies of her song around the beams entwine;
The moon shines upon joys of red lights and green wine.

From ancient times to today,
No woman can exchange hers for a male body;
Yet through a dream, she has created such a wonder.
A lady becomes the Number One National Scholar;
A Skirt-Hairpin boldly steals into the Gown-Cap order.
Her adventures match those of Huang Chonggu;
Her talent and lyrics rank with those of Li Yi'an[8].
Hereafter, her play will be spread
as a holy show among the fair sex,[9]
Beheld with *The Peach Blossom* and *The Swallow*
on the same horizon.[10]

—End of the Play—

---

[7] This commentary poem was written by Zhu Gui (1731–1807). It was included in the play as its ending in the original woodblock print.

[8] A famous woman poet of the Song dynasty, better known as Li Qingzhao (1084–ca. 1151).

[9] *Faqu* (holy music or message) originally refers to music of the Daoist temple and later includes plays on the subject of immortality. Here it simply means Wang Yun's play.

[10] Refer to the two famous plays: *Taohua shan* and *Yanzi jian.*

WANG BAILING'S POSTFACE

This play is written by my mother, Madame Wang. She was born with unique talents and had a good command of history. Out of a constant regret over being unable to gain titles in the imperial examinations and having no opportunity to enter civil service, she wrote this play to express her wish-fulfilling fantasy. I remember the days of my childhood when I was taught by my mother. She often encouraged me by saying, "You must study hard to realize my ambition." Therefore, at the age of eight I was sent to be tutored by my maternal grandfather, Nanpu Gong. When I was twenty-three, I was recommended by the county to take the imperial examination. But I could not afford to travel to the north. My mother lectured me, "I have eaten poor food and worked hard since entering your family. My only wish, as the daughter of a *jinshi*, is to become the mother of a *jinshi*." My maternal grandfather became *juren* in the year of 1738 and gained the title of *jinshi* in 1748.

To fulfill my mother's wish, I studied hard, as though I was charging forward on a chariot in the battlefields, and in 1802 gained *fangkui* (a secondary place) in the imperial examination. I was appointed to serve in the Hanlin Academy. I asked for a leave to pay my mother a visit. Although she was pleased about my achievement, she was disappointed that I had failed to gain *dakui* (first place). In the autumn of 1804, I read my mother's play and wrote this postface to share with the world my mother's strong will and her son's incompetence to live up to her expectation. I would also like to see my mother's collection of poems and her other *chuanqi* play, *Quanfu ji*, published.

Son, Wang Bailing

WANG YUANCHANG'S POSTFACE

My daughter Yun was born with exceptional talents. From childhood, she could comprehend a book or a historical record after a single reading. Out of a long festering regret for being a female, she wrote the play, *Fanhua meng*, to express her desires. After completing the draft of the play, she gave it to me for editing. I deleted some seemingly florid parts and did a little refinement to make it flow well. It was condensed into a publishable play, with my comments inscribed on the head margins. But due to financial difficulties, the manuscript sat hidden away in a small box for a decade. In the third lunar month of 1778, I, by chance, showed it to Judicial Inspector Zhang and he passed it to his sister Madame Bi immediately. They were so excited from reading the play that they wrote a preface and a commentary poem respectively, serving as the introductory part. Inspector Zhang donated sufficient funds to cover the publishing costs. Hence, this humble writing from a boudoir can be released to the world. It will also be a consolation to my daughter that she should no longer regret having been born a female. The printing blocks having been carved, I wrote these words to commemorate this occasion.

Wang Yuanchang of the Southern Garden*
Inscribed at the Locust Hall

* Southern Garden (Nanpu) may refer to the City of Nanchang.

Reference Matter

CHRONOLOGY OF MAJOR CHINESE DYNASTIES AND PERIODS

Spring and Autumn	春秋	770–476 BC
Warring States	戰國	476–222 BC
Qin	秦	221–207 BC
Western Han	西漢	206 BC–AD 25
Eastern Han	東漢	25–220
Three Kingdoms	三國	220–280
Jin	晉	265–420
Western Jin	西晉	265–316
Eastern Jin	東晉	317–420
Northern and Southern Dynasties	南北朝	420–589
Former Qin	前秦	310–394
Northern Wei	北魏	386–534
Southern Qi	南齊	479–502
Sui	隋	581–618
Tang	唐	618–907
Five Dynasties	五代	907–960
Northern Song	北宋	960–1127
Southern Song	南宋	1127–1279
Jin	金	1115–1234
Yuan	元	1279–1368
Ming	明	1368–1644
Chongzhen	崇禎	r. 1628–1644
Qing	清	1644–1911
Shunzhi	順治	r. 1644–1661
Kangxi	康熙	r. 1662–1722
Yongzheng	雍正	r. 1723–1735
Qianlong	乾隆	r. 1736–1795
Jiaqing	嘉慶	r. 1796-1820
Daoguang	道光	r. 1821–1850
Guangxu	光緒	r. 1875–1908

GLOSSARY

Anhui 安徽

Ban Chao 班超
Ban Gu 班固
Ban Zhao 班昭
Baoding 保定
bi shenghua 筆生花
Bi Yuan 畢沅
boshi 博士

Cai Jing 蔡經
Cai Wenji 蔡文姬
caizi jiaren 才子佳人
Cao Cao 曹操
Cao Xueqin 曹雪芹
Chang'an 長安
Chang'e 嫦娥
Chen Duansheng 陳端生
chou 丑
chuanqi 傳奇
Chunyu 淳于
Chunyu Tiying 淳于緹縈
Chunyu Yi 淳于意
Ci Mulan tifu congjun 雌木蘭替父從軍
Ci yuan 詞源
City of Stone 石城

Da Qiao 大喬
da tuanyuan 大團圓
Dai Lanying 戴蘭英
dakui 大魁
dan 旦
daobai 道白

Dong Hunhou (Emperor, Southern Qi) 東昏侯
Du Liniang 杜麗娘

Eastern Sea 東海

fangkui 房魁
fanhua 繁華
Fanhua meng 繁華夢
faqu 法曲
Fengnüci 鳳女祠
Fengnütai 鳳女臺
Fengtai 鳳臺
"Fuxue" 婦學

Ge Hong 葛洪
Gold Turtles 金鰲
Gouling, Mount 緱嶺
Gu Sen 顧森
Guangling 廣陵
guixiu 閨秀
guiyuan 閨怨

Handan 邯鄲
Handan ji 邯鄲記
Handan meng 邯鄲夢
hangyuan 行院
Hangzhou 杭州
Hanlinyuan 翰林院
Hanshu 漢書
Haoqiu zhuan 好逑傳
He Peizhu 何佩珠
He Shuangqing 賀雙卿
Hebei (province) 河北

Henan (province) 河南
Heyang (county) 河陽
hongchen 紅塵
hongfen 紅粉
Honglou meng 紅樓夢
hongya 紅牙
Hua Mulan 花木蘭
Huaiqingtang 槐慶堂
Huaiqingtang ji 槐慶堂集
Huan (Emperor, Eastern Han) 東漢桓王
Huan Liang 桓良
Huang Chonggu 黃崇嘏
Huangdi 黃帝
Huangliang meng 黃粱夢
Hugong 壺公
Huichun meng 回春夢
Huixian ji 會仙記

Ji Junxiang 紀君祥
Jiading 嘉定
Jiang Yujie 姜玉潔
Jiangdu 江都
Jiangsu 江蘇
Jiao Xun 焦循
"Jiaohua song" 椒花頌
jiaopan 椒盤
jieyuan 解元
Jifang yuan 集芳園
jing 淨
Jingwei 精衛
jinlan 金蘭
jinshi 進士
Jinyu yuan 金魚緣
jiuming 九命
juren 舉人

Kong Shangren 孔尚任

Langui 蘭閨
Lanqiao ji 藍橋記
Lantian 藍田
leng 冷
li 里
Li Bai 李白
Li Qingzhao 李清照
"Li sao" 離騷
Li Tiaoyuan 李調元
Li Xiangjun 李香君
Li Yu 李漁
Li Yu'e 李玉娥
Liang Hong 梁鴻
Liang Mengzhao 梁孟昭
Liang Xiaoyu 梁小玉
Lihua meng 梨花夢
lin 麟
Lin'an 臨安
Linchuan simeng 臨川四夢
Liu Chen 劉晨
Liu Dan 劉誕
Liu Shuzeng 劉淑曾
Liu Zhen 劉臻
Liyuan 梨園
liyuan zidi 梨園子弟
Lu Sheng 盧生
luan 鸞
Luoyang 洛陽
Lüchuang nüshi 綠窗女史

Ma Shouzhen 馬守貞
Magu (Immortal) 麻姑
meng 夢
Meng (county) 孟縣
Meng Guang 孟光
Meng Lijun 孟麗君
Menghu yuan 夢虎緣
Mengjue guan 夢覺關
Mengying lian 夢影戀

menyin 門蔭
mo 末
Mo Chou 莫愁
moben 墨本
Mojie 磨羯
Momu 嫫姆
Moxie 磨蠍
Mudan ting 牡丹亭
"Mulan shi" 木蘭詩

Nanchang 南昌
Nanpu 南圃
Nanpu Gong 南圃公
"Niulang Zhinü" 牛郎織女
Nongyu 弄玉
Nü zhuangyuan cihuang defeng 女狀元辭凰得鳳
nüboshi 女博士
nücaizi 女才子
Nüwa 女媧
Nüwa (the daughter of Tiandi) 女娃

Pan Yue 潘岳
Pei Hang 裴航
Penglai 蓬萊
Pu Songling 蒲松齡

Qian Shurong 錢淑容
Qiantang 錢塘
Qin Mugong 秦穆公
"Qing jiang yin" 清江引
qing 情
qing (color) 青
qingshan 青衫
Qintai 秦臺
qiuzhen 秋砧
Qu Bingyun 屈秉筠
Qu Yuan 屈原
Quanfu 全福
Quanfu ji 全福記

Ruan Dacheng 阮大鋮
Ruan Lizhen 阮麗珍
Ruan Zhao 阮肇
ruoshui 弱水

Sanguo yanyi 三國演義
sanhuai 三槐
Shaanxi 陝西
Shandong 山東
Shang Xiaoling 商小玲
Shaohua 少華
Shen Huilan 沈蕙蘭
Shen Jiji 沈既濟
Shen Yue 沈約
sheng 生
shenghua bi 生花筆
Shenxian zhuan 神仙傳
Shi Zhenlin 史震林
Shi'er jinchai 十二金釵
Sima Xiangru 司馬相如
Songping 松坪
Su Hui 蘇蕙
Su Shi 蘇軾
Su Xiaoxiao 蘇小小
Su Yingxue 蘇映雪
Sun Deying 孫得英
Sunü (Goddess) 素女
Suzhou 蘇州

taiben 臺本
tanci 彈詞
Tang Xianzu 湯顯祖
tanhua 探花
Tao Yuanming 陶淵明
Taohua shan 桃花扇
"Taohuayuan ji" 桃花源記
Tianchi 天池

Tianchi shanren 天池山人
Tiandi 天帝
Tiansun 天孫
Tongquetai 銅雀臺
tongxin 同心

Wang Yuan 王遠
Wang Ziqiao 王子喬
Wei Wendi 魏文帝
Wen Yan 文彥
Wu Lanzheng 吳蘭徵
Wu Zao 吳藻
Wucheng 蕪城
Wu'e 巫娥
Wushan shennü 巫山神女
Wusheng xi: Bian nü wei er pusa qiao 無聲戲：變女為兒菩薩巧
Wuyan 無鹽
wuyi 烏衣
Wuyi (county) 吳邑

Xi Peilan 席佩蘭
Xi Shi 西施
Xi'an 西安
Xiang (King, State Chu) 楚襄王
xiao 簫
Xiao Qiao 小喬
Xiao Shi 蕭史
xiaodan 小旦
xiaosheng 小生
Xie Daoyun 謝道韞
Xincheng 新城
xingling 性靈
Xiqing sanji 西青散記
xiucai 秀才
Xiwangmu 西王母
Xiyou ji 西遊記
Xiyuan banxiang ji 西園瓣香集

Xu Wei 徐渭
Xuan (King, State Qi) 齊宣王
Xuanji tu 璇璣圖
Xuanzong (Emperor, Tang) 玄宗
Xue Tao 薛濤

yang 陽
Yanqing 延慶
Yanshi (county) 偃師縣
Yanzi jian 燕子箋
Ye Xiaowan 葉小紈
Yi jing 易經
yin 陰
Yingzhou 瀛洲
Yinjiu dusao 飲酒讀〈騷〉
Yongqing 永清
youren 優人
Youxian meng 遊仙夢
yu 慾
yu fei 于飛
Yuan Mei 袁枚
yuanben 院本
Yuanyang meng 鴛鴦夢
Yuming 玉茗
Yumingtang simeng 玉茗堂四夢
Yun'an laoren 雲庵老人
Yun'an zalu 雲庵雜錄
Yunying 雲英
Yutang 玉堂

Zaisheng yuan 再生緣
zaju 雜劇
Zhang Chang 張敞
Zhang Lingyi 張令儀
Zhang Xuecheng 章學誠
Zhao Feiyan 趙飛燕
zhen 砧
Zhen (Empress) 甄后
Zheng Danruo 鄭澹若

"Zhenzhong ji" 枕中記
zhifu 知府
Zhili (province) 直隸
zhixian 知縣
zhiyin 知音
zhizhou 知州
Zhong Lichun 鍾離春
Zhou Xiang 周庠
Zhou Yu 周瑜
Zhu Bajie 豬八戒
Zhu Gui 朱珪
zhuangyuan 狀元
Zhuangzi 莊子
Zhuge Liang 諸葛亮
Zhuo Wenjun 卓文君
Zhuo Wenjun siben Xiangru 卓文君私奔相如
Zhuyeqing 竹葉青
Zichai ji 紫釵記

BIBLIOGRAPHY

1. Women Playwrights of the Ming and Qing Dynasties

Cao Jianbing 曹鑑冰 (Qing). Style name: Weijian 葦堅. Native of Jiangsu Huating 江蘇華亭. Daughter of Cao Ergai 曹爾垓 and wife of Zhang Yinliu 張殷六. Self-supporting by teaching. Co-published a collection of poems, *Sanxiu ji* 三秀集, with her mother Li Huai 李懷. Play: *Yaotai yan* 瑤臺宴 (The Banquet of Yaotai).

Cheng Qiong 程瓊 (Qing). Lived during the Kangxi and Qianlong periods. Style name: Feixian 飛仙. Native of Anhui Xiuning 安徽休寧. Wife of the dramatist Wu Zhensheng 吳震生 who wrote thirteen Northern dramas. The author of *Xiu mudan* 繡牡丹 (Commentaries on *The Peony Pavilion*). Play: *Fengyue ting* 風月亭 (The Passion Pavilion).

He Peizhu 何佩珠 (ca. 1819–?). Lived during the Daoguang period. Style name: Zhixiang 芷香. Native of Anhui 安徽. Daughter of He Bingtang 何秉堂 and wife of Zhang Ziyuan 張子元. Play: *Lihua meng* 梨花夢 (The Pear Blossom Dream).

Jiang Yujie 姜玉潔 (late Ming). A Daoist priestess. Play: *Jian zhong tian* 鑑中天 (Heaven in the Mirror).

Kong Jiying 孔繼瑛 (Qing). Style name: Yaopu 瑤埔. Native of Zhejiang Tongxiang 浙江桐鄉. Daughter of Kong Chuanzhi 孔傳志 and wife of Shen Tingguang 沈廷光. Play: *Yuanyang pei* 鴛鴦佩 (The Mandarin Duck Pendants).

Li Huai 李懷 (Qing). Style name: Yuyan 玉燕. Native of Zhejiang Jiashan 浙江嘉善. Co-wrote with her husband Cao Ergai 曹爾垓 the play *Shuangyu pu* 雙魚譜 (Twin Fish).

Li Jingfang 李靜芳 (1668–1748). Style name: Youshu 又淑, also Renlan 紉蘭. Native of Changzhou 長洲. Daughter of Li Zhen 李圳 and wife of Jiang Shen 蔣深. Play: *Danjing chuan* 丹晶串 (A String of Vermilion Crystals).

Liang Mengzhao 梁孟昭 (Ming). Still alive during the Chongzhen period. Native of Qiantang 錢塘. Wife of Mao Jiureng 茅九仍. Play: *Xiangsi yan* 相思硯 (A Love Inkwell).

Liang Xiaoyu 梁小玉 (late Ming). A famous courtesan. Style name: Yuji 玉姬. Play: *Heyuan ji* 合元記 (Reunion).

Lin Yining 林以寧 (1655–?). Still alive in 1730. Style name: Yaqing 亞清. Native of Qiantang 錢塘. Daughter of Lin Lun 林綸 and wife of Qian Zhaoxiu 錢肇修. Play: *Furong xia* 芙蓉峽 (The Hibiscus Gorge).

Liu Shi 劉氏 (late Qing). Pen name: Yizong jinü 嬴宗季女. Play: *Liuyue shuang* 六月霜 (June Frost), based on the life of Qiu Jin 秋瑾 (1875–1907).

Liu Shuzeng 劉淑曾 (Qing). Lived during the Guangxu period. Style name: Qingyun 清韻. Native of Jiangsu Donghai 江蘇東海. Daughter of Liu Yuntang 劉蘊堂 and wife of Zhong Meipo 鍾梅坡. Plays: *Xiao Penglai xianguan chuanqi* 小蓬萊仙館傳奇 (Romances of the Little Penglai Abode); *Yuanyang meng* 鴛鴦夢 (Dream of Mandarin Ducks), *Yingxiong pei* 英雄配 (The Heroic Match); *Jingzhong yuan* 鏡中圓 (Reunion in the Mirror); *Nianhua wu* 拈花悟 (Wakening of a Flower Picker); and *Wangyang tan* 望洋嘆 (Sighing over the Vast Ocean).

Ma Shouzhen 馬守貞 (1604–1649). A famous courtesan and painter. Style name: Xianglan 湘蘭, also Yuejiao 月嬌. Native of Nanjing 南京. Play: *Sansheng zhuan* 三生傳 (Three Lives), based on the life story of Wang Kui 王魁.

Ruan Lizhen 阮麗珍 (late Ming). Native of Anhui Huaining 安徽懷寧. Daughter of the famous playwright Ruan Dacheng 阮大鋮 (1587–1646). Plays: *Menghu yuan* 夢虎緣 (Dream of Meeting a Tiger); and *Luanpa xue* 鸞帕血 (Blood on the Phoenix kerchief).

Song Lingyun 宋凌雲 (Qing). Style name: Yixian 逸仙. Native of Suzhou 蘇州. Wife of Li Bo 李博. Play (incomplete): *Yaochi yan* 瑤池宴 (The Banquet of Yaochi).

Wang Yun 王筠 (1749–1819). Style name: Songping 松坪. Native of Shaanxi Chang'an 陝西長安. Plays: *Fanhua meng* 繁華夢 (A Dream of Glory, 1769); *Quanfu ji* 全福記 (Full Happiness, 1779); and *Youxian meng* 遊仙夢 (A Dream Visit to the Immortals), also known as *Huixian ji* 會仙記 (Meeting the Immortals).

Wu Lanzheng 吳蘭徵 (1778–1806). Style name: Xiangqian 香倩, also Mengxiang 夢湘. Native of Xin'an 新安. Wife of Yu Yongji 俞用濟. Plays: *Sansheng shi* 三生石 (A Stone of Three Lives); *Jiang heng qiu* 絳蘅秋 (Purple Berry Autumn); and *Yuanyang meng* 鴛鴦夢 (Dream of Mandarin Ducks).

Wu Shi 吳氏 (Qing). Native of Anhui Luzhou 安徽廬州. Wife of Xu Qian 許乾. Play: *Hongxiao yong* 紅綃詠 (Odes to Red Silk).

Wu Zao 吳藻 (1799–1862). Style name: Pingxiang 蘋香. Native of Zhejiang Renhe 浙江仁和. Play: *Yinjiu dusao* 飲酒讀〈騷〉 (Drinking Wine and Reading "Encountering Sorrow"), also titled *Qiaoying* 喬影 (A Fair Shadow).

Xu Yanzhen 許燕珍 (Qing). Lived during the Qianlong period. Style name: Liqiong 麗瓊. Native of Anhui Hefei 安徽合肥. Daughter of Xu Qizhuo 許其倬 and wife of Wang Renzhen 王人鎮. Had frequent literary correspondences with Yuan Suwen 袁素文 (ca. 1720–ca. 1759), the sister of Yuan Mei 袁枚 (1716–1798). Plays: *Baozhen suo* 保貞蓑 (A Chastity Straw Cape); and *Hongxiao yong* 紅綃詠 (Odes to Red Silk).

Yao Shi 姚氏 (Qing). Wife of Zhu Fengsen 朱鳳森 (1776–1832). Co-wrote with her husband two plays: *Cairen fu* 才人福 (The Fortune of the Talented); and *Shi'er chai* 十二釵 (The Twelve Hairpins).

Ye Xiaowan 葉小紈 (1613–1657?). Died at the beginning of the Qing dynasty. Style name: Huichou 蕙綢. Native of Jiangsu Wujiang 江蘇吳江. Daughter of Ye Shaoyuan 葉紹袁 and wife of Shen Yongzhen 沈永楨 (1611–1646). Play: *Yuanyang meng* 鴛鴦夢 (Dream of Mandarin Ducks).

Zhang Fan 張蘩 (early Qing). Style name: Caiyu 采于. Wife of Wu Shi'an 吳士安. It is said that she wrote a dozen of plays for house troupe performance. But the one play known today: *Shuang kouhun* 雙叩閽 (Double Palace Gate).

Zhang Lingyi 張令儀 (Qing). Lived during the Kangxi and Yongzheng periods. Style name: Roujia 柔嘉. Native of Anhui Tongcheng 安徽桐城. Daughter of Zhang Ying 張英 and wife of Yao Xiangmen 姚湘門. Widowed at mid-age. Plays: *Qiankun quan* 乾坤圈 (A Qiankun Hoop); and *Mengjue guan* 夢覺關 (The Pass between Dream and Wakening).

2. Works Used in Text

Chinese Sources

Cai Yi 蔡毅, ed. *Zhongguo gudian xiqu xuba huibian* 中國古典戲曲序跋彙編 (A Collection of Prefaces and Postfaces to Classical Chinese Play). 4 vols. Jinan: Qilu shushe, 1989.

Chen Duansheng 陳端生 (1751–1796). *Zaisheng yuan* 再生緣 (The Destiny of the Next Life). Zhengzhou: Zhongzhou shuhuashe, 1982.

Gao Xingjian 高行健. *Meiyou zhuyi* 沒有主義 (No-isms). Hong Kong: Cosmos Books, 2000.

Guo Mei 郭梅. "Zhongguo gudai nüqujia de chuangzuo shijian ji xintai" 中國古代女曲家的創作實踐及心態 (The Creative Experience and Psychology of Women Playwrights in Imperial China). *Gudai jindai wenxue yanjiu* 古代近代文學研究 (Studies on Classical and Modern Literature), no. 8 (August 1995): 41–45.

Hu Wenkai 胡文楷. *Lidai funü zhuzuo kao* 歷代婦女著作考 (An Examination of Women's Writings through the Dynasties). Rev. ed. Shanghai: Shanghai guji chubanshe, 1985 (1957).

Hua Wei 華瑋. "Ming Qing funü juzuo zhong zhi 'ninan' biaoxian yu xingbie wenti" 明清婦女劇作中之"擬男"表現與性別問題 (The Problem of Women's Cross-dressing and Gender Identity in the Ming and Qing). In Hua and Wang, *Ming Qing xiqu guoji yantaohui lunwenji*.

Hua Wei 華瑋, ed. *Ming Qing funü xiqu ji* 明清婦女戲曲集 (Anthology of Plays by Women in the Ming and Qing). Taipei: Zhongyang yanjiuyuan Zhongguo wenzhe yanjiusuo, 2003.

Hua Wei 華瑋. *Ming Qing funü zhi xiqu chuangzuo yu piping* 明清婦女之戲曲創作

與批評 (Drama and Drama Criticism by Women in the Ming and Qing). Taipei: Zhongyang yanjiuyuan Zhongguo wenzhe yanjiusuo, 2003.

Hua Wei 華瑋, and Wang Ailing 王璦玲, eds. *Ming Qing xiqu guoji yantaohui lunwenji* 明清戲曲國際研討會論文集 (Proceedings of the International Conference on Ming-Qing Drama). Taipei: Dawen yinshua, 1998.

Jiao Xun 焦循 (1763–1820). *Jushuo* 劇說. In *Zhongguo gudian xiqu lunzhu jicheng.*

Li Tiaoyuan 李調元 (1734–1803). *Yucun shihua* 雨村詩話. 16 vols.

Li Yu 李漁 (1611–1680). *Li Yu quanji* 李漁全集 (Complete Works of Li Yu). Hangzhou: Zhejiang guji chubanshe, 1992.

Liang Yicheng 梁一成, ed. *Xu Wei de wenxue yu yishu* 徐渭的文學與藝術 (Xu Wei's Literary Works and Art). Taipei: Yiwen yinshuguan, 1977.

Sun Deying 孫得英. *Huitu Jinyu yuan* 繪圖金魚緣 (Romance of Gold Fish with Illustrations). Shanghai: Shanghai shuju, Qing Guangxu Guimao 清光緒癸卯 (1871).

Tang Xianzu 湯顯祖 (1550–1616). *Handan ji* 邯鄲記 (The Dream of Handan). In Tang, *Linchuan simeng* 臨川四夢.

———. *Linchuan simeng* 臨川四夢 (Four Dreams of Linchuan). *Nuanhongshi huike chuanqi* 暖紅室匯刻傳奇, vols. 17–20. Reprint, Yangzhou: Jiangsu Guangling guji keyinshe, 1979.

Tan Zhengbi 譚正璧. *Zhongguo nüxing de wenxue shenghuo* 中國女性的文學生活 (The Literary Life of Chinese Women). Yangzhou: Guangling guji chubanshe, 1998. First published 1931 by Guangming shuju.

———. *Zhongguo nüxing wenxue shi* 中國女性文學史 (History of Chinese Women's Literature). 3rd ed. Tianjin: Baihua wenyi chubanshe, 2001.

Tan Zhengbi 譚正璧, and Tan Xun 譚尋. *Tanci xulu* 彈詞敘錄 (Masterplots of *Tanci*). Shanghai: Shanghai guji chubanshe, 1981.

Wang Duanshu 王端淑, ed. *Mingyuan shiwei chubian* 名媛詩緯初編 (Anthology of Poems by Famous Ladies). Qing Kangxi kanben. Vol. 37 (Yaji). Taipei: Shijie shuju, 1985.

Wang Yongkuan 王永寬. "Ming Qing nüxiquzuojia shengping ziliao buzheng" 明清女戲曲作家生平資料補證. *Xiqu yanjiu* 戲曲研究 34 (September 1990): 203–220.

———. "Qingdai Shaanxi nüqujia Wang Yun" 清代陝西女曲家王筠 (Shaanxi Women Dramatist Wang Yun of the Qing). *Shaanxi shifan daxue xuebao* (*Zhexue shehui kexue ban*) 陝西師範大學學報 (哲學社會科學版) (Journal of Shaanxi Normal University), no. 1 (1981): 109–112.

Wu Mei 吳梅. *Zhongguo xiqu gailun* 中國戲曲概論 (Outline of Chinese Drama). Hong Kong: Taiping shuju, 1964.

Xu Fuming 徐扶明. *Yuan Ming Qing xiqu tansuo* 元明清戲曲探索 (Pioneering

Studies on Yuan Ming Qing Drama). Hangzhou: Zhejiang guji chubanshe, 1986.

Xu Muyun 徐慕雲. *Zhongguo xiju shi* 中國戲劇史 (History of Chinese Drama). Shanghai: Shanghai guji chubanshe, 2001.

Xu Wei 徐渭 (1521–1593). *Ci Mulan tifu congjun* 雌木蘭替父從軍 (Female Mulan Joins the Army in Her Father's Stead). In Xu, *Sisheng yuan*, 44–59.

———. *Nü zhuangyun cihuang defeng* 女狀元辭凰得鳳 (The Female Number One Scholar Declines a She-Phoenix and Gets a He-Phoenix). In Xu, *Sisheng yuan*, 62–106.

———. *Sisheng yuan, Gedai xiao* (*fu*) 四聲猿、歌代嘯（附） (Four Cries of An Ape, appended with *Gedai xiao*). Edited by Zhou Zhongming 周中明. Shanghai: Shanghai guji chubanshe, 1984.

Yan Dunyi 嚴敦易. *Yuan Ming Qing xiqu lunji* 元明清戲曲論集 (Essays on Yuan Ming Qing Drama). Zhengzhou: Zhongzhou shuhuashe, 1982.

Yu Qiuyu 余秋雨. *Zhongguo xiju shi* 中國戲劇史 (History of Chinese Drama). Shanghai: Shanghai jiaoyu chubanshe, 2006.

Yu Weimin 俞為民, ed. *Zhongguo gudai sida mingju* 中國古代四大名劇 (Four Masterpieces in Classical Chinese Drama). Nanjing: Jiangsu guji chubanshe, 1998.

Yuan Mei 袁枚 (1716–1798), comp. *Suiyuan nüdizi shi, Suiyuan quanji* 隨園女弟子詩、隨園全集 (Complete Anthology of the Sui Garden: Poems by Female Students of the Sui Garden). N.p.: Wenming shuju, n.d.

———. *Suiyuan shihua* 隨園詩話 (Talks on Poetry in the Sui Garden). Edited by Gu Xuexie 顧學頡. 2 vols. Beijing: Renmin wenxue chubanshe, 1982.

Zhang Hua 張華. "Qingdai nüzuojia Wang Yun" 清代女作家王筠 (Qing Woman Writer Wang Yun). *Xi'an wanbao* 西安晚報 (Xi'an Evening News), March 6, 1987.

Zheng Zhenduo 鄭振鐸. *Zhongguo suwenxue shi* 中國俗文學史 (History of Chinese Popular Literature). Shanghai: Shanghai shudian, 1984.

Zhongguo gudian xiqu lunzhu jicheng 中國古典戲曲論著集成 (Collection of Chinese Classical Treatises on Drama). Beijing: Zhongguo xiju chubanshe, 1959.

Zhongguo xiqu zhi · Shaanxi juan 中國戲曲志 · 陝西卷 (Chronicle of Chinese Theater · Volume on Shaanxi). Xi'an: Zhongguo xiqu zhi, Shaanxi juan bianweihui, 1985.

Zhou Miaozhong 周妙中. "Ming Qing jutan nüzuojia" 明清劇壇女作家 (Ming Qing Women Writers in Drama). *Gudai xiqu luncong* 古代戲曲論叢, no. 1 (July 1983): 57–61.

———. *Qingdai xiqu shi* 清代戲曲史 (History of Qing Drama). Zhengzhou: Zhongzhou guji chubanshe, 1987.

Non-Chinese Sources

Birch, Cyril, trans. *The Peony Pavilion: Mudan ting*. Bloomington: Indiana University Press, 2002.

Chang, Kang-i Sun, and Haun Saussy, eds. *Women Writers of Traditional China: An Anthology of Poetry and Criticism*. Stanford, CA: Stanford University Press, 1999.

Choy, Elsie. *Leaves of Prayer: The Life and Poetry of He Shuangqing, a Farmwife in Eighteenth-Century China*. Hong Kong: The Chinese University Press, 1993.

Edwards, Lee R. *Psyche as Hero: Female Heroism and Fictional Form*. Middletown, CT: Wesleyan University Press, 1984.

Epstein, Maram. *Competing Discourses: Orthodoxy, Authenticity, and Engendered Meanings in Late Imperial Chinese Fiction*. Cambridge, MA: Harvard University Asia Center, 2001.

Furth, Charlotte. "Androgynous Males and Deficient Females: Biology and Gender Boundaries in Sixteenth- and Seventeenth-Century China." *Late Imperial China* 9, no. 2 (December 1988): 1–29.

Gao, Xingjian. "The Case for Literature." Nobel lecture, Börssalen, Swedish Academy, Stockholm, December 7, 2000.

Gilmartin, Christina K. et al., eds. *Engendering China: Women, Culture, and the State*. Cambridge, MA: Harvard University Press, 1994.

Hawkes, David, trans. *The Story of the Stone: A Chinese Novel*. 5 vols. New York: Penguin, 1973–1986.

Hsia, C. T. *The Classical Chinese Novel: A Critical Introduction*. New York: Columbia University Press, 1968.

Hsiung, Ann-Marie. "A Feminist Re-vision of Xu Wei's *Ci Mulan* and *Nü zhuangyuan*." In Zhang, *China in a Polycentric World*, 73–89.

Hua, Wei. "The Lament of Frustrated Talents: An Analysis of Three Women's Plays in Late Imperial China." *Ming Studies*, no. 32 (April 1994): 28–42.

Huang, Martin W. *Desire and Fictional Narrative in Late Imperial China*. Cambridge, MA: Harvard University Asia Center, 2001.

Hutcheon, Linda. *A Theory of Parody: The Teachings of Twentieth-Century Art Forms*. New York: Methuen, 1985.

Idema, Wilt, and Beata Grant. *The Red Brush: Writing Women of Imperial China*. Cambridge, MA: Harvard University Asia Center, 2004.

Ko, Dorothy. *Teachers of the Inner Chambers: Women and Culture in Seventeenth-Century China*. Stanford, CA: Stanford University Press, 1994.

Lennox, Charlotte. *The Female Quixote or the Adventures of Arabella*. Edited by Margaret Dalziel. Cambridge: Oxford Classics, 1998.

Li, Siu Leung. *Cross-dressing in Chinese Opera*. Hong Kong: Hong Kong University Press, 2003.

Lu, Tina. *Persons, Roles and Minds: Identity in Peony Pavilion and Peach Blossom Fan*. Stanford, CA: Stanford University Press, 2001.

Mann, Susan. "Learned Women in the Eighteenth Century." In Gilmartin, *Engendering China*, 27–46.

———. *Precious Records: Women in China's Long Eighteenth Century*. Stanford, CA: Stanford University Press, 1997.

Mann, Susan, and Yu-Yin Cheng, eds. *Under Confucian Eyes: Writings on Gender in Chinese History*. Berkeley and Los Angeles: University of California Press, 2001.

McMahon, Keith. *Misers, Shrews, and Polygamists: Sexuality and Male-Female Relations in Eighteenth-Century Chinese Fiction*. Durham: Duke University Press, 1995.

Ropp, Paul S. "'Now Cease Painting Eyebrows, Don a Scholar's Cap and Pin': The Frustrated Ambition of Wang Yun, Gentry Woman Poet and Dramatist." *Ming Studies*, no. 40 (Fall 1998): 86–110.

———. *Banished Immortal: Searching for Shuangqing, China's Peasant Woman Poet*. Ann Arbor: University of Michigan Press, 2002.

Sinclair, Jo. *The Changelings*. New York: McGraw-Hill, 1955.

Traub, Valerie. *Desire and Anxiety: Circulations of Sexuality in Shakespearean Drama*. New York: Routledge, 1992.

Watson, Burton, trans. *The Complete Works of Chuang Tzu*. New York: Columbia University Press, 1968.

Widmer, Ellen. "Xiaoqing's Literary Legacy and the Place of the Women Writer in Late Imperial China." *Late Imperial China* 13, no. 1 (1992): 111–155.

Widmer, Ellen, and Kang-i Sun Chang, eds. *Writing Women in Late Imperial China*. Stanford, CA: Stanford University Press, 1997.

Willig, Rosette F., trans. *The Changelings: A Classical Japanese Court Tale*. Stanford, CA: Stanford University Press, 1983.

Wilshire, Bruce. *Role Playing and Identity: The Limits of Theatre as Metaphor*. Bloomington: Indiana University Press, 1982.

Wu, Qingyun. *Female Rule in Chinese and English Literary Utopias*. New York: Syracuse University Press, 1995.

———. "Daring to Dream: Wang Yun and Her Play *A Dream of Glory*." *Renditions*, no. 64 (August 2005): 83–95.

Wu, Qingyun, trans. "WANG YUN: *A Dream of Glory*: excerpts." *Renditions*, no. 64 (August 2005): 96–106.

Zeitlin, Judith T. "Shared Dreams: The Story of the Three Wives' Commentary on *The Peony Pavilion*." *Harvard Journal of Asiatic Studies* 54, no. 1 (June 1994): 127–179.

Zhang, Yingjin, ed. *China in a Polycentric World: Essays in Chinese Comparative Literature*. Stanford, CA: Stanford University Press, 1998.

Zhou, Zuyan. *Androgyny in Late Ming and Early Qing Literature*. Honolulu: University of Hawai'i Press, 2003.

INDEX OF *Ci* TUNES

in the order of their appearance

INDEX OF ARIAS

in the order of their appearance

Part Two · The Original Chinese Text

繁華夢

〔清〕綠窗女史王筠 撰
武慶雲 校點

編校説明

此劇依乾隆戊戌槐慶堂藏版校點。原文中稀見的古體字、俗字、異體字、及簡體字統一改為正體字或常見字，但保留了個別同音字借用。除加全文標點外，詩、詞、及道白中的詩句皆按詩體排列。原本有王筠之父王元常眉批數十條，現皆以腳注列出。

張鳳孫序

無涯者海，漫勞精衛之填；有缺維天，亦籍媧皇之補。蓋自陰陽爐炭之既具，哪無通塞屯亨之不齊？尺有短而寸有長，生才本無或歉，兩其足者傅其翼，賦形詎謂非均？偶因所見之偏畸，遂覺彼蒼之顛倒，茫茫此恨，劫劫難消。乃有門陰三槐，生來惠質，地涵八水，長得珠輝。謝庭之柳絮因風，名高詠雪；劉室之椒盤以瑞，才擅頌花；聆琴而雅辨七弦，續史而能成八志。有才如此，偏生閨闥之中。於意云何？合在蓬瀛之上。乍因想以成夢，隨說法以現身。早掇科名，疊逢佳麗。春蘭秋菊，擷秀湖山，歌扇舞衣，怡情風月。迨晨鐘之忽警，覺塵夢之初醒。認變幻於麻姑爪間，喚迷昧於盧生枕上。譜繁華之一夢，證因果於三生。藻采紛披，齊赴生花之管；絲桐迭奏，都成繞樑之音。按紅牙則換羽移宮，自然合度；寫烏絲而媲青妃白，總出無心。此真風雅之餘瀾，足號古今之韻事者矣。嗟乎！蓬萊海水，深淺何常。磨蠍星宮，遭逢若定。非得寄情而解脫，難辭俗累之纏綿。舉足一隅，發予三省。人間富貴，漫思十二金釵；天上神仙，不隔三千弱水。慕古丈夫之風烈，老去無成；藉女博士之文章，閑來自遣。

乾隆戊戌春日，石湖張鳳孫拜題於青門節署，時年七十有三

畢太夫人題詞

秦臺仙子愛吹簫，鳳去臺空不可招。
賸與芳閨傳慧業，清聲譜出葉雲韶。

燕子桃花絕妙詞，南朝法曲少人知。
天公翻樣輕才藻，不付男兒付女兒。

不為海上騎鯨客，暫作花間化蝶人。
是幻是真都是夢，三生誰證本來身？

夙世應知是彩鸞，日抄官韻忘朝餐。
囀喉怪底諧宮徵，玉茗天池學步難。

掃眉才罷襲冠簪，海水蓬萊淺復深。
真倩麻姑抓背癢，聲聲擊節快人心。

東吳歸河間張藻

宮允曹習庵先生題詞

綠窗長日費吟哦，剩有詞壇志未磨。
敲折珊瑚翻一曲，英雄兒女兩情多。

烏衣門第擅風流，自作新詞自遣愁。
一種掃眉才子筆，也應占得鳳麟洲。

翠袖天寒傍玉臺，每憐巾幗困清才。
憑將幾幅雲藍紙，領取書生慧福來。

午夢沉沉翠黛低，睡鄉名字蕊宮題。
大羅天上春方好，懊惱流鶯一霎啼。

有情眷屬總前緣，夙世須生自在天。
金馬班聯金屋侶，耐他一枕小遊仙。

如電如塵枉繫思，空花境界覺來知。
不須辛苦分真幻，付與春風化蝶時。

結習多生詎易忘，漫將九命嘆文章。
青衫慣濕才人淚，不道春閨怨更長。

早玷蓬山侍從臣，鏡臺曾賦夢遊春。
新編小讀添惆悵，可但蛾眉是恨人！

嘉定曹仁虎

卷上

第一齣・開場[*]

(末上)

〔沁園春〕

四海昇平，八紘寧泰，共樂韶光。
醉裏暫開醒眼，幽齋清課，
且抛舊卷，再整新章。
京兆王生，武林謝氏，
鳳麟同夢結鸞凰。
更堪嘉，臨安胡女，吳郡黃娘。

無雙，天緣巧合，
共侍風流御史郎。
佔人間全福，二十年榮貴；
一朝驚覺，百感茫茫。[1]
幸遇麻姑，晨鐘猛擊，
驚醒繁華夢一場。
省得了，一聲長笑，痴恨付東洋。

豪俠女痴心迷幻境，
畫中人情感諧麟鳳。
胡黃氏雙酧花月緣，
麻姑仙單點繁華夢。

來者王夢麟。(末下)

---

[*] 第一齣原題為〈傳概〉，本版據原文之目錄統一改作〈開場〉。

[1] 如聞棒唱。

第二齣・獨嘆

(生女妝，月白披風，束絲，素裙上)

〔繞地遊〕神清骨健，少負雲程願。問蒼天如何發遣？[1] **彩吐霜毫，風生寶劍，**(嘆介) **悵今生雲霄路慳。**(坐介)

〔鷓鴣天〕

閨閣沉埋十數年，
不能身貴不能仙。[2]
讀書每羨班超志，
把酒長吟李白篇。

懷壯氣，欲沖天，
木蘭崇嘏事無緣。
玉堂金馬生無分，
好把心情付夢詮。

自家王氏，長安人也。吾門數代科甲，為關西望族。先祖存日，曾任江西巡道，不幸早故，只存祖母在堂。家君亦登黃榜，職列郎官。家母楊氏，乃江左名家之女，淑德賢明，治家整肅。爹爹作宦半生，惟餘清風兩袖。連枝同氣，只有俺與家兄。俺雖未從師，略知文義。但生非男子，不能耀祖光宗。[3] 身着裙釵，無路揚名顯姓。當此春融天氣，柳媚花妍，鶯啼燕語，總是惱人情緒也。(嘆介) (唱)

〔朝元歌〕花妍柳妍，笑向春爭艷。鶯喧燕喧，聲囀雕欄畔。(白) 對此佳辰，若無題詠，豈不令春光笑我。

---

[1] 一句內已含全旨。

[2] "貴"字伏夢中事，"仙"字伏麻姑事。

[3] 女人不可無此志願。

(作提筆欲寫復放介) 咳，**一付雲箋，一枝彤管，怎生寫得春全？**(拂琴彈介) **欲理冰絃，慵把閑愁指下彈。**(看書念介)

湖光瀲灩晴偏好，山色空濛雨亦奇。
若把西湖比西子，淡妝濃抹也相宜。

此乃蘇公詠湖山之句也。咳，(唱) **我此世見應難還期夢裏緣。**[4] (恨拋書介) 咦，**反助起愁懷無限，惆悵殺事乖心願。**

看書越覺無聊，不免將吳中帶來的美人圖，展開一看，少遣悶懷。(掛畫看，笑介)[5] 咦，妙嘎！你看淡淡丰神，盈盈態度，宛如素女臨凡，不讓飛瓊降世。我若是個男子，定尋這等一位佳人為配。[6] 不免拜告一番，或者真真能降，也未可知？(焚香拜畫介) (唱)

〔前腔〕我心虔意虔，拜請雲英現。(看介) **她神翩態翩，秋水如留盼。**(叫介) 美人美人，**一度高呼，一聲低喚，緣何杳不相憐。要共清談，只好做夢境迷離見麗娟。**(白) 記得那年在邯鄲，遇見的吳下黃姬，臨安胡氏二女，真姝色也。一面之緣，匆匆別去，再會無由矣。**飄渺隔雲山，相思只夢傳。**咳，雖然爹爹現任為官，享受榮華，我身終是女子，焉能出人頭地？(淚介) **念身世倍增悲嘆，**(欠伸介) **驀地裏神迷身倦。**

噯呀，身子一時困倦起來，且自少睡片時，多少是好。(伏几臥介)

---

[4] 伏後夢遊西湖。

[5] 此處掛畫與末折照應，非泛也。

[6] 亦作伏筆。

第三齣・入夢

(小生扮善才跳舞上)

善才善才，侍奉蓮台。

今承法旨，降下凡來。

吾乃善才童子是也。奉菩薩法旨，與下界長安王氏夢中變形。來此已是，待俺與她變者。

(內細樂，小生出鏡引生起，取衣巾與生穿戴介。舉拂塵拂生面身介，復送至原處睡介)(小生白)王生聽者：俺奉菩薩法旨，將你轉女成男。從此後，洞房金榜萬事隨心。[1] 吾神去也。(內奏樂，小生下)(生急起，叫介)神聖請轉，待弟子拜謝。咳呀，怎麼轉眼就不見了？(自看身作驚介)啊呀，當真變了，好奇怪也！

〔香柳娘〕這原由怪哉，這原由怪哉！令人驚駭，原何忽把形容改？(取鏡照，大笑介)**竟居然秀才，竟居然秀才。我本一裙釵，今做衣冠態。**(白)待我搖擺一番。(整衣行介)**整衣巾步階，洒落情懷，任吾搖擺。**

不免速到前堂，說與爹娘知道。(笑介)我好喜也！(行介)(唱)

〔前腔〕我見仙童降齋，見仙童降齋，停雲欄外，何期轉眼歸天界。(笑介)笑盈盈滿腮，笑盈盈滿腮，從此得舒懷，了卻裙釵債。[2] (白)此去說與祖母爹娘呵，定然驚喜也。(急行，笑唱)**去堂前訴來，去堂前訴來，管取顏開，共相稱快。**(下)

---

[1] 細思此數句，真大樂事。而轉女成男，更難。

[2] 了而不了，所以可恨可哭。

第四齣．春綉

(旦扮謝小姐，穿水綠披風素裙；貼旦、丑扮婢隨上) (旦)

〔一剪梅〕日影移花上碧窗，人起蘭房，鶯囀東牆。(貼旦、丑合) **佳人初試薄羅裳，柳鎖池塘，花放階旁。**

〔桃源憶故人前〕

(旦)　碧紗影弄東風曉，一夜海棠開了。

(貼旦)　枝上數聲啼鳥，(丑) 妝點知多少？

(旦) 奴家謝氏，夢鳳，小字瓊真，武林人氏。爹爹在京，官居翰林學士。母親賈氏，誥命夫人。奴家與少弟雲郎相依膝下。當此春光明媚，侍兒們收拾綉床金剪，和你臨軒針指則個。

(貼、丑應) 曉得。(作捲簾放桌介) 安排齊備，請小姐刺綉。

(旦正坐，貼旦、丑侍坐，同綉介)

〔懶畫眉〕風輕雲靜蕩春光，曉起臨軒理綉床。(丑白) 甚麼花兒，這等香嗄？(旦唱) **和風微送海棠香。**(內鶯啼介，旦靜聽介) (唱) **聽黃鸝嬌囀花枝上，**(笑介) **笑他人春日無端惹恨長。**

〔前腔〕(貼旦唱) **柳絲搖曳燕飛忙，花壓闌干春晝長。**(丑背唱) **我停針無緒綉鴛鴦，**(偷看旦介) **怎似她天生一種端方相，任憑這春去春來不斷腸。**

(旦) 刺綉已完，不免到階前閑步一番。(行介) (小生黑三髯同小旦便服上)

〔前腔〕鸞坡休暇暫尋芳，小步名園百卉香。(旦見介) (小生、小旦) 我兒在此何事？(旦) 孩兒刺綉餘閑階前一步。(小生) 好女孩兒家針指女工，乃分內之事。**學一個迴文織錦晉蘇娘，**(小旦) **便天孫巧樣無多讓，**(合) **骨肉相依樂未央。**

（小生、小旦）臨春瑞香，好生伏侍小姐，我們去罷。（丑、貼）曉得。

〔尾聲〕韶光過眼休惆悵，清課閨中佳趣長，（合）**怎負他架上琴書爐內香？**（下）

第五齣・辭親

（生戴巾穿青素圓領，束縧穿靴上）

〔步蟾宮〕文名幸占秋闈首，仗彩筆肯居人後？

（坐介）

數年屈所志，嗟負五車書。
此日登雲路，誰言非丈夫？

小生王夢麟，表字瑞卿。自從變形之後，一意攻書，去歲幸占秋魁。只因久慕西湖之景，今欲往彼一遊，不免請出爹媽，稟問則個。

（請介）爹娘有請。

（外蒼三髯，紗帽，藍圓領；老旦鳳冠，藍圓領；末巾服，黑三髯；小生從隨上）[1]

〔生查子〕（外）**佳氣滿皇州**（合）**共慶昇平候。**

（生）爹爹母親拜揖。（外、老）罷了。（生、末見介）哥哥。（末）兄弟。（各坐介）（外）我兒請我們有何話說？（生）告稟爹媽，孩兒因慕吳越風景，欲往一觀，未知爹娘許孩兒去否？（老旦）嗄，我兒，山水迢遙，你小小年紀，怎生去得？（外）夫人，孩兒雖則年幼，也當教他經歷些世事，去去何妨？（末）西湖風景，果是非凡，兄弟正該看看。（外）既如此，我兒幾時前去？（生）爹爹母親既許孩兒去，今日就是個出行的吉日，就在今日去罷。（末）兄弟，你的行囊可曾打點？（生）兄弟已着瑤琴收拾去了。[2]（外）我兒可去拜別祖母。（生應，下）（老旦）嗄，相公，小孩子家，便許他孤身遠出，放蕩身心，恐誤上進，還是不去的好。（末）孩兒看兄弟志在功名，豈肯放蕩？想他埋頭閨閣，萬種不平之氣；今得揚眉，望母親莫要阻他高興。（外）我兒言之有理，夫人不必過慮。（生上，丑挑行李上）稟上二爺，行李俱已齊備了。（生）既如此，孩兒就此拜別。（外、老旦）罷了。（丑）待小人帶馬來。

---

[1] 派阿兄於巾服，以其不似紗帽中人耳。

[2] 出瑤琴。

(丑下)(生拜介，唱)

〔鎖南枝〕辭親去，浙水遊，山河遠涉風塵走。(外、老旦唱)**我兒，須早轉皇州，在吳中莫浪遊。**

(末背外、老，對生唱)賢弟，**你要訪佳人彼處有，須記古人言，南國色多秀。**

(生點頭介)(丑牽馬上)請二爺起程。(生)爹爹母親，孩兒就此去了。(外、老)我兒須要小心。(生)孩兒曉得。哥哥，兄弟去也。(末)兄弟前途保重。(生)不勞哥哥掛念。(丑與外、老、末叩頭介)小人去了。(外、老旦)路上小心伏侍二相公。(丑)曉得。

(生上馬，同丑左下；外等右下)

第六齣・庵會

(貼旦扮尼姑上)

竹檻繞回廊，城中似外方。

月雲開作片，枝鳥立成行。

小尼乃京都紫竹庵主是也。昨日有謝老爺府中管家，送得綉旛到此，說小姐今日親來降香，不免吩咐徒弟們伺候者。(向內介) 嗄，徒弟們，打點伺候，謝府小姐少刻就到了。(內應) 曉得。

(小生、末同上) 庵主有麼？(貼旦) 哦，在這裏。(生、外) 小姐轎到了。(貼旦) 這等待我迎接。(生外) 請小姐下轎。

(旦穿天青二色錦氅素裙，淨扮老嫗，小旦扮梅香隨上) (旦)

〔引〕風飄仙袂麝蘭芬，才離綉戶，又到山門。(見介)

(貼) 小姐稽首。(旦) 庵主萬福。(貼) 小尼接待來遲，多多有罪。(旦) 好說。(貼) 請小姐拈香。(內敲鐘磬，旦拈香拜介) (貼) 拈香已畢，請小姐駕到荷軒用茶。(旦) 庵主請。(同下) (生、外扮二僕上) 呔，庵主哪裏？(貼急上) 哦，來了。二位是哪府來的？(生、外) 我們是王太爺府中來的。跟隨太太到此降香，轎子已到門首。(貼) 這等請太太下轎。

(老旦鳳冠，月藍圓領，金帶白裙；丑、副淨扮侍女隨上)

〔引〕(老旦) **青松翠竹映沉沉，始識禪林幽韵。**

(貼) 不知夫人降臨，小尼有失遠迎，望乞恕罪。(老旦) 好說。(貼) 請夫人拈香。

(老旦拈香拜介，唱)

〔黃鶯兒〕稽首禮慈雲，爇沉檀紫氣芬，天風繚繞潮音近。(起，看旛介) 這旛是誰家掛的？綉得這等齊整。**看龍文鳳文，羨蘭心蕙心。精工可並雲中錦。費千金，難尋妙手，端不讓天孫。**

庵主，這對旛兒是哪裏來的？

(貼) 這是謝大人府中小姐前來還願掛的。(老旦) 哦，小姐是幾時到此呢？(貼) 就是今日到來，還未去哩。(叫介) 徒弟，看茶來。(雜扮小尼捧茶上) 來了。(貼起送茶介) 太夫人請茶。(老旦) 請。(淨暗上看，扯雜介) 小師父，我問你這位夫人是誰？(雜) 我聽得他們說，是王太爺的夫人，就是去年新解元的母親。(淨) 哦，是王夫人麼？王老爺與我家老爺乃是同年好友，我何不上前一見？(進見介) 喲，這是王太夫人嗄，婆子這裏叩見。(老旦急扶起介) 啊呀，老媽媽不必行禮。(貼) 這就是謝府小姐的乳母張媽媽。(老旦) 哦，原來就是謝小姐奶母，老媽媽且坐了講話。(淨) 啊喲，太夫人在上，婆子怎敢？(老旦) 媽媽說哪裏話來？坐了不妨。(淨) 如此，婆子低處坐坐罷。(坐介) (老旦) 這對綵旛，就是小姐自綉的麼？(淨) 正是。(老旦) 似這般慧心妙手，真是人間少有，世上無雙。(淨) 不是婆子誇口，我家這位小姐，不要講描鸞綉鳳，只她那一付錦心，一枝彩筆，若開女科，錦江拾翠的黃姑，難說個不讓。(老旦) 請問小姐青春幾何？可曾接聘？(淨) 太夫人容稟。(唱)

〔前腔〕美玉隱瓊林，正芳年二九春，鳳樓未卜吹簫信，她文同少君，才欺道韞，便明妃西子也容甘遜。(白) 我家老爺夫人呵，(唱) **為超群難尋佳配，故着急選才人。**

(老旦) 敢問小姐芳名？(淨) 叫作夢鳳。(老旦笑介) 我家二孩兒叫做夢麟。(貼笑介) 鳳麟合是一對。(淨白) 敢問太夫人，二公子青春多少？聘定誰家？(老旦) 與你家小姐同庚，也為佳人難得，尚未結親。(小旦上) 張媽媽哪裏去了？(淨應介) 在這裏。(小旦) 小姐吩咐看轎回府。(淨) 轎子伺候多時了，你請小姐出來。(小旦請介) 請小姐。(旦上，貼迎介) 小尼因接待王太夫人，有失陪奉，萬望小姐恕罪。(旦) 好說。奴家就此告辭了。(貼) 還備有粗齋，敢請少留貴步？(旦) 不消了。(淨) 小姐，王夫人在殿上，可上前見見？(旦點頭介) (老旦白) 丫鬟，吩咐看轎。(丑應，向內介) 太太吩咐打轎，伺候。(內應介) (淨) 小姐來見了年伯母。(旦見介) 老伯母萬福。(老旦見，驚喜介) 呀，小姐萬福。(旦) 不知伯母在此，有失拜望，多多有罪。(老旦) 不敢。[1]

[1] 匆匆一見，不煩再言，最合情事。蓋一切委曲，方才乳母已細言矣。

（生、外上）請太太上轎。（末、小生上）請小姐上轎。（二旦對貼介）庵主，我們在此打攪了，就此告別。（貼）小尼有慢貴人，負罪多多，還乞夫人小姐寬恕。（二旦）好説。（旦）伯母請。（老旦）小姐請。（各上轎介）

〔尾聲〕（合）**拜辭蓮座紅塵近，**（旦顧老旦，背唱）**可怪初逢意便深。**（老旦顧旦，背唱）**怎能勾麟鳳成雙方慰我心。**（分下）

第七齣 · 求麗

(生穿如前解元服色上，唱)

〔新水令〕扁舟游戲任逍遙，似乘槎誤迷瑤島。湖光冰鏡，遠山色翠。雲高雨艷晴嬌巧，丹青難傳照。[1]

(坐介) 小生自到武林，日日閑遊湖上。前日進城，拜望楊家表兄，不期姨娘之子高兄，也在此地。聚談一日，至晚方回。昨日又是端陽佳節，看了一日龍舟。(笑介) 好笑！我朝朝出去，名雖玩景遊山，意在訪求佳麗。雖然士女成行，竟沒有個天然國色，為此心中煩悶。今日懶去行走，不免看書一番，消遣情懷。(上坐看書介) (唱)

〔駐馬聽〕厭聽笙簫，收拾閑心付彩毫。湖山雖妙，悵無秀色與爭嬌。[2] (嘆介) 咳，還不知我功名之事，端的如何？**藍衫雖已改青袍，不知儒巾可換得烏紗帽？一派牢騷，這心事誰能曉？**

(副末冠帶，小生巾服騎馬，雜扮三從隨上)

〔引〕揚鞭過畫橋，咫尺禪林到。

(二雜) 稟爺，已到靈隱寺了。(副末) 上前通報。(雜) 呔，和尚有麼？(淨扮和尚上) 來哉來哉，哪裏來的呀？(雜) 王解元可在寺中？(淨) 在。(雜) 快去通報，城中楊爺高爺來拜。(淨) 曉得哉。(進介) 周阿哥。(丑上) 做甚麼？(淨) 城中楊爺高爺來拜。(丑) 曉得了，你自去罷。(淨下) (丑稟生介) 稟二爺，楊爺高爺來拜。(生) 道有請。(丑轉請介，副末、小生下馬。二雜下) (末白) 你二爺在哪裏？(丑) 在紫雲軒內。

(眾轉行) (生起，整衣見介) 呀，二兄光降，小弟失迎了。(末、小) 豈敢。(各揖坐介，丑送茶介) (小生) 表弟，今日為何不去遊玩？(生) 掃興之極，故此懶去。(副末、小生) 卻是為何？(生笑介) 二兄不知，小弟此來呵，

---

[1] 一幅西湖圖。

[2] 佳句。

〔雁兒落〕一則為玩湖山訪故交，二則為覽秀色尋花貌。又誰知譏桃源路徑遙，因此上懶劉郎把心灰了。

(小生) 哦，原來為此。(末笑介) 賢弟要見佳人，咫尺就有。(生) 在哪裏？(副末) 她的住處，一時忘記了。老弟不要性急，待我想來。

(暗拉小生，背介) 高賢弟，我們何不耍他一耍？(小生) 怎樣一個耍法？(末附耳介) 如此如此，你道好否？(小生笑介) 但憑尊意。(同轉介，生讓介) 請坐。(末、小) 有坐。(生) 表兄想着了麼？(副末) 想便想着了，只是不是個良家。(生) 敢是個風塵中人物？(末) 正是。(生笑介) 只要素徽姝麗，何妨叔夜風流。你且說她有何好處？(副末) 你要問她的好處麼？哪！

〔江兒水〕她丰韵欺蘇小，才華壓薛濤。(生驚喜介) 不信有如此之美。(副末) 還有妙處哩，**俏裙邊猶勝潘家妙。**(生笑，移椅問介) 她叫甚麼名字呢？(副末) **"琵琶錢"美號人爭道，遍江南爭羨如花貌。**(生大笑介) 聽說不禁狂笑。(小生笑，副末急搖手，背生低唱) **他便是多智的周郎，也落吾圈套。**

(生沉吟介) 這美人你可曾見過？不要哄我。(副末正色介) 說哪裏話來，我怎哄賢弟？實是我親眼見過的，果然才色雙全。(小生笑白) 我也曾見過，當真標致。(生喜問介) 如此，請問這位美人住在哪裏？(末) 就在城中西門內。(生) 原來如此，多承指引，小弟明早就去相訪便了。

(副末、小生) 天色過午，我們告辭了。(生) 小弟備有水酒，乞二兄暫留貴步，花前一醉何如？(副末、小生) 表弟客中，怎好取擾？(生) 二兄說哪裏話來，這就是見外小弟了。(副末) 如此說，恭敬不如從命，待我改日回席罷。(生) 又來客氣了。(各笑介) (生) 請。(副末、小生) 請。(各相揖下)

第八齣・誤訪

(丑扮厚脂粉，穿紅衫綠裙青背搭紅女鞋，拿汗巾扇子，作醜態上)

〔普賢歌〕我為名妓壓蘇杭，粉做容顏花做妝。青絲三寸長，蛾眉禿禿光，便石人見了能心蕩。

(坐介) 奴家非別，杭州名妓琵琶錢的便是。[1] 生來容如閉月，漫誇八戒重生；貌似羞花，不讓牛魔再世。妝成對鏡，自號佳人；賣笑倚門，人言鬼怪。(笑介) 想我空有這般顏色，卻再也接不着個年少兒郎，這也苦惱得緊。今日起得早了些，身子有些倦了，不免少睡片時，有何不可。(睡介) (生戴新巾，穿水綠畫花道袍大紅襯衣，挈扇緩步上)

〔懶畫眉〕緩步逍遙整冠裳，(撫心笑介) **初試風流意自惶。昨宵夢斷杜韋娘，咱書生本是無情況，卻被她攪亂蘇州刺史腸。**

小生昨日蒙二位表兄指引，今日早早進城相訪。迤邐行來，此間已是。呀，為何門兒緊閉，車馬全無？不免叩門一問。(叩介) 裏面有人麼？(丑驚醒，緩唱介)

〔前腔〕好夢驚回意癲狂，(作欠伸介) 嗳喲，**坐起神嬌汗似湯。頻頻叩戶是誰行？**(白) 是哪個？(生) 開門。(丑聽，喜介) **耳邊忽聽聲清朗，定是個風流年少郎。**

咦，妙呀！這個叩戶的人兒，必非俗物，[2] 待我開門看者。(舉扇遮面，問介) 小官人，是哪裏來的？(生忽轉見丑，驚介) 呵呀，好一個胖大婦人。一定是美人的使者，待我問來。(揖丑介) 小生是為慕錢娘，特來相訪。(丑背笑介) 咦，我老錢，運氣到了。竟公然有這等少年文士前來下顧。有趣有趣。(對生介) 既蒙光降，請到裏面坐。(生) 請。(同行介) (丑背唱)

---

[1] 琵琶錢，余婢月娥之母也，既老且醜。吾女嘗揶揄之，故譜入戲文，以為笑柄。

[2] 亦自識貨。

〔不是路〕扇底偷張，愛殺他，**骨秀神清傅粉龐。**(笑介) **我魂飄蕩，**這的是**紅裙偏愛綠衣郎。**(生四顧介) **細端詳，看庭中擺設全無樣，自悔尋春到畫堂。**(沉吟介) **沉吟量。**(丑) 相公，和你妝樓上去坐。(引生上介) 嗄，**這神情叫我難猜講，實出人想，實出人想。**

(丑) 相公請坐。(生背介) 且住，看這婦人打扮的極是華麗，為甚麼把扇兒只管遮了面龐，取何原故？(丑叫介) 女兒們，看茶來。(生) 請問足下，是美人的甚麼人？(丑笑介) 活笑殺，則我便是美人。還尋哪個？(生驚急起，問介) 既是美人，請把扇兒收了，待小生一睹芳容。(丑收扇，作嬌態介) 相公請看。(生看，大驚介) 呀，原來是個奇形老嫗。你當真是那個？(丑) 琵琶錢那。(生急介) 果然？(丑) 不錯。(生呆嘆介) 罷了，我被楊兄所誤矣。(背唱)

〔前腔〕猛見花娘，諕得我**魄散魂消汗透裳。真奇狀，便山魈野鬼也勝伊行。**(頓足恨介) 咦，**我恨高楊，害人白日尋魍魎。**咳，**也是我一念貪花沒主張。**[3] (雜捧茶介，丑奉生介) 郎君不要出神，請茶。(生作苦態，接介) (丑笑唱) **我心歡暢，今朝見你多情況。**(作笑近生介) **移身前傍，移身前傍。**

(生笑背介) 這是哪裏說起？看了她的嘴臉，不由人不怕；見了她的醜態，又要發笑，這便怎麼處？(丑笑拍生肩介) 相公為何只管沉吟，不與奴家攀話。請問相公仙鄉貴處？尊姓大名？(生) 小生姓王，西京人也。(丑) 貴庚？(生) 十八歲了。媽媽高壽？(丑急搖手) 啊喲，這是甚麼稱呼？使不得。你們做客的，見了我們妓家，或稱姐姐，或叫美人。若問年紀，或青春，或妙齡，才是個道理。(生笑拱手介) 承教了。請問美人青春幾何？(丑喜介) 奴家叨長郎君四十五歲，今年六十三歲哉。(生笑介) 也還不老。

(丑叫介) 女兒們，看酒來。(生) 天氣炎熱，不勞治酒罷。(丑) 說哪裏話來，豈有不飲之理？快些斟來。(雜應，送酒介) (丑) 相公請酒。(生) 小生素不善飲，姐姐自請。(丑笑介) 又來了，少用一杯。(強生飲介，丑連飲數杯，叫乾，作醉介) 啊喲，吃醉哉！女兒打掃涼床，待我與相公安寢。(生慌介) 啊呀呀，這般高情免了罷，小生就此告別

[3] 然也。

了。(欲行，丑急扯介) 嗳喲，王郎差矣。我和你有緣千里來相會，怎麼倒要做無緣對面不相逢？(扯介，生急介) 啊呀，媽媽這般雅愛，豈敢推辭。但小生此時，賤體有些不快，暫且告別，容明日再來奉伴如何？(丑大笑介) 小王，你這話兒，只好去哄那三歲孩子罷了，怎麼騙起奴家來？我也不管明日後日，只是今日決不放你去了。

(生急揖介) 媽媽姐姐，小生明日一定重來，萬無謊語。(丑) 任你說的天花墜，只當長空亂雪飛。(生急揖介) 媽媽，可憐饒了小生去罷。[4] (丑) 說得這等容易，女兒們一同動手，抬也抬他進去。(二雜應，生慌介) 媽媽姐姐，快請放手，那邊有人來了。(丑回看介) 人在哪裏？(生推倒丑急下) (雜) 啊呀呀，跌壞了媽媽哉。(同扶丑起介) (丑) 啊喲，有這等事，氣死我也。(大叫，起介) 待我趕上去。(欲跑，二雜扯介) 媽媽，那人去遠，趕不上了。(丑) 氣殺我哉。正是：走脱薄倖王公子，惱殺多情琵琶錢。(下)

[4] 如此之苦，乃自取也。

第九齣・投緣

(丑扮瑤琴，笑上)

自家非別，王解元手下一個大總管周瑤琴的便是。自從跟隨來到南方，見了多少美景，看了無數好戲，[1] (笑介) 真非凡之大樂也。好笑我家公子，今日也訪佳人，明日也尋美色。沒來由被楊老爺高相公捉弄了去，訪甚麼琵琶美人。那日起了個清早，打扮得風風流流，欣然去訪。去了半日，氣沖沖跑將回來。進了門不問好歹，說我失誤迎接，着實打罵了一頓。次日獨自進城，和楊爺高爺算賬，鬧了一日回來。

(笑介) 然而此事，區區到底不明。那一日閑暇無事，瞞了主人，悄悄跑到她家一看，(作咬指縮頭介) 啊喲喲，便是無鹽再世，嫫姆重生，也未必有她這般醜陋。你說這等一付嘴臉，怎不教相公着惱？我相公自那日回來，就說身子不快，至今未出寺門。今日用過早饍，忽然不見，問遍了僧房，並無踪影。不免騎了馬，到湖上找尋則個。(作上馬，吆喝跑下)

(小旦青衫白裙，扮胡氏上)

〔海棠春〕蕭條庭院愁多少，驚時序花枝空老。[2] **睡起不勝嬌，慵把雙蛾掃。**

(坐介)

蓬門未識綺羅香，
裊娜腰肢淡薄妝。
最恨年年厭針線，
為他人作嫁衣裳。

奴家胡氏夢蓮，臨安人也。不幸椿庭身故，只與慈母相依。(嘆介) 似這等寂寞荒居，寒微家計，幾時是個出頭的日子也？今日曉起無聊，不免到門前一步。(行介) (唱)

---

[1] 戲中說戲。

[2] 佳句。

〔一江風〕嘆連朝，越覺腰肢小，顧影驚還笑。(淚介)**意而喬，秋月春花，幽怨誰能曉？韶光眼底拋，朱顏暗裏消。**(嘆介)**怕等閑間送去了人年少。**(虛下)

(生巾月藍道袍束絳，緩步上)(唱)

〔前腔〕棄蘭船，步向西山道，幽徑人踪杳。望迢迢衰柳寒雲，總是些悲秋稿。穿林渡小橋，(內吹簫，生聽介)**是誰家弄玉簫？逐西風吹出了淒涼調。**

小生只因曉起無聊，獨到西山閑步。你看林深人靜，鳥語花香，好一派景致也。(小旦上，見生作羞避介)(生背介)啊呀，世上竟有這等美人，豈非天姿國色乎！(作各覷介)(老旦扮胡母上)閑居寂寞無鄰里，鎮日惟聞啼鳥聲。嗄，我兒哪裏？(小旦)來了。(老旦見驚笑介，小旦作微笑回顧下)(老旦)噯呀，原來是位小相公，請到裏面坐。(生)素無相識，怎好造府？(老旦)這有何妨？郎君請。(生)如此，媽媽請。(老旦)郎君請。(進介，生)媽媽，拜揖。(老旦)郎君萬福，請坐。(各坐介)(老旦)請問郎君仙鄉貴處？尊姓大名？(生)媽媽容稟。

〔前腔〕舊槐堂，王姓多名望。(老旦)令尊大人，還是林居？還是現任？(生)**現列朝堂上。**(老旦)呀，原來是位公子，老身失敬了。敢問青春幾何？(生)**念吾行，二九虛生，多愧魁秋榜。**(老旦笑介)是解元公哩。曾取夫人否？(生)**朱門少孟光，乘鸞信渺茫。**(老旦)哦，為何遠來吳地？(生笑介)**為慕湖山，特地來相訪。**

(老旦)哦，是為西湖到此的，好雅興也。(生笑介)(老旦起，背介)且住，我看此生言談儒雅，舉止端祥，異日何愁富貴？想我夢蓮孩兒，年已二八，尚未許婚，他時縱有所遇，哪裏尋這等風流才子？何不面許姻緣，也不負她才貌。有理有理。[3](轉介)(生)媽媽請坐。(老旦)公子請。(生)請問媽媽上姓？(老旦)老身吳氏。先夫姓胡，不幸早年去世，只留母女二人。方才在門首的，就是小女夢蓮。[4](生)原來那位佳人，就是媽媽令愛。(老旦笑介)豈敢。老身有一言奉告，公子容否？(生)媽媽有話請講。(老旦)念小女雖長寒門，卻也粗知文墨，若

---

[3] 其母大有主見。世之覓婿者，能如此乎？

[4] 胡氏乃永清吏人之女，年稚貌佳，未二十而夭逝。

不棄貌醜身微，願奉箕箒。(生) 多承媽媽厚愛，但只是⋯⋯(作沉吟介) (老旦笑介) 公子不必沉吟，老身曉得尊意了。小女身生寒賤，豈敢望正位中宮，得備小星足矣。[5] (生喜，急揖介) 媽媽如此善察人情，只是有屈令愛了。(老旦) 好說。(生) 小生身處客中，不曾帶來聘物，如何是好？(老旦) 古人云，一絲為定。何須厚聘？(生) 既如此，(作解玉介) 小生帶有碧玉絲環一對，送與令愛，權為紅定。(老旦接介) 多謝了。

(轉出，向內叫介) 我兒哪裏？(小旦上) 孩兒在此。(老旦) 嗄，我兒，我們講的話，你可曾聽見？(小旦低介) 孩兒聽見了。(老旦) 這等你意下如何？(小旦笑介) 孩兒有何主意？只是也不該輕易許人為妾。(老旦笑介) 我兒差了，我作娘的，豈肯誤你終身。這王公子呵，

〔前腔〕貌軒昂，出眾風流樣，富貴真難量。他父親啊，**任朝堂，世宦名家，不負你終身望。**(出玉環介) 我兒，這就是他的聘禮，你可收了。(小旦接，背唱) **聞言喜又惶，**(看玉介) **看藍田玉有光，這姻緣端的是從天降。**(下)

(老旦端茶，轉奉介) 公子請茶。(生) 媽媽請。

(丑鞭馬上)

〔水底魚〕覽跡尋踪，加鞭走似風。湖山找遍，不見主人公。

好奇怪，找了半日，不見相公踪影。來到西山，也不見形跡，待我且高叫一番。相公，相公！(生聽介，丑又叫介) 相公在哪裏？(生應介) 瑤琴，我在這裏。(老旦) 呀，公子答應哪個？(生) 是小价前來尋我。(老旦) 哦。(出，招丑介) 這裏來。(丑進，見介) 咦，小人哪處不尋，相公原來在此。(生) 我一時信步至此。蒙這位媽媽相留待茶，故此歸遲。(丑揖介) 老親娘，作揖了。(老旦) 小哥見禮。(丑) 日已過午，相公去罷？(生) 正是，小生就此告別。(老旦) 多多有慢了。公子他日貴顯，幸勿相忘。(生) 媽媽但請放心，小生豈是無義之輩。來年赴罷春闈，一定差人來接。

(生揖別介) 萍水相逢感意深，一言為定重千金。(老旦) 來春紅杏花開日，靜倚柴扉望好音。(生上馬，拱手介) 媽媽請回罷。(各分下)

---

[5] 洞見心事，其母亦聰明。

第十齣・秋砧

(貼旦青衫素裙，扮黃氏上)

〔憶秦娥〕清秋怨，碧天如水冰輪現。冰輪現，玉露無聲，金風拂面。

奴家黃氏夢蘭，姑蘇人也。[1] 不幸慈顏早背，嚴親撫養成人。奴家雖出寒門，性好文墨。有那些俗子求婚，奴家立心斷絕。此世不逢才子，情願祝髮空門。(嘆介) 正是：滿懷幽恨無人曉，訴與天邊皓月知。日間漿洗下幾件衣服，乘此月光之下，不免砧搗一番。

(取衣，坐地砧介) (唱)

〔山坡羊〕靜悄悄荒涼庭院，孤伶伶影兒相伴；慘淒淒階前亂蛩，嚦嘹嘹天外悲鳴雁。夜漫漫含愁人未眠，(淚介) **腸逐砧聲斷。辜負了月朗風清，好夢難。**

(生在內念詩介)

今夜月明人盡望，
不知秋思在誰家？

(貼聽介) 呀，**更殘，甚詩聲隔院傳？疑參，甚書生坐夜闌？**

(生巾，月白道袍，青襯衣上) (唱)

〔前腔〕碧澄澄月光滿院，韵悠悠誰家搗練？亂紛紛秋聲雁聲，冷清清孤館寒燈伴。

自從小生聘定胡姬，即來吳郡。今夜宿在此間，百花洲畔，夜闌人靜。忽聽砧聲，但恨牆兒遮斷，不能目睹其人。

(看介) 呀，且喜牆邊有株垂柳，何不攀枝上去，觀看一番？(作上樹介) **把柳枝扳，身輕不憚難。**(見貼驚介) 呀，**猛見傾城艷，**恰便似**帶月飛瓊下九天。奇緣，步桃源兩遇仙；**[2] **欣然，便鐵心腸也動憐。**

---

[1] 黃氏亦實有其人。

[2] 不脫前事，文法井井。

且住，我看此女妖嬈，不下胡姬。這等良宵月夜，又遇佳人，豈可虛過，待我跳過去。(搖首介) 不可，黌夜入人家，非姦即盜。萬一被人拿住，成何體面？(又看，笑介) 咦，我也顧不得了。壯一壯膽，跳過去罷。(跳介) (貼驚起介) 呀，甚麼人跳過牆來，爹爹兄弟都已睡了，如何是好？待我到前邊去叫。(貼走) (生急攔，揖介) 小娘子，休得驚怕，切莫聲張，小生並非歹人。小娘子請看，世有衣冠之盜賊乎？[3] (貼看，背介) 原來是個文弱書生，待我問來。(轉介) 那秀才既是讀書之輩，豈不知禮？黌夜跳牆，是何原故？(生) 小娘子容稟 (揖介) (唱)

〔金落索〕**躬身告玉仙，**(背介) **我欲語羞無限，為偷花自取身輕賤。**

(轉揖介) **娘子行請聽言，我性非顛，乞恕書生在少年。**(貼) 既是儒門，如此作為，有玷名教。(生) **非關吾把儒冠玷，只怪伊家貌忒妍。**[4] (貼) 一發沒來由了。

(生羞介) (唱) 我**原非慣**，都只為**藍橋咫尺**，豈可**竟無緣**？我自**愧無端，怎奈情牽。**(揖介) **還望卿垂念。**

(貼) 秀才既是讀書君子，奴家怎好聲張。請問貴郡仙鄉，大名高姓，因何到此？(生) 小生王夢麟，表字瑞卿，隨家君赴任燕京，偶遊貴郡。今晚忽聽砧聲，一時大膽，目睹花容，不禁狂喜。感蒙寬恕，(揖介) 深謝高情。(貼答禮介) 豈敢，公子自請尊便。(生笑介) 難道就這等去了不成？還要問小娘子尊姓芳名，青春幾何？(貼) 奴家黃氏夢蘭，賤庚一十七歲。(生) 這等小生還叨長一年。請問堂上尊親在否？(貼) 家母早故，只有家父在堂。(生) 小娘子可曾接聘？(貼低介) 尚未。(生喜介) 咦，妙呀！這個牆兒跳着了。小娘子在上，小生斗膽有一言奉告。(貼) 請講。

(生) 姐姐仙姿玉貌，足稱佳人；小生自愧粗俗，虛傳才子。小娘子若肯位屈副室，自當貯之金屋。[5]

---

[3] 衣冠盜賊，世間多有。

[4] 怪得大奇。

[5] 胡氏係其母求婚，梁氏 (編校者著：該為黃氏) 係王生自求，排場不同。

(貼) 君乃玉堂仙客，妾本田野村姑。萍水相逢，忽蒙垂念，自慚微陋，恐辱朱門。

(生笑介) 小娘子太謙了。既荷見允，小生帶有玉釵一枝，權為紅定。(取釵送，貼接介) 雖荷厚愛，但堂有嚴親，妾難自主。(生) 姐姐不須慮得，小生明日自然着人來講。(貼) 奴家還有一言。(生) 請講。(貼) 恐君異日身榮，金釵羅列，使妾此身置於何地？(生) 小娘子一發多慮了。小生豈是那等薄倖之徒？小娘子如不深信，當此星月之下，共立山盟，[6] 決卿疑念。(生拜天介) 神天在上，王夢麟，若忘黃氏，天地鑒之。(貼) 相公如此深情，使妾感之無盡。

〔前腔〕誠心拜告天，訂結三生願。(看貼，笑介) **和你今宵惟有嫦娥見。**

(貼) 相公請上，受妾一拜。(生旁立，還揖) (貼拜) (唱) **庸姿荷意憐，自含慚。**(背介) **月夜私盟，怕禮欠端。**(生背唱) **風流誰道白司馬，**我如今呵，**楊柳櫻桃也一樣牽。**(貼覷生介) (唱) **我偷斜盼，**看**芳蘭春柳態翩翩。**(生欲近貼復退介) (唱) 待和她**攜手依肩，舉步羞前。**(貼) 因何**紅暈何郎面？**

(生仰看介) 呀，月已西斜，小生就此告別了。(貼) 相公怎生過去？(生笑介) 來從牆上來，去只得還從牆上去。只是無樹可攀，如何上去？(貼想介) 哦，有了。屋後有古槐一株，可以扳越。(生) 如此甚好。(貼) 相公這裏來。(引生轉介) 就在此處。(生) 小娘子穩便，小生去了。(上牆介，生)

〔尾聲〕匆匆欲去還留戀。(貼) 相公此去，何時再會？(淚介) **目斷東牆淚暗彈。**(生) 小娘子保重，後會有期。不須憂慮，**莫為了別後相思損玉顏。**(各分下)

---

[6] 胡黃二氏，一盟一不盟，亦有不同。

第十一齣・菊宴

(外冠帶黑三髯，末扮院子隨上)

〔西地錦〕烏巷槐堂家世，榮叨黃榜名題。曹郎簪筆奉恩時，敢負人臣殊遇。

東壁文章重，西京閥閱高；
有兒能繼起，爭羨鳳凰毛。

下官王文翰，表字圖南；謬忝科名，官居郎署。孩兒夢麟，已魁秋榜。近來聘定謝年兄之女，明春若能再捷南宮，那時金榜洞房，一時並舉，未為遲也。今日乃是重陽佳節，已曾吩咐備酒，與夫人慶賞。院子！(末) 有。(外) 筵席可曾完備？(末) 完備了。(外) 吩咐將筵席擺在園中，請夫人出堂。(末請介，老旦便服，丑、小旦隨上)

〔一剪梅〕庭前玉樹久暌違，幾度尋思，無限憂思。

(見介) 相公萬福。(外) 夫人拜揖。(坐介) (外) 今日乃重陽佳節，下官設宴西園，請夫人同賞。(老旦) 多謝相公，妾當陪侍。(同行介) (外) 青山遠近帶皇州，霽景重陽上北樓。(老旦) 雨歇亭皋仙菊潤，霜飛天苑御梨秋。(外) 夫人你看，園中好一派秋色也。(老旦) 正是。(外) 看酒過來。(眾進酒介)

〔啄木兒〕昇平候，佳節期，看滿目秋光如畫裏。(外) 且同夫人憑欄一望。(同起介) (外整冠笑介) **按烏紗短髮羞吹，玩秋光把危欄同倚。**[1] (老旦嘆介) **猛想起天涯遊子今何處，臨風不覺長吁氣。**(外) 夫人，**你因何樂地生愁鎖兩眉？**

夫人，為何面有不悅之容？(老旦) 妾身也沒有甚麼不悅，只為小孩兒久不歸來。未免懸心。(外) 下官已差人去接，不日便回，夫人何須憂悶？

---

[1] 警策之句，切當不浮。

〔前腔〕你休憂慮，免慘悽，不日龍駒來帝里。(老旦)怕他小孩子家沒主意，身迷花柳，有誤功名。(外笑介)夫人說慣下官了，[2] 難道孩兒也是這樣？**他豈肯為飛絮閑情，灰卻了如虹壯志？**(老旦)還有一件，**他如今雖做男兒體，怕嬌柔終有些裙釵氣。**(外)夫人一發多慮了。(老旦)咳，相公，**我則怕他客舍秋風被病所欺。**[3]

(外點頭介)便是呢。咳，我的兒，(起介)

〔三段子〕你歸鞭整未？早歸來免你娘親慮疑。(對老旦介)夫人，**你愁他怎的？展憂容休拋酒卮，盼嬌兒指日征鞍至，早承歡解卻椿萱慮。**(同舉手介)**共祝蒼穹，只求周庇。**

(老旦)這畜生久遊外郡，浪蕩身心，還不知明歲春闈怎樣哩？

〔歸朝歡〕慮的是，慮的是文荒性痴，怎配那瓊樓鳳侶？(外)**誰不道，誰不道吾兒俊奇，豈不堪為他佳婿？**(合)**兒曹姻事非容易，人間難得無雙配，今喜得王謝名家早為繫赤絲。**

(生扮家人上)稟老爺，有各位老爺相請赴宴，連邀兩次了。(外)知道了，吩咐外邊打轎。(內應介)夫人，下官失陪了。(老旦)相公請。(生、末隨外下)(老旦)侍兒隨我進去。(丑、小旦應，同下)

---

[2] 吾女為我言之也。

[3] 佳句也。

第十二齣・行程

(生戴秀士巾，穿青道袍束絛，騎馬；丑挑擔，同上)

〔勝如花〕(生唱) **秋風動，行客愁，極目雲橫遠岫。望長堤衰草萋迷，逐殘霞馬蹄馳驟。**[1] (作回望，嘆介) **兜底裏關心回首，嘆孤身天涯久遊，累高堂晨昏望眸。**(鞭馬介) **急奔皇州，還恨山川疊湊。**(內吹笛介) **忽聽得笛聲遠奏，**(看介) **卻原來是野渡橫舟。**

(勒馬，叫介) 瑤琴！(丑) 有。(生) 我身子有些倦了，且在此歇歇再走。(丑) 是。(生下馬，坐地介) (丑白) 相公坐在此，小人去放放馬來。(帶馬下)

(生白)

〔減字木蘭花〕

垂鞭日暮，踏遍天涯荒草路。
吹面霜風，回首西湖似夢中。

遠山幾點，牽惹離愁魂欲斷；
衰柳鴉啼，一片殘陽在客衣。

小生自離京師，已經數月。心牽膝下，趨奔燕山。前在臨安，聘了胡氏。復遊吳郡，沒來由乘興登牆，偶遇黃女，一時狂妄，與她月下私盟，後令媒氏通言明，把小星再定。[2] (笑介) 仔細思來，未免有些多事。況黃氏之貌，頗遜胡姬。既已聘定，這也罷了。(欠伸介) 噯呀，一時精神悶倦，不免起身一步。(起，整衣望介) 呀，坐不多時，又早是日西時分也。

---

[1] 曲如風行水上，自然成文。

[2] 補出。

〔泣顏回〕**遠樹淡烟浮，又早斜陽時候。寒雲衰柳，遙看瀑布飛流。望沙灘聚鷗，聽嚦嘹嘹哀雁添眉皺。**咳，看了這深秋景物，令人百感俱生。**為悲秋瘦比黃花，**咳，回念湖山不能無恨，**戀湖山懶上驊騮。**

(丑帶馬上) 相公，日已西斜，上馬趲路罷。(生) 帶馬過來。(丑) 嗄。(帶介) 相公，請上馬。(生上馬介)

流水橋西小徑斜，
馬蹄今夜入誰家？
秋光何處堪消日，
霜葉紅於二月花。

卷下

第十三齣・報捷

(小生紅圓領紗帽，小旦鳳冠圓領，同上)(小生)

〔菊花新〕**佳氣祥烟積帝京，上林春色聚文星。**(小旦)**子尚孩齡，把佳婿捷音先聽。**

(見介)相公。(小生)夫人。(小旦)今日放榜之期，不知王郎中否？(小生)王郎三場試卷，下官俱已看過，必非落人後者。

(小旦)若有佳音，報人也該到了。(小生)便是。(老旦、淨、貼、外扮報人，打鑼上)

〔不是路〕**一片鑼聲，萬里春光上苑生。喧聲競，官衙直入報魁名。**(丑、生扮家丁上)你們做甚麼？(眾白)我們是報喜的。貴府姑爺狀元及第，要見老爺討賞。(生白)住着。(見小生稟介)(小旦下)(生)你們進來。(眾進，叩頭介)恭喜老爺，姑爺高中魁元，小人們特來報喜。(小生)可是真的？(眾)怎麼不真？現有報單在此。(出報單，小生看介)(眾唱)老爺呵，**喜非輕，名魁天下人爭敬，一躍金鰲四海驚。修來命，少年獨占春闈勝。非凡之倖，非凡之倖。**

(小生)左右，將報人領到門房酒飯，打發賞銀。(眾應，小旦同下，復上)相公喜也。(小生笑介)夫人難道不喜？(合唱)

〔前腔〕**喜氣盈盈，年少王郎果俊英。**與吾兒呵，**才容並良緣，端不負今生。笑相稱乘龍佳婿真堪慶，又見朝陽小鳳鳴。威儀盛，天街走馬看紅杏。鳳池名定，鳳池名定。**(同下)

第十四齣・琴訴

(生紗帽月白道袍上)

〔步蟾宮〕微名雖已題金榜，關心事幾回悒怏。

(坐介)

誰家玉笛暗飛聲？
風透湘簾月滿庭。
千里相思何處是？
綠窗昨夜夢分明。

下官一自來京，喜得春闈得手。前者爹娘已為聘定謝年伯之女，尚未完婚，聞說才貌無雙，未知果否。只是我與黃胡二姬，盟約已定，會面無期。原許她得中之後，接取來京。如今欲待差人前去，又恐爹娘知道見怪。(嘆介) 咳，教我如何是好？(沉吟介) (丑捧茶上) 別院笙歌美，書齋月影清。老爺請茶。(生) 放下。我問你，大老爺在哪裏？(丑) 大老爺在花亭上聽他們唱曲。(生點頭介) (小生上) 奉了大爺命，特來請狀元。稟老爺，大老爺在花亭上設宴，差小的來，請老爺聽曲賞月。(生) 你去拜上大爺，說我身子不快，不去罷。(小生) 嗄。(下) (丑) 老爺既不耐煩聽唱，當此月明如晝，何不操琴一曲？(生) 這個使得。(丑取琴放介) (生) 你自出去，呼喚時再來伺候。(丑) 曉得哉。(下) (生撫琴介) (唱)

〔二郎神〕天似洗，夜雲輕花香細，在月下鳴琴權寫意。聽清音絃管，隔牆風送微微，疑是蟾宮歌霓羽，好良宵人生幾遇。何須慕瑤池？看人間別有歡期。(拂袖起，閑行介)

〔集賢賓〕抬身移步臨階砌，向花間竹裏徘徊。遙憶天涯，人似玉倩，誰寄雲中錦字？[1] (嘆介) **心懸兩地，何日得玉樓雙聚？**(背手，搖擺介) **教我茫無計，怕反被風流相累。**(作對月悶坐介)

[1]《紫釵記》中語。

(末微醉上)

〔集唐〕

玉碗盛來琥珀光，
小亭夜靜百花香。
緩歌慢舞凝絲竹，
醉倚東風白玉床。

(見生叫介) 兄弟！(生作不知長嘆介) (末背介) 呀，我看瑞卿對月嗟嘆，必有原故，待我問個明白。(近生後，大叫介) 兄弟！(生驚起介) 呀，哥哥來了。(末笑介) 愚兄來此久矣。(各揖介) (末) 兄弟，愚兄着人相請，為何不去？(生) 多承哥哥厚意，弟因身子不快，故此不去。(末) 方才見你對月長吁，有何心事，何不對愚兄一講？(生) 沒有甚麼心事。(末笑介) 兄弟，

〔前腔〕你**臨風長吁非無意，料來是有尋思。**愚兄看來，你也沒有甚麼不足處了。**金榜題名酬夙志，喜百歲赤繩已繫。你昔懷今慰，更有甚關心憂慮？**(生嘆介) (末) 兄弟，為何欲言又止？(移坐近生，笑介) 兄弟你**休瞞昧，我和你連枝同氣。**[2]

(生) 夜已深矣，我們進去，燈下細談便了。(叫介) 瑤琴看茶來。(生末對坐介) (丑端茶上，送介) (生) 瑤琴，可將院門關了，你自去睡罷。(丑笑介) 妙哉，此言正合學士之意。(關門) (末笑介) 一向不曾問得兄弟前在江南，可有所遇否？(生笑介) 若説起所遇，萬分可笑。平白被楊家表兄，捉弄了去。訪甚麼琵琶美人，弄出一場大笑話來。我也不耐煩講他，昨日備細寫下個冊兒在此，哥哥請看。(取送末介，末細看大笑介) 恭喜兄弟，見了這番勝景，你方才的心事，就是思想她麼？(生大笑介) 豈有此理。我如今將心事，告訴了哥哥罷。

〔黃鶯兒〕惆悵武陵溪，賺劉郎兩度迷，與他萍水留情意。花枝柳枝，緣奇遇奇。(背介) 咳，**意中人，此際成眠未？怎能知為伊憔悴，弱體不勝衣。**

[2] 只如白話。

(末白) 聽弟所言，似有佳遇了？(生白) 正是。前者弟在臨安，寄居靈隱。偶步西山，得遇夢蓮胡氏。(末白) 哦，多少年紀？容色如何？(生白) 一十六歲，容技雙全。兄弟隨解絲環，已將她聘下了。(末白) 佳人難遇，聘下了極是。(生) 此後復至姑蘇閑玩，月夜聞砧，又遇黃姬芳素，亦頗嬌嬈，親贈玉釵，小星再定。(末白) 怎麼又是一個？吾弟好僥倖也。二人容質，必竟誰高？(生白) 公道看來，畢竟胡出黃右。(末笑介) 老弟，你也忒粗心了，萬一遇着河東柳氏，如之奈何？畢竟年幼，所見不到。(生笑介) 這叫做：要知山下路，須問過來人。(各笑介) (生) 兄弟當時曾與她們約下，得中之後，接來完聚。如今欲待差人，又恐爹娘見罪，故此憂悶。(末白) 這便怎處呢？(生作愧笑介) 如今沒奈何，做哥哥不着。(末佯笑介) 教我也沒法呀！(生起揖介) 哥哥，念兄弟呵，(唱)

〔前腔〕幾月費尋思，為蘇杭兩聘姬。(白) 如今呵，(唱) **要煩伊替我堂前啟。**(笑介) **君肯方而便之，我自知而感之。**(揖介) **他時自有酬兄計。**(末白) 酬謝愚兄甚麼呢？(生笑介) 哪 (唱) **我選蛾眉，教成歌舞，相贈捧金杯。**

(末大笑介) 吾弟不必憂心，都在做哥哥的身上；你所許之事，也要在心。

(生) 這個自然。(內打四更介) (生) 呀，說話之間，譙樓四鼓矣，我們也該安寢了。(末) 正是。(起介) (末) 書院無人到，清宵月倍明。(生) 弟兄一夕話，不覺已深更。哥哥請。(末) 兄弟請。(同下)

第十五齣・入京

(老旦翠藍圓領束緣素裙，旦扮侍女隨上)

幼出名家掌上珠，長歸儒士奉孀姑。
而今慚愧沾鸞誥，子貴夫榮樂有餘。

老身楊氏，自隨相公作宦京師，又經幾載。且喜堂上婆婆康健，膝前二子承歡。幸得麟兒功名已就，皆賴祖宗之慶也。已定吉期，與他畢姻，完我一樁心事。前者大孩兒說起，麟兒在南時，聘有二妾，不敢擅取來京，煩他轉告我知。我想既已聘定，豈可棄之？為此着掌家婆、院子、乳母前去接來。去了日久，為何還不見到？(末白鬚青衣，扮院公上) 才離南國地，又到北京城。(見介) 太夫人在上，老奴叩頭。(老旦) 呀，你回來了。二姬可曾接至？(末) 都到了。小人先至臨安，訪問住處，至她家中，備道原由，胡媽媽十分歡喜。母子不忍分離，一同起身。後到蘇州，見了黃老，說了來因，交明聘禮。她父親不願同來，黃姑娘一身到此。昨日天晚，未得進城。如今兩位姑娘的小轎，已到府門。胡媽媽因未得夫人之命，不敢擅入，尚留寓所。(老旦) 你一面着打轎進來，一面就去接胡媽媽入府。(末) 曉得。(向內介) 打轎進來。(內應介，末下) (老旦) 丫鬟出去迎來。(旦應下，引小旦、貼，俱青衣白裙；小淨扮奶媽隨上) (旦)

〔海棠春〕故鄉身別心還戀，(貼) 慢回首親闈目斷。

(淨見叩介) 婆子叩頭。(老旦) 起來。(淨) 兩位姑娘，這就是太夫人，過來拜見。(二旦) 太夫人在上，容婢子叩見。(老旦看，喜介) 罷了。(二旦合唱)

〔鎖南枝〕含羞臉，移步蓮，(拜介) 深深拜倒台座前。生長在蓬茅，規禮何曾慣？念年還幼，恩望寬，侍晨昏求教管。(老旦唱)

〔前腔〕看花容媚，柳態翩，娟娟楚楚並蒂蓮。(白) 哪個是黃氏呢？(貼) 婢子便是。(老旦唱) **細語似新鶯。**(白) 這個是胡氏了。(笑介) 妙嗄！(唱) **嬌小如飛燕，莫怪兒相愛，我亦憐。**他日呵，**待蘭閨真**

良伴。(生紗帽月白圓領上) (唱)

〔前腔〕**朝方罷，日已遷，整衣敬請堂上安。**(見二旦，急退介) 呀，**猛見兩嬋娟，趨步忙回轉。**(白) 啊呀，好生奇怪呀。(拭目再看介) (唱) **此是林中遇，月下緣，自何來華堂站？**(生徘徊偷看二旦介) (小旦作見生驚) (背唱)

〔前腔〕**見雕欄外，一少年，烏紗雪面丰韵翩。**(拭目介) 呀，**此是舊劉郎，**(急避介) **乍見羞無限。**(貼亦見介) 呀，**重見當年面，宿世緣，得與侍衾裯，深謝天從願。**

(老旦見生故問介) 嗄，甚麼人在簾外偷覷？這等大膽。(生急閃下，淨旦笑介，老旦亦笑介) 做了官，還是這等孩子氣。丫鬟，你可領她們去見太老夫人。吩咐收拾後院秀春軒，與她二人安住，令侍兒春英相伴伏侍。(旦) 曉得。(貼) 片帆雲載到京華，(小旦) 似入瑤池阿母家。(老旦) 南國佳人今有二，不須爭把莫愁誇。(同下)

第十六齣・合巹

(外紗帽紅圓領，老旦鳳冠紅圓領，同上)

〔西地錦〕(外) **喜氣照臨庭院，笙歌繚繞堂前。**(老旦) **彩鸞丹鳳兩團圓，佳婦佳兒如願。**

(外) 夫人。(老) 相公。(外) 今日與二孩兒完婚，花轎將至，怎不請婆婆出來受禮？(老) 妾身方才去請婆婆，說是單身，吉時不便相見，明日拜罷。(外) 自家兒女，何須計較？(末、小生扮家人急上，內吹打介) 稟上太老爺，花轎到了。(外) 快叫儐相贊禮。(小生叫介，淨扮儐相，眾扮鼓樂上。照常贊禮，吹打，請介。生紗帽吉服簪花披紅上。淨又請介，旦吉服鳳冠罩面，小旦、丑扮喜娘扶上。淨贊拜介) 禮畢，儐相告退。(下) (合場同唱)

〔畫眉序〕美玉種藍田，百歲良緣鳳鸞眷。喜玉堂學士，金屋嬋娟。看雙星天上諧和，羨二美人間歡忭。[1] **屏開金雀排佳宴，慶當戶，吉星光現。**(外、老旦) 花燭引道，送入洞房。(轉行介) (合)

〔雙聲子〕銀燭燦，銀燭燦，引上蓬萊苑。金屏艷，金屏艷，彩射合歡宴。百年眷，百年眷，真堪羨，真堪羨。看宮袍霞帔，光照瓊筵。(送生旦進房坐介) (眾轉唱)

〔隔尾〕新郎才俊新人艷，是一對玉京仙伴。從今後堂下雙承舞綵歡。(同下)

(內起更介) (生唱)

〔太師引〕畫堂前，方罷合歡宴。早樓頭玉滿聲傳，(起，閉門介) **慢抬身把朱扉自掩。**(看旦，背介) **她背羞容默坐燈邊。**(嘆介) **猛思量蘭閨雙艷，頓令情牽心戀。俺這裏錦鬧鳳鸞，她那裏青燈孤枕伴愁眠。**[2] (悶坐介，內打二更介) (旦唱)

---

[1] 佳句。

[2] 香艷之詞，不讓古人。

〔啄木兒〕銀缸燦，玉漏遷，萬種羞慚憑小扇。（生長嘆介）（旦唱）**耳邊廂短嘆長吁，好教人難猜難辨。莫不是朱陳強結情非願？莫不是章臺別有蛾眉絆？因甚的起坐難安意態顛？**

（生笑介）到是我差矣，眼前坐着位千金小姐，不去看看。沒來由為了二姬，只管煩悶，豈不可笑？（起，剪燭看旦，驚喜）（背介）嗳呀，王夢麟今夕遇仙也。（拭目看，笑介）咦，妙嗄。

〔太師引〕翠雲冠倍顯出如花面，似姑射飛來玉仙。（抖袖介）**天不負風流翰院，特賜與個月殿嬋娟。遂張敞畫眉宿願，效于飛勝似虎榜魁元。**（大笑介）（旦作詫介）（生唱）**難尋這福命時緣，**（搖擺舉手笑介）**問銀河，雙星可羡此宵歡？**

（內打三更介）（生）呀，樵鼓三敲矣。（近旦，揖介）小姐，夜已深了，請安寢罷。（旦不動介，生笑，唱）小姐，

〔餘文〕勸你**抬頭且把羞眉展。**這把扇兒也可去掉了。（奪扇介）妙嗄，**恰便似掃去浮雲現月仙。**[3]（又揖介）小姐，你**看桂影斜窗已是半夜天。**（持燭攜旦下）

[3] 奇句。

第十七齣·春怨

(貼青衫月白背心束緣白裙，緩步上) (唱)

〔步步嬌〕綠楊深鎖梨花院，曉起纖腰倦。妝成只自憐，多病多愁，香消玉減。獨自倚雕欄，眼穿芳草魂應斷。(坐介)

〔阮郎歸〕

杏花零落蕩春烟，
韶光在眼前；
東風如醉草如眠，
畫樓寒食天。

籠茜袖，掠雲鬟，
斜憑鬥鴨欄；
嬌慵無力上鞦韆，
人如春夢間。

奴家黃夢蘭，自與王狀元月下訂盟，蒙他不負前言，與胡家妹子一同接取來京。年光彈指，轉眼新春。(嘆介) 咳，雖然畫閣藏嬌，終是紅顏薄命。妹子年幼嬌痴，懨懨春睡，此時梳洗未完。奴家獨自臨軒，倍難消遣，好生傷感人也。(拭淚介) (唱)

〔醉扶歸〕冷清清淚滴桃花面，意遲遲羞看玉鑑圓。訴幽情鸚鵡語簷前，伴傷春紫燕飛簾畔。傍妝臺，愁多慵整翠雲鈿。警啼鶯心煩，懶舉湘妃扇。呀，妹子出來也。(小旦水綠衫，青背心，白裙束緣，緩步上) (唱)

〔步步嬌〕春閨曉夢驚誰喚？(內鶯啼介) (小旦唱) **原來是柳上黃鸝囀。春山不喜添，瘦不勝衣，腕鬆金釧，嬌怯倩誰憐？**(作捲簾介) **含情自把湘簾捲。**

(見介，貼笑介) 賢妹今日好妝梳也。看你巧挽雲鬟掃翠峰，妝成端的為誰容？(小旦笑介) 姐姐，我天然愛好從來性，不為他人只為儂。(貼) 妹子，我和你蘭房寂寞，形影相依。豈知玉府仙郎，也做人間薄倖。(淚介) (小旦) 姐姐，且自寬懷。(貼) 非是我苦苦縈心，他那裏鼓瑟調琴，郎才女貌。咱這裏空閨晝永，錦帳鸞孤。值此春光，能無傷感？(嘆介) (小旦笑介) 姐姐又來無為了。縱然金屋承恩，玉樓侍宴，不過抱姬妾之衾裯。怎如我倚月吹簫，拈花作賦？(貼) 賢妹之言，自是高人雅見。但朱顏易改，未免難甘。(小旦) 這也憑天聽命，不必縈懷。我們在此，蒙太夫人另眼相看，錦衣玉食，就是家母也得安樂。此身得所，他事無勞我念。王郎宴爾新婚，自然無心我輩。昔既多情，今豈輕棄？姐姐請自開顏，當此春光，不可辜負，且和你花叢一步。(貼) 賢妹請。(起，同步介) (小旦唱)

〔皂羅袍〕春晝寥寥難遣，蕩湘裙小步，花下盤桓。(合) **玉肩相並立瓊軒，恐驚花底鶯和燕。波清影現，卿憐我憐，鸞簫鳳管，朝閑暮閑。**[1] **問天公，春光妝點誰家院？**

〔好姐姐〕(貼) **嘆紅顏生成命慳，**(小旦) 你**休得苦相嗟怨。**(倚几介) **弱身慵倦，拈毫懶拂箋。**(貼) **臨風嘆，朱欄倚遍，情難遣，強把花枝帶笑看。**

妹子有些倦了，且和你進房去罷。(小旦) 姐姐請。

〔意不盡〕翠苔踏遍芳心倦，看雲淡風輕近午天。(貼背介) 少不得到黃昏呵，**也則是綉被焚香獨自眠。**

百花庭院日遲遲，(小旦) 永晝無人鶯亂啼。(貼) 坐久暗生惆悵事，(小旦) 海棠軒外去題詩。(同下)

---

[1] 竟是絕妙好辭矣。

第十八齣・閨聚

(老旦錦鬓素裙，淨扮梅香隨上)

〔引子〕兒曹喜已諧隨唱，慰膝下不勝歡暢。

自次兒畢婚之後，又將一載矣。且喜媳婦才色無雙，賢明絕世。只是夢蓮芳素，久居後院，豈是了休？孩兒正在新婚，又難提起。我看謝家小姐，決非妒婦，今日待她來時，講明此事，也完了老身一樁心事，多少是好。(旦花披風素裙，丑扮梅香上)

〔引子〕嬌癡閨性今成往，學修婦道，暗自慚惶。

(見介) 婆婆萬福。(老旦) 媳婦坐了。(旦坐介) (老旦) 嗄，媳婦我有句話，要對你講，未知你意如何？(旦) 婆婆有話請講，媳婦敢不敬聽？(老旦) 只因你丈夫當初呵，

〔桂枝香〕閑遊南郡，偶逢雙俊。(旦) 是甚麼人？(老旦) **住臨安胡氏娉婷，居吳下黃姬韵韻。**我兒與她們呵，**是三生意深。三生意深，遂把小星雙聘。**(旦) 都是哪等人家子女？(老旦) **都是良家玉潤。**(旦) 如今都在哪裏？(老旦) **現在別院棲身。**如今你丈夫呵，**專望你一身為做東風便**，好教他，**兩朵花枝和笑簪。**(旦起) (背唱)

〔前腔〕我聞言私忖，喜盈方寸忍妒。她玉貌紅裙，教負卻仙郎綠鬢。[1] (笑介) 相公相公，怪你**書生性喬。書生性喬，欺人忒甚，把咱心兒錯認。**我來日呵，**且做個假醋喬嗔。**且看二妾之貌，果是如何；**試認她金屋如花貌，安慰星前月下人。**

(轉介) 既有兩個美人，望婆婆喚來相見。(老旦) 正要叫出與媳婦叩頭。(對淨介) 翠雲，速去叫她們來見夫人。(淨應下，引二旦青衣素裙上) (唱)

〔賺〕似出長門，庭院繁華別是春。徐前進，移蓮繞徑蕩湘裙。(內鸚鵡叫介) 姐姐喜也！(二旦) **暗生欣，嘲人鸚鵡為傳信；**好教咱，**欲笑還羞搵翠襟。**(淨) 姑娘來了。(老旦對二旦，指旦介) 二姬過來，這就

[1] 賢哉謝女。

是你家主母，上前拜見。(二旦) 是。夫人在上，賤妾等叩頭。(旦) 罷了。(二旦拜) (老旦唱) 媳婦，**我把雙紅粉，從今付你香閨訓。**(對二旦介) 你們呵，**須要小心承順，小心承順。**(旦看二旦，笑介) 果然好。(唱)

〔前腔〕貌果超群，兩朵芙蓉出水新。(白) 昔人以美人比香扇墜，今胡姬是也。(唱) **真丰韵，可將嬌小鬥香君。**(二旦看旦，背介) **暗驚心，仙姿萬種描難盡。**羞殺我，**癡負蛾眉不讓人。**(旦背介) (白) 王郎王郎，你好僥倖也。這樣女子，一個也足矣，還要成雙做對。(唱) 咦，**好個花星運，兼取蜀隴貪何甚。思之堪哂，思之堪哂。**

(老) 媳婦，幾時領她們見你丈夫？(旦) 今日欠好。待媳婦另選吉日，收拾房室衣妝，諸事齊備，方可完聚。(老旦點頭喜介) 使得。(起，背介) 好嗄，媳婦見了二姬，不但沒有分毫妒意，更且欣然喜笑。小小年紀，這等賢明大量，難得難得。

(轉介) 如此說，二姬且歸後院，媳婦自去打點便了。(旦) 正是。(同下)

第十九齣・雙圓

(旦鳳冠紅圓領素裙上)

〔虞美人〕文魔故態真難料，怪殺喬圈套。教人堪笑又堪嗔，且自令他疑假復疑真。

(坐介) 奴家自從于歸王郎，一載有餘。只道琴瑟同心，誰料小星先定。若非婆婆講起，奴家哪裏得知？且喜那兩個女子，態度幽閑，儀容秀麗，依依身畔，甚是可人。但怪相公少年狂性，既有此事，就該實告我知。為甚麼一意欺瞞，片言不露。我如今欲令相見，教他看得太容易了，因此袖了他昔日聘二姬的雙玉。待等朝回，且做個假意兒，難為他一番，有何不可？(下)

(外、末、小旦、淨扮從，引生紗帽紅圓領上) (唱)

〔懶畫眉〕九重春色醉仙桃，丹鳳池頭潤彩毫。回瞻天闕五雲高，咱**書生慚愧登廊廟，父子承恩佐聖朝。**

(到，下馬介) (丑、小生上，眾下) (生坐介)

紫陌雞鳴赴早朝，
花迎劍佩露初消；
老天不負男兒志，
贏得天香染絳袍。

(小送茶介) 老爺今日下朝卻早。(生) 正是。今日朝中無事，故而早歸。左右，擊雲板。(丑應，敲介) (老旦扮婢上) 呀，老爺進來了，有請夫人。(旦上，背坐介；生進見介) 夫人拜揖。(旦不睬介，生詫，背介) 嗳呀，奇怪。下官往日歸衙，夫人必定笑臉相迎，今日為何不瞅不睬？必有原故，待我問來。(轉介) 嗄，夫人，看你無言默坐，似有不悅之容，何不說與下官知道？(旦不理介) 夫人只管不言不語，豈不悶壞下官。嗄，夫人！

〔前腔〕你**匆匆怒氣鎖眉梢，**(背笑介) 咦，妙嗄，**越顯出萬種丰神費畫描。**(轉介) 夫人，**莫怪我頻頻向你問根苗，**(笑拍旦介) 小姐端的是為甚麼呢？**望你把衷情且對吾行告，**(旦作拂袖起介) 咦，**聽了這巧語花言意倍焦。**

(背立介，生背介) 咳呀，細看夫人光景，似有些惱着下官了。(想介) 我沒甚麼不是嗄？(轉介) 不才細看夫人尊意，似有哪個得罪了？(揖介) 實是想不着，求夫人說了罷。(旦) 你且去想來。(生) 想甚麼呢？哦，敢是見怪下官麼？(旦冷哂介，生急揖介) 夫人，下官若有得罪夫人之處，望夫人明示其非，使下官自知其罪，也好與夫人陪話。(旦) 你既要我明講，這也不難。(生急揖介) 正是，夫人請講。(旦唱)

〔前腔〕狂生心意太蹊蹺，你當初功不成，名不就，便想着，**銅雀春深鎖二喬。**(生大驚介) 噯呀，這這這是哪裏說起？事要三思，不可屈了平人。(旦) 你還賴到哪裏去？(出雙玉介) 你且看這件東西從何而至？(生看，急，背介) 啊呀，這是我當初聘二姬的玉釵玉佩，怎生得到夫人手中？咳，機關已露，只得招認了罷。(頓足介) 事到頭來，也顧不得羞恥了。(對旦揖介) 夫人既已知之，下官不敢再辯。果是下官不是，只求夫人寬恕。(連揖不起介。旦冷笑介) (唱) **你本是狀元骨氣自然高，咱這寒微何福沾鸞誥。**(生笑介) 夫人別話不提，如今只求大德寬恩，容留了那兩個女子罷。(旦) 這個麼實對你說，萬不能夠。(生) 所有不是，下官自甘認責，其實與二女無干，還望夫人憐念。(旦怒介) 好不知羞，只管憨臉歪纏，難道我就罷了不成？(生又揖介) 夫人請息怒，下官也不思別事了，只教她們過來，早晚伏侍夫人罷。(旦) 我自有人伏侍，何勞你費心？[1] (生急，背) 這便怎麼處？咳，沒奈何，只得跪了。(趨前跪介，旦急閃開，笑介) 羞死羞死，為了兩個妮子，自甘屈膝與人，好生可笑。(生笑，揖介) 好夫人放賢惠些，不要學世人的俗套。(旦) 我生成的性兒，終不然為你改了罷？(生) 咳，你不容也罷。(旦) 你不罷待怎麼？(生背嘆介) 正是萬事易明，人心難料。誰知絕世佳人，竟是非常妒婦。看她的主意，是決難移轉的了。咳，我豈可因妾姬之愛，有乖夫婦之情。咳，二姬嗄二姬！是下官負了你也。(唱) **莫怪我薄倖書生，還是你薄命招。**

[1] 其口角光景，頗似作者乃堂。

咳，二姬不能到手還可，夫人只管不理，卻有些不妙。做我不着還去陪個小心，求她息氣罷。(轉介) 夫人，既然不用她們伺候，待下官明日尋兩分人家，打發她出嫁便了，只求夫人不要生氣罷。(旦冷笑介) 你把這話兒哄誰？我不是痴子。(生笑介) 夫人，下官的性兒，從來是說得出，就做得出，再不說謊的。(旦) 不要反悔呀！(生) 豈有此理？(旦) 既然說過，我也不計較了。(生) 如此說，夫人拜揖了。(旦) 罷了，相公請坐。(各坐介，旦叫介) 丫鬟看茶來。(老旦捧茶上，送介) (旦) 相公，我看你有些口是心非嗄。(生笑介) 夫人忒煞多心了，下官此心，惟天可表。(旦) 當真不生事了？(生) 實是再無他念。(旦點頭介) 這便才是。(背生，對老旦介) 你速去喚二位姨娘出來，拜見老爺。(老) 曉得。(下。引小旦水綠畫花披風，貼月白畫花披風，同上) (唱)

〔引子〕重整翠雲翹，自愧羞花貌。

(旦起介) 隨我進來。(引二旦入介) 相公，有兩個故人在此，你可認得？(生起看，驚喜介)

〔解三醒〕分明是舊時花貌，(拭目再看介) **我拭雙睛再認丰標，**好叫咱，**疑真疑假神顛倒。**(扯住旦介) 夫人，**望解說巧根苗。**(旦笑) 這有甚麼解說？相公方才說打發她們出嫁，妾身已備有妝奩，單等擇配。[2] (生作愀然介) 既如此，卻又教她們過來則甚？(旦) 相公，當初相愛一場，今日分手，豈有不來拜別之理？(生呆介) 這這這兩兩分人家，哪裏能夠便有？也待慢慢打聽，夫人忒也性急了。(旦) 既然兩處難尋，便是一家，使她二女同歸也罷。(生急介) 就是一家，目下也不能便有。(旦笑介) 還是相公不用心，若把奴家，保管現成。(生) 夫人又來取笑了，你又不去外面走動，卻從何打聽呢？(旦) 已有在這裏了，相公不信請看。(生驚介) 哦，在哪裏？(旦笑介) 遠在天邊，近在眼前。(生想介) 天邊眼前？(忽悟介) 夫人眼前，定是下官了。(旦) 難道是我不成？(生大笑介) 夫人夫人，則被你瞞殺下官也。[3] (唱) **我已把青青柳色憑她挽，怎承望玉臼玄霜倩我敲？**(旦笑介) 你如今放心了。(生搖頭介) **我還驚跳。**(旦) 卻是為何？(生) **怕的是忙中有錯，浪裏生濤。**

---

[2] 弄之於股掌之上。

[3] 如脫面具。

(旦笑介) 如今輪到你多心了。(生笑介) 非是下官多心。常言道得好：事不三思，必生後悔。(旦) 如今但請放心，決無他變。(生喜揖介) 下官敬謝。(旦) 二姬過來，拜了老爺。(二旦) 是。老爺請上，妾等拜見。(生) 罷了。(生傍立，二旦拜，旦看生笑介) 相公相公，你好僥倖也。(唱)

〔前腔〕攀仙桂將金鰲獨躍，今日個**占春光又把玉貌雙招。天教便宜你個喬京兆，綠窗下黛同描。**[4] (生看二旦大笑介) (唱) 不枉咱**幾屈金膝求德耀，頻倒烏紗為阿嬌。**(旦) 相公相公，你**且休歡笑**，還怕咱，**醋風可畏妒罪難逃。**(生愧笑，急揖介) (旦) 侍兒們，將酒宴設在百花亭上，與老爺慶喜。(老旦) 曉得。(旦) 相公請。(生) 夫人請。(合唱)

〔尾聲〕風流占斷人間好，問此福啊誰能效？奪盡了海內繁華第一標。[5] (同下)

---

[4] 真人生難得之事。

[5] "繁華"二字，又逗夢境。

第二十齣・喬議

(生戴巾，水綠道袍紅襯衣，上)

〔繞池遊〕**花飛鶯老，轉眼春殘了，困人天薰風初裊。酒渴思江，詩狂欲嘯，共青蓮同心意交。**

(坐介) 下官當初一時乘興，如今二美兼收，嬌妻艷妾，足快平生。深感夫人毫不見妒，這也是人生之大幸也，。想我當初曾對哥哥許下，若與二妾完聚之後，定然買個美人相贈。前已尋下兩個女子，叫做賽紅勝雪。下官曾交付二姬，習學歌舞。我這段意思，夫人還不曉得。二女子住居別院，許多時不曾看見，未知教的如何？今日清閑無事，不免進去問問夢蓮芳素，若是精熟了，便與夫人商議，明日送去便了。(起，行介) (唱)

〔玉芙蓉〕**荷錢水上飄，翠竹窗前繞，喜人間清晝，景遇逍遙。**呀，妙嗄！看那欄外榴花開得鮮艷可愛，何不折取兩枝，與二姬簪戴？(作捲袖折花，放扇上介) (唱) **笑將素扇擎紅玉，親向佳人點翠翹。尋歡笑，得桃妍杏嬌，又何須金釵十二樂昏朝？**(下)

(小旦水紅衣素裙，貼旦水綠衣素裙，同上) (唱)

〔前腔〕**寥寥清晝迢，拂拂南風裊。乍湘簟睡起，枕印紅消。**(小旦倚桌翻書介) **閑翻名媛蘭閨集，**(貼弄簫介) **笑弄飛瓊碧玉簫，**(貼倚小旦介) **把香肩靠。**(小旦笑，推介) 啐，**你向誰行獻嬌？**[1] (內鶯啼介) (二旦唱) **聽簷前鶯聲，嚦嚦轉花梢。**(坐介)

(貼) 妹子，你我荷蒙夫人見喜，老爺多情，處此錦綉叢中，可為幸矣。(小旦) 正是。(生潛上，笑介) 二姬好洒落也。(二旦) 呀，老爺來了。(福介) 老爺萬福。(生) 罷了。你們在此做些甚麼呢？(二旦) 妾等因理綉工餘，偶向南窗少寐，忽被啼鳥驚回，在此閑話。[2] (生) 你們雖然清趣，未免近乎寂寞，得我來也好添些熱鬧。(二旦笑介) 老爺請

---

[1] 閨中韵事，描寫畢盡。

[2] 雅詞出香口，不亞康成婢。

坐。(生) 你也坐了。(二旦) 老爺在此，賤妾怎敢？(生笑介) 説哪裏話來？只管坐了。(扯二旦坐介) (二旦) 老爺到此有何貴幹？(生) 我因公事餘閑，特來看你們一看。(出花介) 方才偶見榴花開得可愛，剪得兩枝在此，好與美人生色。(親與二旦戴介，左右看，笑介) 嗳呀，妙嗄！簪上這絳色花兒，越顯得玉容耀彩，雲鬢生輝，可不愛殺人也。偶成小詞二首，寫來相贈。(小旦拂箋磨墨，貼打扇，生寫念介)

幽窗綉倦眠初醒，金釵斜溜依人整。和笑點雲翹，穠花可助嬌。

搖風揮小扇，嬌倚香几畔。蘭麝拂輕紗，飛來萼綠華。

右調菩薩蠻
題贈芳卿黃姬夢蘭妝次

(又寫念介)

少小輕盈似燕身，花妒丰神，柳妒丰神。啼鶯警夢惹嬌嗔，若與溫存，儂與溫存。

一朵紅霞點鬢雲，蜂解依人，蝶解依人。溫柔足可老儂春，生也消魂，死也消魂。[3]

右調一剪梅
題贈芳卿胡姬夢蓮妝次

(二旦各看，喜介) 多謝老爺。(生) 罷了。(各坐介) (生) 我且問你們，前者命你教那賽紅勝雪的歌舞，可曾習會？(二旦) 妾等正要稟知老爺，那兩個女子卻也心靈，都已精熟了。(小旦) 請問買此兩人何用？(生笑介) 我自有用處，你不要管。(貼) 老爺也忒無厭了。(生大笑介) 怎麼這兩個妮子，也會吃起醋來？(二旦笑介) 妾雖不敢奈何老爺，

[3] 詩餘大佳，黃絹幼婦。

卻也要與夫人助力。(生笑指二旦介) 好好好，明日將你們分在夫人名下，我再也不敢來管你了。(小旦) 不管也罷，我們隨着夫人，還怕少了甚麼哩？(生) 阿素，去請了夫人來。(貼) 曉得。(貼下，小旦欲行，生拽介) 你不許去，在此伴我。(小旦笑立介) (生) 看杯茶來我吃。(小) 曉得。(取茶送生飲介) 你母親這些時在哪裏住，怎的不見？(小) 夫人命在那邊老太夫人房中做伴。[4] (生點頭介) 這個卻好。(貼) 夫人來了，(生慌起迎介) 夫人在哪裏？(貼笑介) 少刻便到。(生笑拍貼介) 原來是你這妮子諕我一跳。你為何去了這半日方來？夫人怎的不見？(貼) 妾去時，夫人正在水閣上操琴，妾待曲終方敢相請，故此來遲。(旦月白披風素裙上) 閑消白日拈彤管，欲引清風理玉琴。(貼) 夫人到。(生整衣迎介) 夫人來了，夫人拜揖。(旦) 相公萬福。(小) 夫人萬福。(旦) 美人少禮。(生、旦坐介) (旦) 相公，相喚有何話講？(生) 下官因晝長無事，奉請夫人閑敘，兼有一事相商。(旦) 請教何事？(生) 就是前者買的那兩個女子之事。(旦) 奴家正欲動問，相公置此二姬何用？(生) 夫人何等聰明，怎麼這點小意思兒就猜不着了？(旦) 奴家哪裏猜得着，還是相公明說了罷。(生) 說出來夫人不要惱嗄。(旦) 妾身怎好惱相公？(生笑揖介) 求夫人早定良辰，使下官一發完完心願，感恩無盡矣。(旦) 前者曾說要贈人，為何忽發此念？(生笑介) 夫人忒也老實了，那不過是句話兒，怎麼認起真來？(旦作色介) 相公差矣。(生搖扇佯笑介) 何差？(旦) 你如今凡事須當尊重，須比不得當初了。

〔前腔〕你，**扶搖上九霄，佐政登廊廟。**正應把**經綸才展，風月情抛。**(生大笑介) 好不中聽。難道這頂紗帽倒會管起人來了！趁着咱**五陵豪興三千價，**必須要**買斷燕城廿四橋。**(旦唱) **真輕佻，**(指二旦介) 你**列金屋二嬌。**(生) 只要夫人不妒，何妨廣列金釵？(旦唱) 咳，**這其間，便入宮不妒也恐人嘲。**

(生) 哪裏顧得甚麼外人議論，只要夫人容恕。(旦) 這卻決難從命。(生笑介) 別人家金釵十二，我只三五小星之願，你就容不得了，可笑可笑。[5] (旦) 這等不知足盡的狂人，我也管不得許多了，由你去

[4] 安頓極妥。

[5] 前是旦哄生，此是生哄旦，固是相報，亦文法也。

罷。(貼、小旦) 這些事全在夫人，怎麼由得老爺？只怕沒有這般規矩。[6] (旦) 是呀。(生大笑介) 怪不得這兩個丫頭，在我面前作惡，原來卻是夫人慣壞了。夫人請自三思，你這等的勢力，下官哪得不怕？(旦笑介) 相公，可還記前番的利害麼？(生) 啊喲，若提起那段光景，使下官心膽生寒。(各笑介) (生) 如今把這原故，告訴夫人罷。(旦) 請講。

〔前腔〕我明珠聘阿嬌，深意無人曉。(旦) 是甚深意？(生) **與吾兄昔日，戲語相邀。**(旦) 相邀甚麼？(生) 下官當初曾對哥哥許過，我若納了二姬，定然買妾相贈，故此今日與夫人說知，再到堂上稟過，來日打點請他到來相贈。(旦) 原來如此，沒來由哄人則甚！(生笑介) 實是有累夫人吃這一場寡醋。[7] (三旦同笑介) (生) 不知我**嫁衣本為他人做；**皆認着**翠黛留將我自描。相煩告，要整金釵玉搔；更鮮明，明璫綉服翠雲翹。**

(旦) 這些物件，有何難處？妾身即與打點便了。(生) 如此卻好。一言為定豈移更，不惜明珠聘嬝婷。(旦) 閑聚幽軒相共話，(二旦) 茶烟輕颺午風清。(同下)

---

[6] 二妾撚酸，亦是情理。

[7] 有趣。

第二十一齣・贈妾

(丑青衣羅帽上)

書房承值已多年，
守得儒生中狀元。
衣食兩般皆足意，
只有姻緣一事尚懸懸。

學生非別，瑤琴大叔的便是。想我當初伏侍公子，磨墨洗硯，掃地燒香，吃了許多苦，方得他功成名就。(笑介) 小子如今鮮衣美食，人稱二爺，好生快活。(皺眉介) 只是孤身獨睡，豈是個常法？今早老爺吩咐叫廚下安排酒席，要請大老爺來贈妾。[1] 我想有的雙雙對對把來送人，何不嫁與區區一個，也是個人情。氣他不過，待老爺出來，說上一番，有何不可？(生紗帽錦氅，搖扇上) 昔日片言邀貴客，今朝一笑贈佳人。瑤琴，酒宴可曾齊備？(丑) 齊備多時。(生) 可着人去請大老爺？(丑) 已請過了。(跪介) 小人有話稟上老爺。(生) 你有甚話講？(丑) 老爺容稟。(叩頭介) (唱)

〔園林好〕喜爺台名成志全，嘆小人緣慳命蹇，(叩頭介) **求恩主早生憐念。**(生) 教我憐念你甚麼來？(丑唱) **賜一個好丫鬟，成一段好姻緣。**

(生大笑介) 這狗才好沒廉恥，自己要起老婆來了。(丑) 人皆如此，豈獨區區？(生) 不勞你着忙，我早與夫人商議定了。(丑喜，聽介) 哦，商議下甚麼呢？(生唱)

〔嘉慶子〕我替伊早把紅絲綰，已向那金雀屏中定小鬟。(丑) 是哪一位阿姐？(生) 就是夫人贈嫁臨春。(丑大喜，急叩頭) 多謝老爺。

---

[1] 照應。

(生) 只是一件…… (丑) 哪一件？(生唱) **可惜配伊行花面。**(丑) 老爺這個不相干，(唱) **曾記得古人言，巧妻伴拙夫眠。**[2]

(生笑介) 既然如此，今日就是吉日，與你花燭成就便了。(丑叩頭介) 小人叩謝老爺天恩。(生) 你去打扮，不消在此伺候。(丑應，跳笑搖擺下) (小生上) 稟爺，大爺到。(生) 有請。(小生請介，末巾錦氅上，生迎介) 哥哥請。(末) 兄弟請。(各揖坐介，小生送茶介) (末) 兄弟今日相招何事？(生) 哥哥記得兄弟當初呵，(唱)

〔尹令〕為雙姬調琴寫怨，(舉手介) **感吾兄玉成心願。**[3] **今日裏華堂開宴，**(末) 哦，排宴酬謝愚兄了。(生笑) (唱) **非止開筵，妙處中藏別有緣。**

(末笑問介) 有何妙處呢？(生) 昔日燈前一語，小弟刻記於懷。今已選得雙艷，贈待衾裯。(末) 可是真的？(生) 兄弟怎好哄哥哥？(末急揖介) 多謝兄弟。(生) 豈敢。(對小生介) 吩咐將酒擺在內書房。(小) 嗄。(生末轉介，外、小生送酒介) (生白) 院子敲雲板，傳與掌家婆，領二位新姨出見。(外應，傳話介) (生) 你們退去，不必在此伺候。(外、小生下) (生) 哥哥請酒。(末) 兄弟請。(旦扮賽紅，貼扮勝雪，各盛服艷妝。小丑扮婢，副淨扮掌家婆上)

〔品令〕(二旦同唱)[4] **忽聞傳語，整妝移步蓮，私心自喜相隨出畫欄。**(見末，急退介) 呀，**抬頭猛見，趨步忙回轉。**(小丑) 怎不進去？(二旦) **卻原來設宴留賓，險教人拋頭露面。**(副淨笑介) 那就是大老爺喲。(丑、副淨醜臉笑介) (二旦唱) **古禮曾聞，早難道喚出紅妝佐玳筵？**(生) 怎麼還不見到來？待我去看。(作出看介) 呀，怎不進去？

〔玉交枝〕為何站立欄畔，背湖山雙雙懶前？(小丑) 姐姐說怕大老爺看見，不肯進去。(生大笑介) 一發奇絕了。**哪曾聞巫娥反怕襄王見？**(二旦詫介) (背唱) **這話兒難教猜辯。**(末潛出，偷覷介。生回頭見，大笑介。末羞，以扇遮面急坐介。副、丑笑) (生唱) **這壁廂含羞推**

---

[2] 現成妙句。

[3] 開口說出，直截了當。

[4] 必須另派二旦扮二妾，方不混人眼目。

整鳳頭簪，那壁廂潛身偷覷如花面。(二旦作背唱)**好教人左難右難。**(末唱)**好教人立難坐難。**

(生正色介)二姬過來，我前者買伊之時，原非為己。汝等今日還是我家人，明日即為大爺尊寵，須要小心侍奉。(二旦駭介)(背唱)

〔么令〕聽言來心中驚閃，默地裏沉吟自憐。別東家再侍西家，知他苦甜。(淚介)**真可嘆，飛花同類，任風捲旋。**(生白)紅姐，雪姐，不必生悲。大爺之為人，兒女情長，汝等侍彼衾裯，勝似吾家多矣。(唱)**休錯認紅顏命蹇。**隨我進來。

(小丑)二位姐姐到了。(末急看介)在哪裏？(生迎介)在這裏。(末看生，作愧色。各大笑介)二姬過來拜了大老爺。(末笑，容謙介)不消不消。(二旦拜，末作欲扶復止謙恭不安介；生笑，以扇拍末肩介)老兄放尊重些，這是甚麼嘴臉？(末作惶恐，拈髯佯笑介；生大笑)(唱)

〔江兒水〕顛倒兄堪笑，痴狂弟亦然，而今各遂風流願。(白)哥哥，今將此二姝奉贈，亦須好好看承，莫使她們落後。(唱)**這花枝兩兩憑君戀，休教紅粉悲秋扇。**(末唱)老兄弟，**此事無勞懸念。**我，**這風月班頭，豈比那尋常村漢？**

(生)兄與二姬就此同歸便了。(二旦)妾還不曾拜夫人。(末)正是正是。(生)既如此，侍兒相隨進去。(小丑、副淨應，同二旦下。外上稟介)稟老爺，鼓樂儐相，俱已齊備，請老爺去看拜堂。(末白)呀，今日哪個完婚呢？(生)就是瑤琴。(末)瑤琴幾時定了親事？倒不曉得。(生)就是弟婦的侍女臨春，配他為妻。(末)原來如此，愚兄也去看看。(生)哥哥請。(轉介，眾扮鼓吹，淨扮儐相，吹打請介。小生引丑新衣帽上，立介。又請老旦扮喜娘，扶小旦紅衫罩頭上，拜天地介)(淨)禮畢。(生)送入洞房。(鼓樂引下，生、末吊場。小丑、副淨引旦、貼上)移步離香閣，含悲別玉人。(生)你們來了，吩咐侍兒們，掌燈送老爺與新姨歸去。(副應介)(生)兄弟粗備妝奩，明日送去。(末急揖介)吾弟一發費心了。(生)好說。(老旦、小旦扮婢，執紗燈上)(生)哥哥請行罷。(顧二旦介)你們好生伏侍大老爺，去罷。(二旦)老爺請上，待妾等拜別。(生笑介)如今是二位如嫂了，豈可還行舊禮？(二旦)老爺言重，我們呵，

〔川撥棹〕居庭院，一年來蒙恩眷。(背介)**雖不曾侍宴調衾，雖不**

曾侍宴調衾，也算做琵琶再彈。[5] (淚介) **念夫人德萬千，恨無緣中道捐。**

(末) 愚兄告辭，明日再來相謝。(生) 豈敢。(唱)

〔尾〕黃金不惜教絃管，贈與君家樂少年。(末大笑介) **從今後笑擁紅妝醉綺筵。**(分下)

[5] 佳句。

第二十二齣·賞春

(丑青服鸞帶，戴八字黑髯上)

小子周瑤琴的便是。[1] 這幾年衣食豐足，夫妻和順，十分快樂。昨日老爺吩咐教人打掃花園，安排酒宴，要玩賞春光。不免叫眾夥伴們來，大家料理。(叫介) 眾兄弟哪裏？(副末、淨、雜青衣上) 有福人伏侍，無福伏侍人。(見丑介) 呀，老周，你不去陪着老婆，這時候就起來了！(丑) 取笑取笑，學生豈是那樣人乎？(眾笑介) 嘴臉，你哪一日不如此？今日又改起調來了。(丑笑介) 閑話少說，昨日老爺吩咐的話，列位可曾料理？(眾) 不勞你管，我們俱已收拾齊備了。(丑拱手笑介) 動勞列位，自在了學生。(各隨意渾耍介) (淨) 不知今日，是家宴，是請客？(丑) 不請甚麼外客，就是我們老太夫人，太老爺，太夫人，大老爺，請謝老爺謝夫人與探花小老爺。(眾) 哦，原來都是自家人。(丑) 天氣尚早，我們且在此坐一坐，再去伺候。(眾) 正是。(各坐地介) (副末) 咳，想這位謝公子，也算難得，小小年紀就戴了紗帽。(雜) 便是呢，我們老爺當初，是十九歲的狀元，謝公子又是十八歲就中了探花，果然難得。(丑捻鬚介) 咳，提起來，又是些舊話了。想我當初隨老爺下江南的時節，都是小孩子，如今不覺做了個美髯丈夫也。(眾笑渾介) (副末) 他們還是後來人，不曾看見，老爺娶夫人的時候，探花來送姐姐，只得四歲。屈指算來，已是十四五年光景了。(丑點頭介) (淨) 我們老爺的官運也算罷了，年紀不上四九，就做到吏部侍郎。(雜) 更妙的是父子翁婿，共列金階。(淨) 便是呢！我們這位大老爺，偏是不耐煩做官的。(雜) 卻是為甚麼呢？(副末) 咳，有了老爺做官，大老爺落得自在了。(淨) 如今處在富貴場中，不要說老爺，就是老周，也足夠受用了。(雜扮門公上) 你們眾位好消閑哪。(眾) 有甚麼話說？(雜) 謝太老爺和探花老爺都到了。(眾急起介) 如此我們快去通

---

[1] 周有姐，永清周氏女也。隨伊父母役署中。黠而慧，吾女愛之，名之曰“瑤琴”。未幾，以疾夭。故譜入曲中。蓋一切嬉笑之詞，皆斷腸聲也。

稟。(丑) 太老爺有請。(外戴紗帽，穿香色蟒袍；末戴方巾穿錦，開場；生戴黑三髯紗帽月白圓領上) (外) 春光臨宅院，(生、末) 佳氣滿皇州。(丑) 謝太老爺到了。(外) 快啟中門。(丑眾應，作開門介，內作樂。雜扮從人，小生紗帽天藍蟒袍，小旦扮探花，紗帽大紅圓領，同上。外、生、末同出迎介，各揖讓進介) (外) 老親家光臨寒舍，小弟未得遠迎，多多有罪。(小生) 豈敢。荷蒙親家見邀，小弟來遲，有勞久待。(外) 好說，請坐。(小生) 請！(各揖，坐介) (外) 看茶。(丑、淨送茶介) (外) 小弟昨見小園春色頗佳，聊設粗筵，奉邀親家一敘。老親母為何不見光臨？(小生) 寒荊承老親母見召，焉敢有遲？愚父子先來，寒荊少刻便到。(外) 如此甚好，請到小園。(小生) 請。(同行介) (小生) 妙嗄，這園真好景致也。(雜) 酒筵齊備。(外) 看酒。(內細樂，外把盞，小生攔介) 老親家，我和你昔為同譜，今叨至戚，理應去此客套了。(外) 年翁説哪裏話來？豈有不把敬一杯之禮？(小生) 如此説，是見外愚父子了。(外) 既然老年兄尊意不允，小弟只得從命了。(顧生介) 我兒把盞。(生) 是，看酒過來。(丑眾捧杯，生先送小生席，次送外席，再送小旦、末。小旦、末回送生，各揖坐介，丑眾跪介) 請上酒。(起介) (合唱)

〔駐馬聽〕日麗風清，無限春光繞鳳城。園林美景，盈眸錦綉瑞雲生。夢中何必羨瑤京，人間亦有蓬瀛境。[2] (外) 左右看大杯來。(眾) 嗄。(淨取杯酒奉，外敬小生介) 老親家請。(小生) 老親家請。(各照飲介，合唱) **盞換杯更，當此會須豪興。**

(外) 左右！(眾) 有。(外) 速到曉春軒內，另設酒筵，我與謝太老爺賞玩，可喚梨園子弟承應。(雜、副末應，同下。外對小生介) 嗄，老年兄，我們且到小軒，杯酒談心，好讓他兄弟們洒落。(小生笑介) 小弟正有此意。(同起介，生、末、小旦揖送介) (外) 親家請。(小生) 請。(同揖讓下) (生) 左右，謝府太夫人到了不曾？(丑) 早已到了。(生對末、小旦介) 老舅，哥哥，我們都把大衣卸了罷。(末、小) 正是。(丑、淨伏侍更衣介，末換藍錦氅，生換月白錦氅，小旦換銀紅錦氅，各坐介) (生) 瑤琴，喚歌姬們伺候。(丑應，喚介) 歌姬們走動。(旦、

[2] 點逗"夢"字。

貼、老旦、小丑各艷妝，扮四歌姬上）（白）舞殘楊柳樓心月，歌盡桃花扇底風。（叩介）歌姬們叩頭。（生）起來，好生唱曲奉酒。（眾）曉得。（生）看大杯來。（丑、淨遍送酒介）（生白）老舅請。（小丑）姐丈請。（末）老賢弟請。（小旦）老世兄請。（各飲介，四歌姬合唱）

〔畫眉序〕花裏喚神仙，幾曲園林芳徑轉。正春光滿眼，桃李能言。鋪翠陌茸嫩平莎，拂畫簷垂楊金偃。春成片無人見，平付與鶯捎燕剪。

（小旦）妙嗄，真繞梁之音也。（四妓送酒，生、末、小旦合唱）

〔駐雲飛〕絃管悠揚，嘹亮清音繞畫梁，欄外花相向，林內鶯隨唱。（生起，送酒介）（唱）**㗇，自起奉霞觴，把舅兄同讓。美景良辰，飲酒當豪放，必須要盡量開懷入醉鄉。**歌妓們再歌一曲。（眾）曉得。（小旦）久聞老世兄精於玉笛，小弟從未領教，意欲奉煩吹和一曲，未知尊意如何？（末笑謙介）粗俗小技，怎敢在老弟面前獻醜？（小旦笑介）太謙了。（生）瑤琴，取我紫玉笛過來。（丑應，取笛送末介）（末）老弟不要笑嗄。（小旦）豈敢。（四妓唱，末吹笛和介）

〔黃鶯兒〕偷眼艷陽天，帶朝雲暮雨鮮，一枝低壓宜春院。芳心半點，紅妝幾瓣，和鶯吹折流霞茜。糝香肩春纖袖口，拈插鬢雲邊。

（生、小旦各笑贊介）（白）妙嗄，笛韵悠揚，歌喉婉囀，可為雙絕矣。（末笑介）見笑見笑。（生）看酒。（丑斟酒介）（生白）兄弟奉哥哥一杯。（小旦）小弟借花獻佛，也敬老世兄一杯。（末）二位老弟，亦當陪我一杯。（生、小旦）這個自然。（各飲照乾介）（生）快斟來。（眾斟，末、生、小旦同飲照乾，各大笑介）今日之遊，可為樂矣。（生）左右，將酒宴移到茜雲亭上，去看桃花。歌妓們奏樂引道。（眾應介）（生）老舅，哥哥請。（末、小）請。（作樂，同揖讓下）

（貼穿粉紫畫花衣，小旦穿水綠畫花衣，各擎扇，同小丑、丫頭上）

〔駐馬聽〕同步園林，素手相牽踏翠茵。香風徐引，（小旦整鬢笑介）**怪荼蘼抓住了鳳頭簪。**（內鶯啼介）（二旦）**鶯聲巧囀上林春，花枝笑奪天公錦。**（小旦）咦，好對花蝴蝶也。（各撲介）（二旦唱）**彩扇揮頻，驚鳳子分飛陣。**

（小丑）二位小夫人，請到那邊去，打鞦韆耍子。（小旦）姐姐，我

和你去來。(貼旦) 請，紅杏花中聞笑語，(小旦) 綠楊影裏效飛仙。侍兒，隨我來。(小丑) 曉得。(二旦攜手下，丑同下)

(貼改扮祖太夫人，鳳冠香色錦氅；小旦改扮謝夫人，鳳冠天藍錦氅；老旦扮王夫人，鳳冠紅青錦氅；旦鳳冠月白錦氅；二雜扮梅香，同上)[3] (四旦合)

〔駐雲飛〕春滿名園，青帝臨空萬象鮮。花底排筵宴，柳外鳴簫管。嗏，人醉杏花，天和風乍暖，芳草紅橋，繞過了梨花院。(雜笑指介) 哪，夫人，請看二位小夫人，在鞦韆上起的那們高，好看好看。(旦望，笑介) 果然有趣。(唱) **笑指飛來雲外仙。**

(小丑上，跪) 稟上太夫人：兩位小夫人，在鞦韆架邊錦霞亭上，請列位夫人賞玩海棠。(貼) 知道了。(小丑起介) (貼白) 既是她們敬心，請親家母同往一觀。(小旦) 太親母請。(貼) 親母請。(小旦讓老旦介) 親母請。(老旦) 說哪裏話，親母先請。(小旦、貼) 竹裏登樓人不見，(老旦、正旦) 花間覓路鳥先知。(同讓下)

(外換青錦氅，小生亦換天藍錦氅，各搖扇。外先上) (唱)

〔前腔〕醉解宮袍，笑傲花前宦態消。(小生作醉態上) (唱) **側帽狂吟調，不脱風流套。**(旦、貼、老旦、小丑照前扮四妓；小旦復照前扮謝公子；生、末同上) (唱) **嗏，絃管送春醪，紅妝前導，看西轉金烏，閃閃晴霞照，長笑春風醉碧桃。**

(生) 呀，爹爹岳丈在此。(各整衣立介) (小生) 天色將晚，小弟要告辭了。(外) 老年翁又來了。當此良辰，我和你知音聚會，奈何飲興未闌，即欲見棄？(小生笑介) 既承老年翁雅愛，小弟亦非興淺者，達旦之歡，敢不如命。(外) 如此甚好。左右！(丑、雜) 有。(外) 可到望仙樓上，[4] 另整酒筵伺候者。(眾) 嗄。(外) 歌妓們隨去承應。(妓) 曉得。(外、小生攜手行，生、小旦、末隨) (小生唱)

〔前腔〕花月同酬，良友多情約醉遊。(白) 老親翁，想小弟呵，(唱) **半世躭詩酒。**(作醉態，彈冠介) **奈彼烏紗紐。**(外) 便是。想我輩少年時節，於風月場中，頗亦放誕。今為宦路牽身，(拈鬚笑介) 覺道

---

[3] 所用腳色頗雜，若臨登場，必須多備生旦數人。

[4] 逗下仙化。

歲月無多，早又鬢髯蒼矣。(小生) 弟想人生呵，(唱) **嗏，得做個洒落醉鄉侯，陶然自有，轉得個五柳栽門，煞勝似黃金綬。**(外) 閑話慢講，莫要冷落了杯中竹葉。(小生) 正是是是，我們今日呵，(合唱) **須飲到紫陌雞鳴，好同去拜冕旒。**(同下)

第二十三齣・省舊

(場中桌上先要掛簾，為改妝之地)

(生紗帽月藍圓領，緩步上，唱)

〔一江風〕甚因緣？數載神仙眷，記不起風流案。任狂顛，彩筆生輝，怕扭不得天心轉。徘徊情悵然，(內鵑啼介)**聽催歸枝上鵑，一聲聲叫的咱心撩亂。**

(作歪坐介)

〔南鄉子〕

獨自坐書齋，
欲話因緣意已呆。
來往紛紛拏不住，
疑猜，恰是新懷觸舊懷。

運數有安排，
萬事何須問泰乖。
身後身前茫不認，
嗟哉！造物何曾解愛才？

今日曉起，情懷好是無聊賴也。(作懶態，背手閑行介)

〔前腔〕步盤旋，把往事沉吟遍。(欠伸介)**恍惚神魂散，猛相關，似假如真，兜底來心畔。搖搖意若懸，呆呆眼望天。**(撫心嘆介)**揣心頭似續還如斷。**[1]

想當初此身呵，

〔紅衲襖〕本是個**着裙釵綉閣娟**，今做了**戴烏紗皇朝宦**。(指筆介)這一枝**小霜毫**，只不過**題心怨**，怎承望**掃千軍把社稷安？**(抖袖介)一般兒**佩金章惹御烟**，又何必**拜相榮封侯顯？**(呆想介)猛想起這二十載**的富貴繁華，也怕做了一枕邯鄲午夢酣。**[2]

---

[1] "斷"者，夢將醒也；"續"，此愁正多也，故用此二字。

[2] 古往今來，大都如此。

(作倦倚几睡介，旦穿月白圓領束緣，小旦、貼穿花披風同上)(旦)

〔前腔〕一則為**聽鶯啼出翠軒，**二則為**踏春陽來書院。**(小旦)呀，為甚的**靜悄悄把朱戶掩？**(貼)敢則是**怕春歸不捲簾？**[3] (同進，見生介)(旦白)為何衣冠不整，獨臥空齋？卻原何**倦懨懨依書案？**(淚介)**嘆殺人今朝了夢緣。**[4] (二旦作下簾與生脫冠帶去鬚，原穿前〈獨嘆〉齣服色；生昏介，二旦扶至原處睡介)(旦)嗳呀，相公嗄，(各悲介)(唱)今日裏**好交割了二十載的恩情也。**(三旦哭介)啊呀，王郎嗄，**苦殺你自鎖重重離恨天。**(三旦同下，生在場)

[3] 仍是佳句。

[4] 一語櫽括已盡。

第二十四齣・出夢

(生急立起，叫介) 夫人轉來，二姬慢去！(作呆狀，四顧，忽驚介) 咳呀，好奇怪。啊，這是甚麼所在？我方才身在書房，怎麼得到此處？(起身四望介) 咦，看此情境，竟是閨閣中的光景了。(看自身驚介) 呀，我的鬚髯冠帶，怎麼都不見了？好生奇怪，是甚麼原故呢？(作呆想介，忽大叫介) 哦！我省得了，原來半世功名竟是一場大夢。[1] (作悶倒介，坐地緩唱)

〔端正好〕夢迷離，神顛倒；猛驚回，魂魄飛搖。俺向那睡鄉中覓了些虛歡笑，怪轉眼乾坤悄。[2]

(起，嘆介) 咳，可惜我二十年的愛眷，竟逐浮雲空矣。(淚介) (唱)

〔滾綉毬〕痛花枝空裏簪，嘆月光水底撈。未卜得再生緣今生已了，思量起恨茫茫蝶翅飛飄。(哭介) **俺撇了效齊眉的孟光，抛下了抱衾裯的二喬，眼睜睜問不着故人消耗，閃殺咱地遠天高。看了這一庭花影簾前轉，恰似我半世功名醒後消，只落得怨氣沖霄。**

(拭目看畫，驚介) 呀，我看這畫上佳人，分明是我妻房謝氏。(拍桌哭介) 啊呀，夫人嗄！(唱)

〔叨叨令〕這姻緣魂招和那夢招，一靈兒赴天台乘風到。這莽紅塵誰識得舊藍橋？空望你鸞飛鶴去三山杳。曾記那夢裏的情苗，伊是咱金蘭琴瑟的真同調。今做了花殘和那露消，斷送得啼鵑頻向斜陽叫。[3] 兀的不痛殺人也麼哥，兀的不恨殺人也麼哥！閃得我形影蕭條，似這等悲悲切切的悼。

想起胡黃二姬，甚因緣竟為我妾？(悲唱)

〔脫布衫〕醒無緣月下吹簫，睡偏能金屋藏嬌。空和恁夢魂中紅依翠靠，只落得覺來時影形相弔。

---

[1] 大似《邯鄲》盧生光景，真實不虛。

[2] 大言炎炎。

[3] 悲壯淋漓，不亞蔡姬曲。

(拍書恨介) 咦，則被這案上詩書誤了我也。[4] (擲硯筆) (唱)

〔小梁州〕恨忡忡擊硯拋書擲彩毫，(泣介) **做不得投筆班超，空向那夢裏占金鰲。虛榮耀，回首處淚滔滔。**

咳，我如今便對人言，有誰相信？不若隱之於心罷了。[5] (嘆介) 天哪！從此後宵長晝永，無賴無聊，好夢成空，風流難再，教我如何捱得過也？(泣唱介)

〔么篇〕沒來由花前午夢迷心竅，枉添番怨緒與愁苗。忘不了二十年風流調，嘆茫茫人間天上此恨怎能消？噯呀，我那夫人嗄，我那二姬嗄！(唱)

〔快活三〕念前緣愁冉冉，追往境恨迢迢。(白) 如今畫圖雖識春風面，只是環珮難歸夜月魂了。(唱) **問嫦娥，何時再降碧雲霄？可念我一點癡心兒臨風弔。**

〔朝天子〕慕淳于境迢，羨盧生入道，這鬧塵中尋難到。似這等一枕浮雲遊魂的飄渺，怎能彀了塵緣歸玄妙？夢去難招，愁來誰掃？此日淒涼，慘東風落照殘霞老。(泣介) **淚洒衣袍，魂消芳草。好把這一覺繁華，做一個天荒地老的痴情稿。**(下)

---

[4] 真堪痛哭。

[5] 大是。吾之所以再不提為官時也。

第二十五齣・仙化

(旦扮麻姑，戴仙翹，穿雲錦服束絲，執拂。小旦、貼翠衣鳳翹，扮仙娥，執幡引上) (同唱)

〔點絳唇〕海上遨遊，天風盈袖。玄關透與世無求，明月清風友。[1]

〔集唐〕

細環清珮響叮噹，
花底真人道姓王；
省得壺中見天地，
世間名利久相忘。

小仙麻姑是也，身居蓬島，位列仙班。今因下方王氏女，痴心感夢，醒後生悲，意欲下凡指點一番，度她入我玄門。女童與我更衣者。(二旦應，伏侍更衣。內細樂，旦去仙翹，換水田衣束絲，執拂) (旦白)

你們不須隨往，待俺獨向紅塵走一遭也。(二旦下) (旦唱)

〔新水令〕一聲長嘯下瑤京，駕長風拂開塵徑。天香雲外靜，桂子月中清；鶴唳鸞鳴，暫離卻清虛境。(飄然下)

(生穿青衣束絲，青帕包頭，作病妝上) (唱)

〔步步嬌〕急煎煎夢去無踪影，底事難追省。秋來病轉增，咄咄書空，神魂不定。(內雁叫介，生淚介) (唱) **聽天外雁悲鳴，一聲聲似讚咱殘生命。**[2]

(伏几坐介)

[1] 大夢醒後，如痴如醉，不死不活。不得不以仙佛作收科，亦無聊之極思也。

[2] 回思夢中之紗帽圓領，能不令人氣死！猿聲三咽，聲淚俱下。

〔集唐〕

傷心不獨為悲秋，
夜思千重戀舊遊。
此際斷腸人不見，
任他明月下西樓。

俺自仲春一夢，日夜追思，寢食悠悠，染成一病。[3]今乃中秋節令，教人觸景傷懷，倍難消遣。(掩淚嘆介) 咳，天哪！似這等不生不死，如醉如痴，多應不好矣。(泣介) 正是：永夜角聲悲自語，中天月色好誰看？(伏几假寐介)

(旦上) (唱)

〔折桂令〕乍離了玉闕金扃，回首瑤台，霞鎖雲橫。任飄然獨步青霄，眼觀滄海，三度塵生，誰識俺玉壺中乾坤鎖定？嘆殺那莽人間歲月頻更，誰肯將名利休爭？着意修行，也得個跨蒼鸞朝來碧落，舞黃鶴暮去蓬瀛。(下)

(生緩起) (唱)

〔江兒水〕過雁魂應斷，敲砧夢自驚。[4] **慘淒淒，蛩吟砌畔和愁聽；虛飄飄，行來月下徘徊影。**(內吹笛介) (生唱) **韵悠悠，誰家玉笛臨風弄？**(對月長嘆介) (白) 對此清光，橫生百慮，偶成小詞一首，寫來聊寄愁衷。(入坐，寫介)

〔右調滿江紅〕

搔首呼天，呼不應茫茫一片。嗟顛倒弄權，造化故生缺陷。紅粉飄零今古恨，才人老大千秋怨。問乾坤心劍倩誰磨？揮愁斷。

論萬事，從公判；安時命，達人見。嘆河陽鬢改，隱侯腰倦。孽夢徒嘗人造福，痴文枉奪天成案。搵青衫咄咄日書空，沉吟遍。[5]

(長嘆投筆起，悲介) (唱) **離恨天高無徑，倚月題箋，做不得吹笙緱嶺。**

---

[3] 觀其口角神氣，都全無女人意思。

[4] 律中佳句。

[5] 沉雄流麗。

(旦暗上，立桌上，吟介) 自脱紅塵不記年，(生驚聽介，旦又吟介) 幾看滄海變桑田。誰能打破三生夢，便有雲梯引上天。(生) 呀！聽此一詩，大非凡人口氣，是甚麼人呢？(抬頭見旦，驚介) 咳呀，你看那朵彩雲裏面，明明顯出一位仙姑。想因念我悲傷，前來度脱。急速上前禮拜，莫教錯過。(急整衣跪拜介) 上仙上仙，弟子下界愚人，不知是哪位大仙降臨？望乞少留仙駕，念弟子孽夢糾纏，要求上仙分明指點。(旦笑介) 爾好痴也！

〔雁兒落帶得勝令〕伊只待佩鳴珂把紫禁登，卻原何**倒烏紗將山人敬？**怎不見**列金屏二孄婷？倒去了賦〈關雎〉伊的賢尊正。**(生掩淚介) 這都是些夢話，上仙提他則甚？弟子如今拜告真人，要求度脱。(叩頭介) (旦唱) 呀，恁自去**把筆佐朝廷，又何必崎嶇上玉京？**(生) 上仙端的是哪位真人？(旦唱) **恁這蠢凡夫要問咱的真名姓，早難道神仙不肯明修行？這些時懶踏紅塵徑，恁可也知也麼名，俺曾在漢桓時鞭蔡經。**[6]

(生) 呀，原來是麻姑大仙。咳呀，大仙哪，(忙叩介) (悲唱)

〔僥僥令〕我誠心求妙訣，再拜問長生，咱這一枕魂遊冤家境，端的是甚來由有此情？甚來由有此情？

(旦) 這有何說，皆汝平日不忿身為女子，每每自悲自恨，一點痴心，參成世界耳。[7] (生) 可惜我半世功名，一生愛眷，就是這等罷了。(哭介) (旦) 你休得悲啼，恁看世間真榮真貴，亦不過野馬浮雲，誰保百年長在？況空虛幻境乎！[8] (生) 弟子再問尊師，畢竟那班人物，從何來往？(旦) 總因汝之一念，夢去即生，醒來即滅，有何來往！(生呆，醒作忽悟介) 弟子醒悟了，原來二十年恩愛榮華，皆出一念，沒來由為生為死，可不羞死人也。(叩頭介) 弟子悟徹痴緣，不貪名利，望乞大仙收為門下。(旦) 汝今省得了麼？(生) 是，省得了。(旦唱)

〔收江南〕呀，**俺看那世間人的榮辱呵，誰不是夢中情？打不破貪嗔愛痴死和生，陷名坑利坑。陷名坑利坑，怎似俺無愁無礙萬緣清。**

(生) 弟子就此拜了師父罷。(起，整衣復拜介) (唱)

---

[6] 隸事千妥萬妥，押韵更極自然。

[7] 揭出正旨，女人不可無此志氣。

[8] 世人急宜猛省，木清泰所以出家也。

〔園林好〕感真言迷醒夢醒，悟因緣今生再生。弟子呵，**欲拜識大羅仙境。**(叩介) **望師父憫微誠，垂慈念許同登。**

(旦笑介) 這卻早哩。[9] 爾今痴念雖消，塵心未淨。待你見性明心之後，吾當引汝超凡也。(生揮淚叩頭介) 多謝尊師。

(小旦、貼扮前二仙娥執幡暗上，立旦左右介) (旦) 你看月斜河轉，夜色已闌，俺就此去也。[10] (唱)

〔沽美酒〕見雙鬟雲路迎，見雙鬟雲路迎，俺跨青鸞上玉京。(生) 仙師當真去了？(旦唱) **早難道斜倚祥雲不肯行。**(生淚介) (旦) **伊休得淚零，終有日輕身飛去伴雙成。**(生拜介) (唱) **感恩師點開迷境，睹仙儀不勝肅敬；受玄機性明心領，似晨鐘睡魔初警。**俺呵，**修得個身清念清，**(旦唱) **要心堅志誠**呀，**俺引恁朝元果證。**

(內細樂，旦、貼、小旦同下)

(生大笑介) [11] 不料俺今夜當真遇仙也。(唱)

〔清江引〕無端一覺消春夢，夢裏空馳騁。三生情枉痴，一笑今何用？方曉得女和男一樣須回省。(下)

花光蕉影映窗紗，知是多才道韞家。
獨向書中尋旨趣，還從夢裏譜繁華。
百年眷屬原同幻，三島追隨尚未遐。
一曲繞梁爭擊節，燈紅酒綠月痕斜。
形軀變換古今難，夢裏何妨作是觀。
巾幗居然登甲第，裙釵一任襲衣冠。
行蹤不讓黃崇嘏，才藻真同李易安。
從此閨中傳法曲，桃花燕子好同看。

北平年愚叔朱珪題

—終—

[9] 四字有幾十年俗事在內。

[10] 思之可悲可恨。

[11] 《南柯》之淳于生，成佛後亦曾大笑，與此笑同。

王百齡跋

此劇為齡母王太孺人之作。太孺人秉異質，通書史，常以不獲掇巍科取顯宦為憾，因譔是編以抒胸臆。憶齡幼受書於母，即勗之曰："汝當努力功名，以成吾志。"故齡八歲就傅於外祖南圃公，二十三領壬子鄉薦，無資艱北上，母曰："吾於汝家食貧作苦，所望者，為進士女，復為進士母爾。"蓋外祖公係乾隆戊午舉人，戊辰進士也。齡迫於母命，襆被公車六戰，而於嘉慶壬戌掇房魁，旋入詞桓。請假歸，太孺人欣慰之餘，尚以不能大魁為憾也。甲子秋，讀是編，因記數語，以見太孺人之志，與齡之不肖也。至太孺人所編詩集，及《全福記》各傳奇，俟續刊焉。

男王百齡謹識

王元常跋

女筠，幼稟異質，書史過目即解。每以身列巾幗為恨，因撰《繁華夢》一劇，以自抒其胸臆。草創就，即呈余勘正。其中有涉於繁冗者，為細加刪潤，綴以評語，勒為一編。因剞劂無力，藏諸篋中者已十年矣。戊戌三月，偶出以就正於觀察息圃張公，公即轉呈畢太夫人，共為激賞，各賜序及詩，以弁冊首。觀察公仍獨力捐金，趣付梓人，俾閨中小言得以出而問世。吾女亦可欣然自慰，不復以巾幗為恨矣。刻成，為志其緣起如此。

南圃王元常題於槐慶堂